T0311393

"This is a truly wonderful work, scholarly, readable, comprehensive and concise, with transparent headings and an invaluable glossary. Juliane House is a gifted educator with a passion for her subject. This gem of a book will benefit students, practitioners and lay readers who want to get across the field of translation studies."

Charles Denroche, *University of Westminster, UK*

Praise for the first edition

"Juliane House presents a thorough overview of the practice of translation and of the academic field of translation studies. As well as providing an introduction to basic concepts and practices, the book offers a readable and cogent analysis of the different theoretical perspectives and recent trends which make translation such a powerful linguistic and cultural phenomenon."

Jeremy Munday, *University of Leeds, UK*

"This book offers a comprehensive and practical set of essential ideas and a most up-to-date account of trends in Translation Studies. Juliane House is able to make abiding issues in Translation Studies authentic, clear and reader-friendly, and most importantly of all, using innovative and critical viewpoints. A valuable reference book for scholars and students in both translation teaching and translation research."

Meifang Zhang, *University of Macau, China*

"An essential book for anyone who researches, studies or is interested in translation."

Yuanyi Ma, *Guangdong Polytechnic of Science and Technology, China*
Bo Wang, *Sun Yat-sen University, China*

TRANSLATION

THE BASICS

Translation: The Basics is an accessible and comprehensive introduction to the study of translation. This revised edition includes two new chapters on culturally embedded concepts and translation in global business. All references have been updated with additional references and new quotes added.

Combining traditional text-based views with the context of translation in its widest sense, it presents an integrated approach to methodology in order to critically address influences such as power and gender, as well as cultural, ethical, political and ideological issues. This book answers such questions as:

- How can translations be approached?
- Do social issues and culture play a part in translations?
- How does a translation relate to the original work?
- What effect has globalization had on translation?
- What are the core concerns of professional translators?

Key theoretical issues are explained with reference to a range of case studies, suggestions for further reading and a detailed glossary of terms, making this the essential guide for anyone studying translation and translation studies.

Juliane House is Professor Emerita of Applied Linguistics at the University of Hamburg. She is the author of *Translation Quality Assessment: Past and Present* (Routledge, 2015) and *Translation as Communication across Languages and Cultures* (Routledge, 2016).

The Basics

The Basics is a highly successful series of accessible guidebooks which provide an overview of the fundamental principles of a subject area in a jargon-free and undaunting format.

Intended for students approaching a subject for the first time, the books both introduce the essentials of a subject and provide an ideal springboard for further study. With over 50 titles spanning subjects from Artificial Intelligence to Women's Studies, *The Basics* are an ideal starting point for students seeking to understand a subject area.

Each text comes with recommendations for further study and gradually introduces the complexities and nuances within a subject.

For a full list of titles in this series, please visit www.routledge.com/The-Basics/book-series/B

TRANSLATION

THE BASICS

Second Edition

Juliane House

Routledge
Taylor & Francis Group

LONDON AND NEW YORK

Designed cover image: © Shutterstock

Second edition published 2024
by Routledge
4 Park Square, Milton Park, Abingdon, Oxon, OX14 4RN

and by Routledge
605 Third Avenue, New York, NY 10158

Routledge is an imprint of the Taylor & Francis Group, an informa business

First edition published by Routledge 2017

British Library Cataloguing-in-Publication Data
A catalogue record for this book is available from the British Library

Library of Congress Cataloging-in-Publication Data
Names: House, Juliane, author.
Title: Translation: the basics / Juliane House.
Description: Second edition. | New York, NY: Routledge, 2024. |
Series: The basics | Includes bibliographical references and index.
Identifiers: LCCN 2023014292 |
Subjects: LCSH: Translating and interpreting.
Classification: LCC P306 .H68 2024 | DDC 418/.02—dc23/eng/20230404
LC record available at https://lccn.loc.gov/2023014292

ISBN: 978-1-032-41014-2 (hbk)
ISBN: 978-1-032-40711-1 (pbk)
ISBN: 978-1-003-35582-3 (ebk)

DOI: 10.4324/9781003355823

Typeset in Bembo
by codeMantra

Access the Support Material: www.routledge.com/9781032407111

CONTENTS

ACKNOWLEDGEMENTS

Every effort has been made to contact copyright holders. Please advise the publisher of any errors or omissions and these will be corrected in subsequent editions.

INTRODUCTION

This book is designed to familiarize you with some basic ideas and trends in the field of translation studies. You do not need any previous knowledge of translation. This does not mean, however, that the presentation of issues in the field of translation in this book will be oversimplified, thus distorting the information you will be given. Rather, what you will read here will be authentic, clear and reader-friendly.

In the first part of this book, translation is characterized and defined. So, Chapter 1 looks at common negative and positive aspects of translation and describes the nature of translation as a basically secondary type of communication involving two phases: a first phase where the translator receives and comprehends the source text, and a second phase where the interpretation of the first phase is rendered in a target text. In the second part of this chapter, translation theory and practice over time are reviewed. Here, you learn about the rich tradition of translation, how the reputation of translators has changed over time and what impact translations have had on the development of vernacular language. The dichotomy of literal versus free translation which cropped up under different labels over time is described, and its relevance for translation is shown. A more sinister aspect of translation is its use in the conquest of indigenous populations in many parts of the world.

In the last part of this introductory chapter, two other dichotomies are deconstructed: translation as art or science and translation as product or process. Literary translation is often regarded as an art of 're-creation'. Other text types, often lumped together as 'pragmatic texts', are explored in a more scientific manner.

Discussions in translation studies often make a distinction between translation as a final product and translation as a process that occurs inside the translating individual. Another popular distinction concerns two basic types of mediation: (written) translation and (oral) interpreting. Apart from a brief characterization of interpreting, this book is about translation.

A further dichotomy concerns human versus computer-mediated translation. Here, we look at recent advances in computer-aided translation facilitated by technological progress. The question of whether computers will make human translators redundant in the near future is answered with a clear 'No'.

We will then look at translation as a cross-cultural and intercultural phenomenon. Translation is a type of intercultural communication because it involves not only two languages but also two cultures. Culture-specific items in original texts are often difficult to translate. However, cultural differences should not be exaggerated.

The final part of this introductory chapter tells you that translation activities are today growing at an astounding pace and explains why this is the case.

Chapter 2 explains the concept 'translation competence' – an ability every professional translator must have. Translation competence consists of three parts: an ability to understand the original text; an ability to transfer the message from the source language to the target language; mastering target linguistic resources. The core competence is the second one: transfer competence. The translator's ability to work **between two languages** implies that not every bilingual is automatically a competent translator. The role of knowledge in its various forms is further revealed as a central part of translation competence.

In the third chapter, we look at translation from different perspectives. The first perspective is linguistic, a perspective with a long and venerable tradition. The second perspective is on literary and cultural systems, and we here look at the different translation schools that investigate literary translations. A third perspective is on the socio-cultural context of a translation. Here, we examine schools that emphasize the role of this particular context: post-modernist, post-structuralist, post-colonial and functionalistic schools. Finally, a perspective on translation as an act of re-contextualization is discussed. Pragmatic and systemic-functional schools as well as discourse analysis are here described, and it is shown that they are particularly useful for explaining exactly what happens in translation.

The fourth chapter discusses the role of culture and ideology in translation. Here, we first describe the concept of 'culture' in different disciplines, and we examine how 'culture' has been related to notions such as mentalities, national characters or stereotypes – notions that are shown to be of limited importance for translation. More useful concepts are 'small cultures', 'community of practice' and superdiversity as well as a recent psycho-social view of culture. In this chapter, we also examine what 'ideology' means for translation. Ideology is currently a fashionable notion, to the point that revealing ideological biases now occupies a central space in translation studies. Complementing the idea of an ideological bias by the original author is a concern for recipients of a translation. The concept of 'audience design' taken from stylistics is relevant here.

The second part of this book examines several much-discussed concepts in translation theory. Chapter 5 looks at the age-old question of when and why translation is possible. The discussion centres around 'linguistic relativity' – an idea which can be traced through the past centuries. Linguistic relativity implies that the language you speak influences your thinking and behaviour. If the 'strong linguistic relativity hypothesis' were true, translation would be impossible. However, this hypothesis has been refuted, and there are also other arguments for the possibility of translation. But there are exceptions, and these are the true limits of translatability.

Chapter 6 then asks the question: Do translation universals exist? We first examine the literature on language universals and then move on to answering the title question. The question is answered in the negative and several reasons are given to support this view.

The question of how we know when a translation is good is explored in Chapter 7. Here, you find both an overview of approaches, each of which in their own way tried to find answers to the evaluation of translations, and a detailed account of the only existing fully worked out model of translation quality assessment.

Chapter 8 then asks: What goes on in translators' heads when they are translating? Various methods of looking at the process of translating are discussed, ranging from thinking-aloud protocols to experimental methods (keylogging, eye-tracking) to neuro-linguistic attempts to examine the translator's 'black box'. This chapter is not only descriptive but also tries to evaluate the various methods applied in this cognitive research strand.

In Chapter 9, the use of corpora in translation studies is explained, tracing its development from the early 1990s to the present time. Examples of corpus work are given, highlighting the function of different types of corpora. The current fashion of using corpora should not be mistaken for a new theory; rather, it is simply a method facilitated through the power of computers to store and manipulate vast quantities of data.

In Chapter 10, we look at how translations have changed as a result of globalization and digitization, and how the worldwide spread of global English affects translation today. The fear that the dominance of one particular language marginalizes translation is refuted, and examples are given to illustrate the continued importance of translation.

The final part of this book is devoted to translation in 'the real world'. Chapter 11 looks at translation in globalized business; concretely we will examine how the global furniture company IKEA manages the use of address forms in their multilingual catalogues.

Chapter 12 discusses the important question of the (im)possibility of translating deeply culturally embedded notions. Here, readers are introduced to a concept that is peculiar to the Chinese linguaculture and its many possible translations into English.

Chapter 13 takes a critical look at how translation has been used in language learning and teaching. We first trace the role of translation through the centuries to illustrate the continuous misconception of the nature of translation. The chapter closes with examples of alternative uses of translation that bank on its communicative purposes.

The final chapter of this book, Chapter 14, deals with translation as a professional practice in different situations. The chapter covers first translation in use in multilingual institutions, and in multilingual and multicultural societies where translation has become increasingly important given recent massive migration. New trends in translation studies, such as 'micro-history', are also mentioned, where translators' manuscripts, revisions, notes and interviews about actual translations are studied. We then look at the translator's working environment, including modern translation practices such as computer-assisted translation (CAT) tools, localization practices and project management. An important facet of translators' work today has to do with ethics and the need to accept responsibility for their work, which may mean rejecting the translation of racist, sexist and otherwise offensive texts. Translators also face ethical problems when they work in situations of conflict and war. Finally, this chapter explores an increasingly important practice for translators: audio-visual translation, a field of action in which non-professional translators are also now active in different media.

The book also offers an extensive glossary and reference section.

PART 1

BASIC ISSUES IN THE FIELD OF TRANSLATION

This part of the book discusses some of the most important issues in translation studies: Chapter 1 introduces you to the nature of translation, Chapter 2 asks what it means to be a competent translator, Chapter 3 describes several influential perspectives on translation and Chapter 4 looks at the much-discussed role of culture and ideology in translation.

DOI: 10.4324/9781003355823-1

WHAT IS TRANSLATION?

In this introductory chapter, we look at what translation is and how it has been described over its long history. Then, we will examine a number of age-old questions about translation.

HOW CAN WE DEFINE TRANSLATION?

Translation is a procedure where an original text, often called '**the source text**', is replaced by another text in a different language, often called the '**the target text**'. This book is concerned with translation, the written mode, with a brief discussion of interpreting, the oral mode. Over the centuries, translation has been regarded both positively and negatively. Positively, because translation can provide access to new ideas and new experiences that stem from a different language community, opening horizons that would otherwise remain unknown behind the barrier of another language. Negatively, because translated texts can never be 'the real thing': they remain something second-hand, a kind of inferior substitute for the original. From the positive perspective, translation has often been compared to an act of building bridges or extending horizons. Translators are valued because their act of mediating between different languages, cultures and societies provides an important service for people who only speak their mother tongue.

Seen from a negative perspective, any translation clearly lacks originality: it merely gives people access to a message that already exists in another language. So translation is, of its nature, a type of secondary communication. In the process of translating, an original

DOI: 10.4324/9781003355823-2

communicative event is repeated in order to enable persons to understand and appreciate the original event, from which they would otherwise be excluded.

In translation, there is always both an orientation backwards to the original's message and an orientation forwards towards the communicative conditions of the intended readers, and towards how similar, 'equivalent' texts are written in the target language. This basic 'in-betweenness' of a translation can be called a 'double-bind relationship', which is a defining characteristic of translation. Backwards orientation means that generally the content of the original text needs to be kept equivalent in the translated text. This type of equivalence is called semantic equivalence. If we now take the forward orientation into account, we notice that semantic equivalence is often not sufficient: we also need another type of equivalence, one that takes account of the style of the translated text, its level of formality and the way its different parts hang together. We may call this **pragmatic equivalence**. Generally speaking, pragmatic equivalence characterizes the way language is used in a text. So, in saying that in translation the two texts – the source text and the target text – are equivalent, we mean that they are comparable in both semantic and pragmatic meaning.

Translation generally involves two phases: a first phase in which the translator understands and interprets the source text, and a second phase in which the translator's interpretation is rendered in the target language. In other words, it is not the case that the translated text is simply a reproduction of the original text. Rather, the translated text is a rendering of an interpreted version of the original.

A BRIEF GLANCE AT THE HISTORY OF TRANSLATION THEORY AND PRACTICE

Translations have existed for a very long time. They have been important for the invention and spread of writing conventions, for the development of national languages and national literatures, for the spread of knowledge and political power and influence across national borders. Translations have also provided support in many diplomatic and scientific exchanges; they are instrumental in the extension of religions and in the transfer of cultural values as well as the compilation of dictionaries.

In the following, we will take a brief look at the development of translation practices and theories from a Western perspective – with occasional brief remarks about other areas of the world. Readers interested in what happened in the non-Western world may fruitfully turn to the relevant chapters in the *Routledge Encyclopedia of Translation Studies* (Baker and Saldanha 2019).

Some of the oldest extant translations are Babylonian religious inscription tablets in Sumeric and Akkadian languages that date back to the third millennium bce. Pictures of the surviving tablets show that the social position of translators tended to be rather low, despite the importance of their mission, since the names of the translators are generally rendered much smaller than the originators of the translated texts. Translators were regarded as not much better than servants. They were generally not allowed to act independently, but had to follow strict orders and their work was heavily censored. Their work was conducted, to a large degree, anonymously. When the name of a translator was known and his translation was not up to the required level of fidelity to the original text (particularly important in religious texts), serious consequences followed. For example, in the sixteenth century, one French translator was executed as a heretic because in his translation of a Plato dialogue, he had added a phrase that did not exist in the original: he had written that there was 'nothing at all' after a human being dies. This was regarded as questioning the immortality of the soul.

The first well-documented period in the history of Western translation is the era of Greek-Roman Antiquity. When the Romans started translating texts from Greek into Latin, their main idea was to use translations for enriching the Latin language, taking advantage of the many literary genres that already existed in Greek at the time. Early on, Greek texts were often liberally expanded or reduced, following translators' personal preferences or their assumptions about their readers' expectations. The result was that a given Greek text may turn out to be very different in its Latin translation depending on who happened to translate it from Greek into Latin. The works of the Roman playwright Terence, for example, were largely based on the Greek plays by Menander and Apollodorus. What Terence did was to freely combine translated passages from several Greek originals.

Later, when authors such as Cicero and Horace rose to fame in the Classical Roman tradition, translations became increasingly independent from Greek models. Cicero famously claimed that word-for-word translation is not a suitable practice for translation at all, rather translators should try to find in the language they translate expressions that are able to reproduce as far as possible the strength of the original text. Of similar importance for translation practice and theory is Horace, whose *Ars Poetica* influenced translators over the centuries to come. One of his major principles was that, while translators should certainly strive to imitate the original author, they should also aim to express their own individuality – an idea that greatly increased their prestige. The post-Classical era had nothing much to add to this, and it became clear that translators in antiquity were confronted with similar translational difficulties to those of modern translators, e.g. divergent linguistic systems, lexical gaps, semantic ambivalences, non-translatable idiomatic phrases and so on.

Essentially, new ideas about translation arose in the Christian era of late antiquity, where a distinction was first made between texts embodying different degrees of 'authority'. In the case of 'holy texts', such as the Bible, no part of the text was to be changed in any way – a desideratum that resulted in what was called 'interlinear versions', i.e., a type of word-for-word translation, where new text was written in between lines of the original, a practice that characterized early medieval handwritten documents. Noteworthy here is a letter written by Hieronymus (St Jerome, 348–420) to Pammachius, where the Latin Bible translator admits that in translating Greek texts other than the Bible it is often impossible to render one word through another word. He suggests that translators should rather aim for a sense-for-sense translation. For the translation of the Bible, however, St Jerome did not dare to abandon the assumption that the original's word order be regarded as an unalterable mystery.

In medieval times, the German translator of the Bible, Martin Luther, openly dared to challenge the dogma of complete faithfulness to the original, suggesting instead a much freer formulation whenever necessary. In Luther's view, the translator needed to be close to the content of the text to be translated, and to watch out for the rhythm and melody of the text to be able to produce the desired effect. In his famous 'Sendbrief vom Dolmetschen' (An open letter on translating), Luther vigorously defended his new liberal translational procedures against his many critics, who accused him of producing an altogether too free translation of such a holy text as the Bible. Luther's Bible translation was instrumental in shaping Modern High German. In fact, he is often called the father of Modern High German. The success of Luther's Bible translation may be attributed to his creative use of the German vernacular and to his principles of 'sense translation' rather than word-for-word translation. Luther's decision to express the word of God in the Bible in the language of the common people (German) found its limits, however, whenever essential theological truths were touched upon. Here, Luther would regularly sacrifice the 'principle of intelligibility' to a much more faithful word-for-word translation.

The difference between **word-for-word and free translation** turned out to be a recurring theme of reflections on translational activities across the centuries. While the search for basic 'principles' to guide translators continued, it became clear that such principles were nothing but ideals, and that these ideals would have to be compromised in any individual act of translating. General principles were often formulated as demands on individual translators. For example, for producing a 'good' translation, translators had to have knowledge of the two languages involved, knowledge of the subject matter, stylistic competence and knowledge of the original author's intention.

In the nineteenth century, it was the German philosopher Friedrich Schleiermacher in his well-known essay 'Über die verschiedenen Methoden des Übersetzens' (On the different methods of translating) (1813) who famously formulated (or rather re-formulated) the age-old dichotomy between 'verfremdender' (alienating, i.e., word-for-word) and 'verdeutschender' (integrating, i.e., free) translation. This dichotomy has influenced translation theory and practice up to the present day. We will see in the following parts of this chapter, and indeed in this book as a whole, how far-reaching these opposing poles in fact turned out to be.

Interestingly, the same concerns about 'literal' and 'free' translation can also be seen in the rich ancient translation tradition in

China and in the Arab world. In the Chinese translations of Buddhist sutras, the very same dichotomy could also be detected. However, it is essential to also question this issue: such presumably stable concepts as 'the original text' or the 'source language' may well be thrown into doubt and relativized because oral recitations abounded of which there existed very many different versions. In the rich tradition in the Arab world, and here especially in the famous ancient translation centre in Baghdad, we again notice these two poles, literal and free (or word-for-word and sense-for-sense), with translation from Greek philosophical and scientific writing into Arabic being at the centre of discussions about translation. Another way of looking at these two poles is to emphasize the way these two translation strategies were instrumental in exporting and establishing new systems of thinking that were to become the foundation of Arabic–Islamic thinking as something distinct and clearly independent of the Greek model.

As we can see from the brief review above, the history of translation has focused on translations of literary, philosophical, scientific and religious texts. While the concern about these text types holds true for cases of conquest and invasion into foreign territories, here we also find many translations of administrative and legal texts. For example, when Europeans invaded what they chose to call the 'New World', i.e., South America, they needed many translators and interpreters to make themselves understood by the native population. Here, the direction of translation was overwhelmingly from European languages (Spanish, Portuguese) so as to 'educate' 'the natives' and, above all, to ensure that the power of the invaders was consolidated and remained uncontested. Sadly, much of the indigenous literature, as well as more mundane texts, were irretrievably lost in the process. This was also the case in North America, where the languages of the American Indians were similarly neglected, despised and left to die. The translation direction was again nearly exclusively from English into the native languages – mostly with the intention of missionizing the native population and to exert efficient administrative control. The same (sad) story can be told about many other parts of the world (Africa, Asia), where invading and colonizing Western forces superimposed their own languages onto the indigenous peoples, using translation activities as ready instruments for establishing and securing their administrative and military power. Given the long history of European domination of other linguistic, social and cultural domains, a new field of research – postcolonial translation studies – was to gain ground in the twentieth century. Here, much attention has been paid to the important role that translation has played in colonial contexts across the world. We will look at this field of translation studies below.

SOME RECURRENT ISSUES: TRANSLATION AS ART OR SCIENCE, AND PRODUCT OR PROCESS

Over and above the issue of literal versus free translations discussed above, there are other recurrent questions in the history of thinking about translation. One such question relates to whether translation is to be looked upon as an art, in which case – often with regard to literary translation – the worth and success of the translation is said to depend to a very large extent on the intuition and the competence of the translator. However, if one looks upon translation as a subject to be studied as a science, the person of the translator and his or her capabilities will not be the centre of attention. Rather, more objective criteria for producing and testing a translation will need to come to the forefront.

Another abiding question about translation has regularly revolved around whether the content of a text is to be of prime importance or whether it is the form of the text that deserves most attention. In this connection, a distinction is often made between translation of literary texts and translation of 'pragmatic' or non-literary texts. In the case of literary texts, the linguistic form is never arbitrary. This means that the form needs to be considered essential in any translational act. In the case of non-literary texts, it is the content that needs to be preserved, often at the expense of the linguistic form. Language is here believed to be a mere vehicle transporting the content. In the case of literary texts, on the other hand, the linguistic form and the content are seen as a single inseparable unit.

In discussions about translation, a distinction between **translation as a product** and **translation as a process** is also often made. Translation viewed as a product refers to the text that results from the process of translation, which happens in the translator's mind. Later in this book, we will look in detail at theories about translation as both a product and a process.

TRANSLATION AND INTERPRETING

A basic distinction in writings about translation is the one concerning oral translation and written translation. Oral translation is generally referred to as interpreting, and when we talk about translation, we generally mean the written form. The term 'interpreting' is here to be distinguished from the type of interpretation that applies to understanding and explicating the meaning of a text. As mentioned earlier, this book is about translation, not interpreting. However, a few words about interpreting may be in order here, too, as this can throw light on the characteristics of (written) translation.

In written translation, a fixed, permanently available and, in principle, unlimitedly repeatable text in one language is transformed into a text in another language which can be corrected as often as the translator sees fit. By contrast, in interpreting, an oral text in one language is changed into a new text in another language, which is, as a rule, available to the interpreter only once. Since the new text emerges chunk by chunk and usually does not stay permanently with the interpreter (or the addressees), it is only correctible by the interpreter to a limited extent. While some phases in the act of interpreting are handled quite automatically, requiring little conscious attention or reflection, others may be more difficult and take more time. This extended time requirement may then lead to problems because the interpreter must listen and interpret at the same time. Due to the absence of such time constraints in written translation, the translator can generally read and translate chunks of the source text at her own pace. Another important difference between interpreting and translation is that, in translation, the source text is available to the translator in its entirety, whereas in interpreting, it is generally presented and interpreted bit by bit. A further crucial difference between the two modes of mediating is that in written translation neither the author of an original text nor the (potential) addressees are usually present, which means that no overt interaction or direct feedback can take place. In interpreting, however, both author and addressees are usually present, so interaction and feedback may occur.

HUMAN AND COMPUTER-MEDIATED TRANSLATION

Translations can be performed not only by a human being but also by a computer. **Computer-mediated translation** can be fully automatic or semi-automatic. In the former case, a source text is fed into a computer, and the translation is exclusively performed by a computer with no human involvement whatsoever. At present, fully automatic machine translation usually produces texts that need some degree of further editing **('post-editing')** by a human translator or editor. Computer-mediated translation output can, however, be very useful and very often sufficient in quality for highly specialized scientists, for whom the exact wording and stylistic finesse is less important than quickly getting access to the meaning of a (technical) text. As a specialist in a particular subject, the expert who is familiar with the subject matter is usually in a position to easily disambiguate any clumsiness resulting from machine-produced formulation and other linguistic oddity as long as he is able to grasp the meaning of the translated text. However, whenever the addressee of a machine translated text needs perfect quality, pre-editing and post-editing will often be still carried out by a human being, rendering the translation in a semi-automatic one.

A growing number of continuously improved computer programmes that assist the human translator in different ways are now available: advanced translation software can help the translator solve complicated translation problems by offering either extensive lexical assistance through work stations that provide access to huge online dictionaries or by offering useful grammatical help in the form of empirically derived, co-occurrence patterns of words and phrases stored in very large linguistic corpora. Today, computers can also assist translators in their attempt to retrieve a host of idiomatic and otherwise routinized, and thus highly predictable, target language structures that enable translators to slot these structures into their emerging target texts. Computers can further assist translators by giving them access to ever-growing encyclopaedic knowledge banks and corpora of various kinds, and by offering translators useful search procedures with which they may be enabled to overcome linguistic and conceptual knowledge gaps that occur with highly specialized terminology. So we can say that in many computer-assisted translation activities today there is some degree of division of labour between human and computerized translators. Computerized translation programmes can relieve human translators of repetitious, boring and time-consuming tasks by giving them access to large translation corpora and a variety of reference works and terminology dictionaries. Computers thus liberate human translators for more worthwhile, more interesting, more creative and less mechanical parts of the translation process, such as the more demanding tasks of decision-making, problem-solving and fine-tuning of stylistic choices.

The idea of using 'a machine' for translation goes back to the 1950s and the so-called Cold War, when US scientists first attempted to use computers to translate from Russian. Researchers at IBM and at Georgetown University under the direction of Leon Dostert programmed as few as six rules and a vocabulary of some 250 words into a computer. In 1954 they presented 60 automated translations. However, the initial optimism regarding automated translation soon led to disappointment, and after more than ten years' intensive research, much more modest goals, such as the development of automated dictionaries, were suggested as more worthwhile and achievable. Work on 'machine translation' – as it was then and is even today often called – stalled for the next 20 years or so. The reason for the disillusionment with the early work on automated translation was its rule-based approach: when researchers tried to base automated translation on many more rules than the original six, the system became prone to produce nonsense clauses. Apart from the enormous difficulty of programming the entire rules of a grammar, an important conceptual difficulty also became apparent: the complex problems of meaning, context and knowledge of the real world – problems that researchers involved with automated translation battle with to the present day.

The quality of computerized translation improved substantially when researchers switched from rules-based approaches to the statistics-based system in the new millennium. Statistics-based approaches banking on statistical probabilities depended on improved computers that could process and store vast amounts of data, which could then be used to train translation systems. Google Translate is one system that is based on such an approach. It still makes mistakes, particularly with language pairs that are structurally very different, such as English and Japanese, but it more often than not provides users with basically acceptable approximations. And already now Google Translate and Microsoft's Bing Translator and DeepL Translate are capable of producing near-perfect translations since the software can be assisted by 'deep learning' from digital neural networks. In fact, neural-net-based computer translation systems are to date the most promising development: for example, Google uses for instance a neural-net-based engine for eight language pairs. It is, of course, most efficient in the case of closely related European languages, where a large volume of training data is already available. However, the truth is that fully automated, high-quality computerized translation is still not possible today. Current approaches proceed clause by clause; long clauses as well as preceding co-text still create problems. The best results in the use of computerized translation systems can be achieved today in the case of highly specialized textual domains, such as medicine, engineering, law, etc. Extremely useful in such clearly defined fields are also so-called translation memories, i.e., software which stores textual chunks previously translated by human beings. Translation memories are now employed as standard with recurring routine materials.

To summarize, currently available computerized translation systems are today constantly being improved upon. They are based on empirical findings of research into the human translation process, i.e., documented translation behaviours and insights from expert human translators. In this way, computers are today enabled to imitate typical translation strategies employed by human translators and programmed to consistently learn from them. This new translation expertise that computers now have is the manifestation of their power of 'deep learning' – an artificial intelligence technique, in which a software system is trained using billions of examples, usually taken from the Internet and cloud storage. Deep learning empowers computers so that they are now nearly equal to humans in computerized translation systems, and they improve rapidly. Some people even predict that computerized simultaneous translation systems may soon render the need to learn a foreign language superfluous...

So, we can ask: will maximally improved software make human translators redundant in the near future? At the present time, this is not likely, certainly not for every kind of text. Computer-mediated translation will continue to be highly useful for translations of specialized texts, where content and form are routinized and predictable. This is the case, for instance, for business communication, such as market reports, documents detailing goods, sales and financial statistics or technical texts replete with highly specialized terminology. However, when it comes to literary texts and other texts based on creative writing, it seems difficult to imagine that computers will completely replace human translators in the near future. Connotative meanings, cultural associations and a strong reliance on contextual cues make it unlikely that this will happen in the foreseeable future.

For the practising translator, the development in computerized translation means that her professional profile will gradually change in that she will have to devote considerably more time to pre- and post-editing of texts.

TRANSLATION AS A CROSS-CULTURAL AND AN INTERCULTURAL PHENOMENON

The idea of 'difference' lies at the heart of translation, and this difference not only relates to the two languages involved in acts of translation but also relates to the two cultures in which these languages are embedded. So we can say that translation is also an act of communication across cultures. Languages are culturally anchored in that they both express and shape cultural reality. The meanings of linguistic units – words, phrases, paragraphs, texts – can only be properly understood when considered within the cultural context in which they come to be used. So in translation, not only two languages but also two cultures come into contact, and translation can then be defined as a kind of intercultural communication (see here for instance Bührig et al. 2009). In translating, we need to pay attention to conventions that are shared or not shared in the source and target cultures, and to take account of how culture-determined conventions and knowledge sets characterize the two languages involved in translation. The translator needs to be aware of differences in conventionalized meanings that derive from their cultural embeddedness. As a simple example take the meanings of certain dates that derive their particular meaning from the historical tradition in a particular country: 11 November in the UK, 3 October in Germany, 28 October in Greece, etc. These dates are linked to important events that belong to the 'cultural memory' of a nation. As such, they do not travel freely across different languages. The translator may either need to add a brief explanation or try to find an 'equivalent' date in the target culture. There are of course many such culturally embedded items in texts to be translated. These items not only include all culturally embedded idioms but also expressions that relate, for instance, to particular sports fashionable in one culture but virtually unknown in another: for example, the many expressions related to cricket in the English language that have no equivalent expressions in other languages; or references to particular customs – putting out stockings on Christmas Eve in the Anglophone countries or references to well-known fairy tales and the canon of classic literature in one culture unknown in another. The translator needs to be aware of the cultural associations and implications of the language used in the original text, and she needs to understand the cultural context in which the translated text is to live. We will look more closely at the role of culture in translation in Chapter 4.

THE GROWTH OF TRANSLATION PRACTICES WORLDWIDE

Translation is today more important than ever before. Just as globalization has had an enormous impact on the world economy, on international relations in science and politics, so translation has also experienced a boost beyond expectation. Translation is used today to enable fast and efficient information distribution, and more than ever before, it relies on new technologies that promote a worldwide translation industry. Translation plays a crucial role in multilingual news writing for international press networks, television channels, the Internet, the World Wide Web, social media, blogs, Wikis, etc. The BBC, Al Jazeera International, Deutsche Welle, Press TV and many other globally and multilingually operating TV channels today heavily rely on messages being translated simultaneously into many different languages. Whenever information input needs to be quickly disseminated across the world in different languages, translations are indispensable. Translation is also essential for the ever-increasing global tourism industry, and for the worldwide information flow in globalized companies, where the idea that information available in a local language will substantially improve sales potentials has of course boosted translation activities.

There is also an ever-growing demand for translation in what is called **'localization'**, i.e., adapting a product to the local conditions of the receiving linguacultural community. Software localization covers diverse industrial, commercial and scientific activities ranging from CD productions, engineering, testing software applications to managing complex team projects simultaneously in many countries and languages. Translations are needed in all of these. Indeed, translation is part and parcel of all worldwide localization and glocalization processes. In order to make a product available in many different languages, it must be effectively localized via translation. Producing a localized version of a product is essential for opening up new markets across the world, since immediate access to information about a product in a local language increases its initial demand. An important offshoot here is the design of localized advertising, again involving massive translation activity. Translation can thus be said to lie at the very heart of the global economy today: it tailors products to meet the needs of local markets everywhere in processes of glocalization.

Translation is also increasingly propelled by the World Wide Web, whose development has spread the need for translation into e-commerce globalization. And the steady increase of non-English speaking Web users naturally also boosts translation.

Another important factor contributing to the ever-growing importance of translation is e-learning. The expansion of digital industries centred around e-learning and other education forms spread over the Web in many different languages again shows the intimate link between translation and today's global economy. In sum, globalization has led to a veritable explosion of demand for translation. Translation is therefore not simply a by-product of globalization: it is an integral part of globalization in the modern world.

TRANSLATION COMPETENCE

Now that we have some idea of what translation is all about, and how it has developed over time, let us briefly look at what it means for a person to be able to translate and to become and be a competent translator.

First of all, we can say that in order to know how to translate and how to be competent in translating, a person needs at the very least to possess linguistic knowledge of the source language and the target language involved in the act of translation, i.e., she needs to be bilingual. However, this is not enough; clearly, not everybody who is bilingual can also translate. In what follows, we will look at what else a person needs to know and be able to do in order to be a competent translator (see here, for instance, Göpferich and Jääskeläinen 2009).

COMPONENTS OF TRANSLATION COMPETENCE

Translation competence encompasses three elements: first, source language receptive competence, i.e., a translator's ability to understand the source text; second, an ability to transfer the message from the source language to the target language; and third, a mastery of target linguistic resources. In other words, not only does a translator need to know his two languages, he must also have the ability to transform a source text into a target text. Necessary for translation are therefore three basic skills: source text processing skills, transfer skills and target text-related skills. To this basic tripartite competence, we can add other components, such as extra-linguistic

DOI: 10.4324/9781003355823-3

competence, professional competence, strategic competence and cultural competence. What one may call the 'core translation competence' is often said to refer to **'transfer competence'**. And it is this transfer competence which distinguishes a translator from a bilingual person: translation competence is essentially about mediating *between* two languages and cultures rather than simply knowing and being competent *in* two languages and cultures. While bilingual competence is a prerequisite for translation competence, the latter always contains a crucial added bit, i.e., transfer competence. Put differently, a translator needs to possess bilingual *and* interlingual skills over and above competence in the source and target languages. While languages are the raw material with which translators need to conduct their work, knowledge of this raw material is clearly not sufficient for what the translator needs to know because she is working **between two languages**.

For a translator to be competent in working **between** two languages, she needs to be aware of lexico-grammatical and pragmatic differences and similarities between the two languages she is dealing with in translation (see here already Wilss 1996). This includes knowledge and awareness of language use in discourse, i.e., a translator needs to be aware of the role of context in language use, of register and genre similarities and differences between the two languages; she needs to be aware of the rules of textual coherence and cohesion in the two languages. And over and above all this, the crucial transfer competence needs to be added, i.e., knowledge and awareness of the equivalence relationships between the two languages. The latter is a prerequisite for being able to appropriately match units of the two languages in acts of translating. This is very different from an individual's competence in using the source and target languages individually, this bilingual competence is merely the starting point in the journey towards what we may call transfer competence that lies at the heart of translation competence.

A BILINGUAL PERSON IS NOT AUTOMATICALLY A COMPETENT TRANSLATOR

A frequently heard lay opinion is that all bilingual persons can translate because they all 'naturally' possess translation competence within the limits of an individual's competence in the two languages. This idea can also be traced back to Brian Harris (1976), who coined the terms 'natural translation' and 'natural translator'. Harris believed that for bilingual persons, translation is a sort of natural, innate skill just as the acquisition of bilingual children's two languages is innate. Harris got his ideas from observing young bilingual immigrant children who, when needed, would frequently, spontaneously and in an entirely unsophisticated manner act as 'language brokers' for their families and friends in simple everyday situations. Everyday situations where one is called upon to translate personal letters, instructions, etc. do not demand more than a low level transfer competence with which a bilingual person can normally make sure the message gets across. Bilingual persons produce here what one may call a 'version' of the original text (see Chapter 7). In general, one can say that bilingual individuals clearly have a predisposition for translation, a natural capacity for translating. Bilingualism may thus be called a necessary, but never a sufficient condition for fully developed translation competence.

True translation competence as exhibited by professional translators embodies transfer and interlingual text production competence, and it results from a kind of 'cognitive interspace', i.e., a constant mental interaction of the two linguistic systems in the translator's mind. It also involves a constant monitoring of the similarities and differences at all levels of language.

TRANSLATION COMPETENCE IS CONTEXT- AND SITUATION-DEPENDENT

Translation competence does not operate in a void. Just as acts of translation need to be seen as embedded in a situation where the translation happens, so a translator's competence needs to be judged with reference to the demands made by the context of the translation situation. Such a view is in line with the model for assessing translation quality to which you will be introduced in Chapter 7. So to develop translation competence from the rudimentary competence in 'natural translation' with which bilinguals are normally endowed would involve widening the range of contexts of situation in which an individual produces a translation that fulfils a certain communicative function. In other words, experiencing exposure to an ever-growing range of translation situations is of crucial importance for developing translation competence. A situation-driven approach to translation competence thus means that the scope of contexts which a translator is competent to handle is maximally increased. Such a view is also in line with current ideas of the development of linguistic competence in a second language which stresses the benefit of experiencing the broadest possible range of contexts of situation in which a language is used and reflected upon, and where similarities and differences between one's mother tongue and the new language need to be 'noticed' and registered.

The notion of 'situation' is thus crucial for fully grasping what translation competence involves. Translation situations create certain expectations on the part of the addressees of a translation. 'Situation' covers a multitude of items that can have an influence on the act of translation and its reception by addressees: the agents involved, the function of the translation, existing norms and constraints, etc. The more complex a translation situation is, the more complex the task will become for the translator. Simple informal everyday translation situations, for example, involve fewer constraints on the translation to be produced. Lexico-grammatical correctness, for instance, is here less important than it would be in the case of a translation of a legal contract.

THE IMPORTANCE OF KNOWLEDGE IN TRANSLATION COMPETENCE

Translation competence also includes knowledge and awareness of extra-linguistic phenomena which include knowledge of the world, knowledge of a special field, ability to search for information, ability to use different translation tools, socio-cultural knowledge, knowledge of cultural similarities and differences relevant to the translation situation on hand.

We have seen how important the factor 'knowledge' is in translation competence. Knowledge is a property of the human mind, and in order to fully understand translation competence, we need to understand how knowledge is acquired, stored, accessed and retrieved in the human mind. The most famous assumption about knowledge in cognitive psychology is the division into declarative and procedural knowledge originally suggested by Anderson (1976).

Declarative knowledge is knowledge *that* something is the case; it refers to factual information. It is use-independent and embodies theories, concepts, principles, ideas and schemata. It belongs to long-term memory. **Procedural knowledge**, on the other hand, is knowledge of *how* to do something. Procedural knowledge is knowledge used in the performance of some specific task, and it is linked to the particular situation in which it is applied. Procedural knowledge occurs in executing a skill that is situation- and context-specific; it is use-specific and consists of associations between situations, goals and actions. Procedural knowledge complements declarative knowledge.

To understand the knowledge base assumed to underlie translation competence, it is fruitful to go deeper than this standard dichotomy between declarative and procedural knowledge. With particular reference to translation, we may distinguish between knowledge types that can be made explicit and those that are left implicit or tacit. **Explicit knowledge** refers to knowledge about translation, about theories of translation, ethics, norms of professional practices, etc. but also to specific subject or special-field knowledge as well as general and language-pair specific intercultural knowledge. For professional special-field translators, it is essential to have as much special-field knowledge at their fingertips as possible, although they are, of course, never really specialists in a specific field, acquiring just as much knowledge as they need for the translation of a particular text.

Another type of explicit knowledge a translator needs is constantly updated knowledge of translation technology. Many translation tasks nowadays must be carried out with a specific translation memory tool designed to assist the translator in making her translation more efficient, saving time and effort. The reader is here referred back to the discussion of computer-mediated translation in Chapter 1.

Implicit or tacit knowledge refers to knowledge that is gained through experience and is difficult to define in precise terms. It develops together with experience in many different situations of language in use in translational situations. Implicit knowledge often leads a translator into automatic performances because of repeated and thus routinized instances of transfer.

Another type of knowledge is **intuitive knowledge** which may also be referred to as 'Sprachgefühl' (German for 'a feeling about language') which is even harder to grasp or define than tacit knowledge. Intuitive knowledge arises out of a sense of appropriateness of language use in certain social situations.

A third important part of the knowledge component necessary for translation is **metacognition** and **monitoring**. This is knowledge which subtly controls the translator's activity, regulating deficiencies and correcting her performance. Important in this respect is the capability to conduct systematic information search which the translator needs in case she initially lacks specific knowledge in a given translation situation. A translator needs sufficient information search knowledge in order to compensate for any gaps she recognizes in her knowledge.

An individual translator's knowledge base is of course highly personal, based on his prior experiences and the cumulative experiences he has gone through as a practising translator. And a translator's knowledge is always dynamic and open to being reorganized as the need for such reshuffling arises through recognition of knowledge gaps of various kinds. In case of difficulties with understanding some parts of the source text, a translator may need to resort to online dictionaries; in case of comprehension difficulties due to technicalities of the source text's special subject, the translator may turn to texts in a comparable text corpus or ask subject field experts for their opinion. Whenever the translator is uncertain about the use of special terminology, she may use parallel corpora for information about the use of lexical and textual conventions as well as connotations in the special field. For all these tasks, the translator needs to possess digital and information literacy.

An optimal combination of the various knowledge components necessary for translation should result in a highly developed strategic competence on the part of the translator. Such strategic competence is equivalent to the translator's ability to make optimal use of a combination of the different knowledge types in the target text production in a specific translation situation.

If the knowledge accrued by a translator is to be readily available for use in her manifold translation tasks, it needs to be 'proceduralized', i.e., converted into translational skill in handling actual translation situations. Translational skill is thus, in a way, the other side of the coin of translational competence. While the knowledge base making up translational competence cannot be observed, translational skill in actual acts of translation can.

EMPIRICAL RESEARCH ON TRANSLATION COMPETENCE

In relation to the acquisition and evaluation of translation competence, the PACTE Group (Process of Acquisition of Translation Competence and Evaluation) (see, for instance, PACTE 2009, 2011) has for a number of years been conducting empirical-experimental research into translation competence and its acquisition as well as translation directionality. Data have been collected on both the translation process and translation products with translations in both directions involving the languages English, German, French, Spanish and Catalan. By comparing measurements between groups of competent professional translators and groups of language teachers in tasks of translations into and out of a foreign language, the PACTE Group found significant differences in translation competence between these two groups. And the concept of a 'dynamic' approach to translation developed by the PACTE group was seen as an important characteristic of translation competence. They understood 'dynamic' as textual, communicative and functional. And they also found that there is a close link between this dynamic approach to translation and the acceptability of the final translated product.

In summary and to conclude, translation competence can be conceptualized as a dynamic transfer and interlingual text production competence gained through experience in manifold translation situations and relying on a multifaceted, ever-growing knowledge base which the translator needs to put into practice such that it becomes a workable skill. The more experience a translator has in as wide a repertoire of situations as possible, the more automatic and routinized her performance will become thanks to her highly developed translational skill, leaving room for the more creative parts of her tasks to be optimally carried out.

LOOKING AT TRANSLATION FROM DIFFERENT PERSPECTIVES

In this chapter, we will look at how translation scholars have viewed and explained the phenomenon of translation. The chapter also gives a critical account of several influential approaches and translation schools.

GIVING PRIORITY TO LANGUAGE AND LINGUISTICS IN TRANSLATION

From a linguistic perspective, an important characteristic of a translation is its specific relationship to a source text. Translation is embedded in the paradoxical situation that the translator is in one and the same situation both speaker and non-speaker. In the translation situation, the translation is the translator's utterance, but at the same time *not* his utterance. So the translator is never really autonomous in formulating her utterance, rather she is bound in a particular way to the source text. And this tie to the source text is indeed particular to translation.

Following the Czech-American linguist Roman Jakobson (1959), a distinction is often made between intersemiotic translation ('translation' between different semiotic systems), intralingual translation (commenting, paraphrasing, summarizing, changing the style of a text and so on) and interlingual translation. The latter type is the one which is commonly understood as translation or 'translation proper'.

One of the earliest schools of translation studies in the Western world is the Leipzig school of 'translation science', as it was called.

DOI: 10.4324/9781003355823-4

It originated in the 1950s in the East German city of Leipzig and was from its inception a strongly linguistically oriented school of translation. Many of the terms and concepts which Leipzig scholars developed have influenced translation studies to this day. It is interesting to note that some of the early insights of the Leipzig scholars coincide with the ideas independently developed by scholars in Britain, the United States and France. Unfortunately, the work of the Leipzig school was not recognized early on due to the Iron Curtain and the Cold War that lasted until the late 1980s.

In the Leipzig school of translation, translation was regarded as an act of bilingual communication where the translator as 'the person in the middle' is mediating between a sender (the original author) and a receiver (the reader of the translated text) who, as a rule, does not know the language in which the original text is written. Under the influence of the then emerging discipline of sociolinguistics, the early focus of Leipzig scholars on system-based linguistics soon turned to the embeddedness of original and translated texts in different socio-cultural situations. Such a focus led to a communicative conception of the notion of 'equivalence', which implies that texts differ in terms of their communicative value in the contexts of the source and target linguacultures. Communicative equivalence was also often called 'functional equivalence'. Functional equivalence means that two texts are equivalent – but of course never identical – in their semantic and pragmatic meanings, including the structuring of the information to be conveyed.

Functional equivalence was also understood to hold whenever the translation of a text that belongs to a certain text type and a concrete communicative situation has the same communicative effect as the source text. Text type was recognized as overridingly important in helping translators decide whether their translations should be faithful to the original or rather appropriately adapted to the conventionalized text types in the target language community.

Another lasting influence in linguistically oriented translation studies was text linguistics. Text linguistics has its roots in the study of rhetoric, a branch of knowledge that, since Aristotle, has dealt with the means by which language is tailored to a certain situation and to specific addressee(s). As a system for producing texts, rhetoric traditionally comprised a number of different phases, such as *inventio*, in which ideas suitable for a certain purpose were discovered in a text producer's mind, *dispositio*, whereby these ideas were ordered to fit the text producers' intention, or *elocutio*, involving the realization of ordered thoughts with appropriate linguistic expressions. We need to keep this tradition in mind, since it links with many later developments in linguistics and stylistics, speech act theory and linguistic pragmatics that have strongly influenced translation studies later on. In general, one could not stress enough the importance of the discipline of linguistics and applied linguistics (House et al. 2022) for translation and translators as well as students of translation.

Influential in the framework of text linguistics has been the work of de Beaugrande and Dressler (1981). In trying to determine what it is that makes a text a text, i.e., a unified meaningful whole rather than a mere string of unrelated words and sentences, they set up seven standards of textuality: cohesion, coherence, intentionality, acceptability, informativity, situationality and intertextuality. These were later famously picked up and made relevant for translation by translation scholars Hatim and Mason (1990, 1997), and can be briefly characterized as follows. **Cohesion** is the network of lexico-grammatical and other relations that link various parts of a text. These relations organize a text by requiring readers to interpret expressions by reference to other expressions in the surrounding linguistic environment. **Coherence** is the network of conceptual relations that underlie the 'surface text'. It expresses the logical consistency of the sentences in a text in terms of content. While cohesion is a feature of the text, coherence relates to a reader's response to the text. The coherence of a text is the result of the interaction between knowledge presented in the text and readers' own knowledge and experience of the world. While **cohesion** and **coherence** are to a large extent text-centred, **intentionality** is clearly user-centred, referring to the purpose a text producer intends. **Acceptability** is equally user-centred, but relates not to the text producer but to the addressees and their socio-cultural background, which predisposes them to 'accept' a text as coherent and cohesive on the basis of their ability to infer missing items. **Informativity** refers to new information presented in a text or to information that was unknown before, and **situationality** concerns the relationship of a text to a particular socio-temporal and local context. Finally, **intertextuality** is the relation between a given text and other relevant texts encountered in previous experience – obviously highly relevant for a translator.

Several of these textuality standards imply that in producing and understanding texts in translation, one must go beyond language and look at a text's psychological and social basis. So a text needs also to be viewed as a cognitive process that underlies its production and comprehension. Characteristic of this strand of text linguistics is its dynamic view of a text as part and parcel of human psychological and social activities. There is of course a great affinity between this paradigm and the practice of translation, the latter being never solely concerned with texts as linguistic strings but also with the human beings involved in selecting, comprehending, reconstituting and evaluating texts. On this view, then, the nature of a text is not found in the text itself as a static, independently existing artefact, rather one must look at the kinds of actions translators can perform with a text as a communicative event. Especially influential in this paradigm of text linguistics have been models of cognitive-semantic relationships in the form of scripts, plans, schemata or frames in the human mind – concepts that go back to early twentieth-century psychological Gestalt Theory as well as Piaget's developmental psychological work. More recently, models of cognitive-neurological networks have been suggested, where general mental activities together with lower level text linguistic activities are assumed to shed light on translation processes.

Other early, unfortunately often ignored in Western translation studies, linguistically oriented studies of translation were conducted in Russia by Fedorov (1958) and in the Prague school of Functional Linguistics with its emphasis on so-called functional styles. One of the members of the Prague school was Roman Jakobson (1959) who, following his move to the United States, made a seminal contribution to the linguistically oriented view of translation in the late 1950s.

The most important early complete linguistic theory of translation was presented by J. C. Catford (1965). For Catford, meaning cannot be simply transferred from a source text to a translated text. Rather, meanings can only be replaced by something different but equivalent, such that the target text with its new meanings can function in a comparable way in the new context. While the idea of a transference of meaning implies that meaning is actually *contained* in the original text that can then somehow be 'taken out' and then given a new and different expression in another language. Catford's idea of replacement suggests that a text's meaning is a function of the relationship between the text and its context, and can thus only be replaced by somehow replicating this crucial relationship. The recognition that it is only through relating linguistic items to their context of situation that meaning replacement can take place, was indeed very new at the time. Catford is thus a pioneer in applying a functional-linguistic theory to translation, the basis of which is the assumption that translation is possible because both original and translated texts can be relatable to functionally relevant features of the socio-cultural situation that envelops the two texts.

Catford also made a distinction between what he called **'formal correspondence'** and **'textual equivalence'** in translation. Formal correspondence is a matter of the language system, and textual equivalence concerns the realization of that system in an actual situation. Formal correspondence between linguistic units in the original and its translation exists when a target language category has approximately the same position in its system of langue as the corresponding category in the source language. However, in many cases involving very different languages, translation shifts will be necessary. Such shifts involve departures from formal correspondence using shifts from lexis to grammar or grammar to lexis. For example, translations of English verbal aspects into German commonly involve shifts from grammar to lexis. For instance, the clause 'She was leaving the house, when the telephone rang' would normally be translated as 'Sie ging gerade aus dem Haus, als das Telefon klingelte', where the English aspectual form is expressed by the German lexical item *gerade*.

Another influential early functional-linguistic theory of translation is Eugene Nida's (1964) and Nida and Taber's (1969) account of translation. They stated that 'Translating consists in reproducing in the receptor language the closest natural equivalent of the source-language message, first in terms of meaning and secondly in terms of style' (Nida and Taber 1969:12). Important here are both the emphasis on the source-language message and its style, and the recognition of the importance of the language of the receptors, specifically that the chosen equivalent renderings be 'natural'. The authors further state that in the process of translation the translator

> first analyses the message of the source language into its simplest and structurally clearest forms, transfers it at this level, and then restructures it to the level in the receptor language which is most appropriate for the audience which he intends to reach.
>
> (Nida and Taber 1969:484)

Nida's interest in translation stems from Bible translation. In his view, translation is first and foremost an act that is directed at certain readers or 'recipients', whose different knowledge sets, cultural conventions and expectation norms need to be taken into account in translation. In Nida's view, only when a translated text is adapted to the needs of the new recipients can it have the effect intended by the author. But despite the necessity of adaptation, the original message still remains important and must be somehow maintained in the translation – clearly a dilemma. In order to resolve this dilemma, Nida identified two different measures for making and evaluating a translation: **formal equivalence** and **dynamic equivalence**. Nida suggested a three-phase process – analysis, transfer and reconstruction. He suggested that the message presented in the source language is first linguistically analysed and broken down into observable grammatical relationships and the meanings of individual words as well as word combinations. The translator then mentally transfers this analysed material from the source language to the target language. Finally, the translator restructures the transferred material so as to make the message adequate for reception by the intended readers in the target language.

The early linguistic approaches described above can all be characterized by a focus on the original text to be translated, and the idea that this original text undergoes analysis, transfer and remodelling in the process of translation. In linguistically oriented translation approaches, the original text is important in that one needs to analyse it in detail and systematically link its forms and functions to reveal the original author's motivated choices.

FOCUSING ON LITERARY AND CULTURAL SYSTEMS

Literary texts make special demands on the translator, and the translation of literary texts is often described as an art that defies generalization. However, **literary translation** has also featured as a subject of detailed empirical description with existing literary translations. Translations are here viewed as part of the system of the receiving national literature.

One of the best-known theories of literary translation is the so-called **Polysystem Theory** (see Even-Zohar 1990), which regarded literature as a system functioning in the larger social, literary and historical systems of the target culture. Polysystem theory originated in Israel and built on ideas from the literary theories developed in Russia and Czechoslovakia in the first half of the twentieth century. The key concept here is the idea of a 'system' in which an ongoing dynamic of change occurs in a culture's literary canon. Translated literature is considered to make up a system in itself in the way members of the target culture select works to be translated and in the way translation norms are influenced by other co-existing systems in the cultural polysystem. The position of translated literature is not fixed; it may have a primary or secondary position in the polysystem. If it is primary, it is often innovative and linked to important events or a period in the literary history of the target culture; translations then become key players influencing the centre of the literary polysystem, creating new models, techniques, stylistic conventions and poetics for the target literature. Examples of a situation where translated literature attains an important position in the target culture are cases where:

1. young' target literature is being newly established and looks for models in more established literatures (an example is Hebrew literature in the newly founded state of Israel);
2. the target literature is 'peripheral' and lacks standing such that the need for more established traditions arises (an example is Galician literature importing from Spanish literature); and
3. a vacuum seems to exist in the literature of the target country (examples are the genre of science fiction imported into many other national literatures via translation, or the genre of the self-help book from American English).

The position which translated literature takes up in the target culture determines the translation strategies used by translators. If the translated literature takes on a primary position, translators tend to come up with a target text that is close to the original text, thus introducing new conventions into the target culture. If the translated literature occupies a secondary position, translators will fashion their translation according to existing target culture norms. Polysystem theory made important contributions to translation studies in the area of literary translation in that it looked not only at isolated individual texts but rather fitted these texts into an entire literary system in its more encompassing historical and socio-historical context.

A predominantly comparative literature-oriented, but also target text-oriented, approach to translation grew out of the work of a group of translation scholars who focused on the position and function of translations in the totality of the target language literature. This approach has come to be known as '**descriptive translation studies**'. The late Gideon Toury (2012), a major proponent of this approach, starts from the assumption that a translation is to be taken as any target language utterance presented or regarded as such within the target culture, on whatever ground. The existence of a source text that served as a basis for the translation is here tacitly assumed.

Descriptive translation studies scholars suggest approaching translation analyses in three steps:

1. placing the translated text inside the target socio-cultural system and determining its acceptability and significance;
2. analysing both source text and translated text so as to identify obligatory and non-obligatory deviations – or translation shifts – of the target text from the source text; and
3. arriving at tentative generalizations about the nature of the translation process in this particular source and translation text pair. This generalization might then be extended to pairs of similar texts leading to a gradual building up of a corpus of translated texts with which to identify certain 'norms of translation'.

Another literature-oriented translation school with close connections to comparative literature was set up in the 1970s and 1980s in

Belgium and the Netherlands, which suggested analysing literary translations in detailed case studies and then drawing theoretical conclusions with reference to literature and society in general. The most famous publication connected with this school is Theo Hermans' anthology with the telling title *The Manipulation of Literature: Studies in Literary Translation* (1985). Hermans suggested that all literary translations – from the point of view of the target literature – imply degrees of manipulation of the original text for a certain purpose. Literary translation which involves necessary manipulation is to be given an important status as it has always been a major force not only in shaping the target literature but also in developing a world culture.

Another literature-oriented approach to translation focuses on the process of interpretation of the source text by a reader and her subjective understanding of the text given her personal background, knowledge of the world, knowledge of specific domains and genres, etc. Eminent scholars such as George Steiner (1975) have propagated this '**hermeneutic school of translation**'. In understanding and interpreting a text, readers actively engage in making their personal sense of the text. This means that texts do not have a life of their own, they are only brought to life ('constructed') in the process of understanding and interpretation by a reader. And in the process of translation, the translator 'as first reader appropriates' the meaning of the text, constructing an individual mental representation of the text's meaning which she then reformulates in the target language. What is of prime importance is the (constructed) representation of the text in the translator's mind. The translator as understander and interpreter of the original text is given pride of place, and his creativity reigns supreme.

In interpreting an original text, a translator engages in a cyclical interpretation process, from the text to its interpretation and back again. This cycle will finally lead to a so-called melting of horizons between the person of the translator and the text she is interpreting. In the neo-hermeneutic tradition it is also often stated that a translator 'identifies' with the message of the text, because it is only through such an act of 'identification' that a translator can be successful (see here, for instance, Vermeer 1994). Understanding and interpreting an original text and the ensuing process of translation are seen as individual creative acts that defy systematization, generalization and rule giving. And there is no objectively restitut-able meaning of a text. On this view, then, translation appears to be, in the last analysis, an intimate and private affair.

STRESSING THE SOCIO-CULTURAL CONTEXT OF TRANSLATION: POST-MODERNIST, POST-COLONIAL, POST-STRUCTURALIST AND FUNCTIONALISTIC VIEWS

Translation scholars in these mostly cultural and literary studies inspired approaches look at translation from the outside, so to speak, i.e., from philosophical, psychological, political or sociological viewpoints. The main idea here is to discover and unmask ideolog-ical twists and unequal power relations reflected, for instance, in translation directions from and into English as a 'hegemonic lan-guage' or in consistent (and wilful) misrepresentation of the beliefs and conventions of non-mainstream, marginalized parts of the pop-ulation of a country, such as refugees, migrants, women or ethnic minorities. Other domains of interest include complaints about the undeservedly insignificant status of translator, her 'invisibility' (Venuti 1992, 1995), and an attempt to make transparent hidden processes of selecting texts for translation (and omitting others) and the (often also hidden) reasons for, and effects of, favoured strategies of translation. Translation theories are also critically reviewed and translation exemplars are scrutinized as to whether they perpetrate 'imperialism' and lack critical assessments of a country's colonial past. Thus, translation scholars embracing post-colonial translation studies (see here, for instance, Bassnett and Trivedi 2002; Robinson 2014) look upon (mainly literary) translations as sites of necessary intervention mirroring the intersection of language and power, and they set out to explain new perspectives on translation with regard to post-colonial societies in the Americas, Asia and Africa.

In the opinion of members of a group of **post-modern trans-lation** scholars following the Brazilian cannibalistic theories of lit-erary transfer designed by the revolutionary Brazilian poet and 'translator-cum-transcreator' Haroldo de Campos, for instance, translating means devouring the original, cannibalizing, hijacking, transforming and 'transcreating' it such that the original text is 'eaten up' and the boundaries and hierarchies between original and translation tend to disappear (see, for instance, Vieira 1999). The translator, vampire-like, takes the original as his nourishment, and in losing his former self-effacing role acquires a more important role as 'trans-textualizer' and creator of something new.

Post-structuralist scholars have often been inspired by Walter Benjamin's ideas about translation in his famous essay 'Die Aufgabe des Übersetzers' (1923) (The Task of the Translator), arguing that it is from its important function of providing an 'afterlife', that a translation gains its true value. Neither original nor translation can be thought of as constituting some kind of coherent semantic unity, rather they embody sets of different pluralistic meanings. Further, as the French philosopher Jacques Derrida (1985) famously maintained, the dichotomy of 'original' versus 'translation' needs to be 'deconstructed'. (Readers interested in a different position may look at the critique of Derrida's stance by the American philosopher and linguist John Searle 1977.)

Even the notion of 'original author' is often deconstructed, such that the author of a text is not conceived of as an actual, living person but as a series of 'subjective positions', characterized by breaches and discontinuities (see here, for instance, Foucault 1977). The author's creative role is thrown into doubt, as is the origin of any particular text.

In much of post-modern and post-structuralist thinking, an attempt has been made to upgrade the status of the translator, elevating him to the status of an original author. However, such blurring of the relationship between author and translator is more complex. One can make a distinction between the roles of animator, author and principal, following the sociologist Erving Goffman (for instance 1974, 1981), where it is only the role of 'principal' that carries ethical responsibility with it. Given this 'deconstruction' of the concept of authorship, clearly there is a difference between authors of original texts and translators of these texts.

An influential offshoot of post-modern and **post-structuralist thinking**, and in particular the idea of increasing the visibility of the translator, is feminist translation studies (see here, for instance, Simon 1996; von Flotow 1997). The main idea here is that female translators (but not only these) should no longer be reticent about openly showing their gendered voice in translation. Translators are urged to proudly accept their identity and its ideological implications and to feel liberated enough to 'subvert' passages in texts they are to translate which run counter to a feminist stance, always acting against 'invisibilization' and 'essentialization'.

Debates about gender and translation have a long history and often reach back into the history of ideas and civilization, where the foundations of current gender relations are to be found in ancient philosophical and religious works. The Bible and the Qur'an, which to this day set norms and rules of gender relations, have been translated numerous times into many different languages. These translations are then used to provide rules for managing human sexual differences in different countries (for further discussion see here von Flotow and Scott 2016).

Another school of translation in which the larger context of a translation plays an important role is functionalistic and action- and reception-theory. These approaches can be summed up as follows: the most important thing for any translation is the purpose of a translation, often also called the **Skopos.** Given the primacy of this purpose, it follows that the end of a translational action justifies the means. A translation counts as a 'felicitous action' when it is interpreted by an intended recipient as sufficiently coherent for her situation. Given the crucial role of the purpose of a translation, the original is of minor, secondary importance, it is 'de-throned', in fact, it is reduced to a mere offer of information, which implies that it can be accepted, rejected or changed and 'improved' as the translator sees fit. The translator is given an important new role of 'co-author', and here we see the affinity of this approach with the post-modern, post-structuralist ideas about translation.

In functionalistic views of translation, **'function'** is equated with the real-world effect of a text in a certain context. This target-oriented focus on the real-world effect of a text goes hand in hand with a relativistic view of the meaning of the original text, which is in fact assumed to emanate from the minds of the readers of the translation. As opposed to the literary theorists who focused exclusively on literary texts and their translations, functionalistic translation theorists mostly turn their attention to texts designed for quick consumption, such as advertisements, instructions, leaflets, manuals, tourist brochures, business correspondence, sales slips and the like, which may indeed have so little 'core-value' that they can easily be completely re-fashioned for new recipients.

VIEWING TRANSLATION AS AN ACT OF RE-CONTEXTUALIZATION

Looking at translation as an act of **re-contextualization** means viewing it as a stretch of contextually embedded language. We can assume that whenever communication is possible between speakers of the same language, it is also possible between speakers of different languages, and for the same fundamental reasons, i.e., through relating a text to the enveloping **'context of situation'** (Malinowski 1935 and see House 2016). For a theory of translation as re-contextualization to be valid, it has to fulfil at least the following three criteria regarding the relationship between text and context:

1. it has to explicitly account for the fact that source and translation texts relate to different contexts;
2. it has to be able to capture, describe and explain changes necessitated by the act of re-contextualization with a suitable metalanguage;
3. it has to explicitly relate features of the source text and features of the translation to one another and to their different contexts.

For a view of translation as re-contextualization, the context-oriented approaches of discourse, pragmatic and functional analyses are particularly important for translation (see here, for instance, Baker 1992/2011; Steiner 1998, 2004; Mason 2014). The historical roots of discourse analysis range from classical rhetoric, Russian formalism and French structuralism to semiotics. In the 1970s, discourse analysis began to establish itself as a discipline in its own right. It was influenced by sociolinguistics with its emphasis on language variation and the crucial role of the social context; speech act theory, where a discourse is seen as a form of social action and cooperative achievement such that a speaker's intention and her relationship with her addressee(s) are taken into account as added features of meaning; anthropology, where studies on the 'ethnography of speaking' link up with linguistics and stylistics – all these played an important part in widening our understanding of the role of discourse in human life.

Branches of discourse analysis that are of immediate relevance for translation are contrastive rhetoric and contrastive discourse analysis.

They compare underlying text conventions holding in different linguacultures and examine their influence on the production and comprehension of different discourse types. Cross-cultural discourse analysis examines discourse organization, use of cohesive devices and the presence of reader or writer perspective. Findings suggest differences in the sequencing of topical strands in texts (linear or circular), presence or absence of digressions and other marked arrangements of textual parts in different genres and languages. **Contrastive discourse analyses** are crucial for translation because they provide translators and translation evaluators with the necessary empirical foundation for explaining changes in the target text. There is a need for more language-pair specific contrastive discourse research. Translation studies would greatly benefit from its findings.

Another part of discourse studies that has had an important influence on translation studies for the past 20 years or so, is critical discourse analysis. Here, power relations and ideology and their influence on the content and structure of texts are regarded as of primary importance for the analysis of discourse.

Another important research field with high relevance for translation is contrastive pragmatics or cross-cultural pragmatics – a field which originated with the volume (Blum-Kulka et al. 1989) summarizing the results of the famous **cross-cultural speech act research project (CCSARP),** and which has seen many related studies up to the present day (for recent work see House and Kadar 2021). Contrastive Pragmatics and its relevance for translation has also recently been emphasized by Baumgarten (2022) and it can be found in many publications in the new (2022–) open access Brill journal *Contrastive Pragmatics. A Cross-Disciplinary Journal.*

The importance of the socio-cultural environment enveloping a text has been captured early on by the anthropologist Bronislaw Malinowski (1935) in his concept context of situation, which strongly influenced **British Contextualism**. The concept embraces the human participants in a situation, their verbal and non-verbal actions, the effect of these actions and other relevant features, objects and events. Detailed descriptions of the context of situation in which a given text functions involve the notions of Field (the general sense of what the text is about, its topic and social actions), Tenor (capturing the interpersonal and role relationships, the writer's stance and the participation of the addressees) and Mode (referring to the particular part played by the language used in the text, i.e., if and how a spoken or written medium is used, and how coherence and cohesion are manufactured). These categories have influenced what came to be known as Register, i.e., the variety of language according to use. Register is a semantic concept referring to configurations of meaning typically associated with particular situational constellations of **Field, Tenor and Mode**. In **Register analysis**, texts are related to context such that both are mutually predictable, the outcome being the isolation of different text types or genres. Register analysis has been fruitfully used in translation studies for several decades, as has systemic-functional analysis in general to the present day (see e.g. Kim et al. 2021; Wang and Ma 2022).

Other suggestions for types of texts – a popular quest in translation studies – have involved the concept of **'function of language'**. Many different views of functions of language have been proposed. Although they vary greatly, a basic distinction between an informative, cognitive function and an interpersonal function to do with the 'me' and 'you' of language use can be found in all functional classifications. Classifications of language functions were often used to devise 'text typologies' following the equation 'one function–one text type'. This equation has been very popular in translation studies, since it is often assumed that knowledge of a text type is an important prerequisite for effective translation procedures. However, preferable to any externally motivated text typology seems to be a view of a text as being in principle multifunctional (i.e., not embodying a predetermined function), such that each text is to be analysed and translated as an individual 'case', considered in its particular context of situation and culture on the basis of an explicit set of text linguistic procedures for describing and explaining how a text is what it is, how it fares in translation, and what the effect of the translation is in each individual case (see here, for instance, the discussion in Steiner 1998, 2004, and see the contributions in Kunz et al. 2021).

CULTURE AND IDEOLOGY IN TRANSLATION

This chapter presents some basic insights into the role of culture and ideology in translation.

In translation, it is not only different languages that are important but also different cultures and different ideological positions taken up by translators. Here, we will first look at the important concept of culture.

WHAT IS CULTURE?

The concept of '**culture**' has been the concern of many different disciplines, such as philosophy, sociology, anthropology, literature and cultural studies, and the definitions offered in these fields vary according to the particular frame of reference invoked. In 1952, Kroeber and Kluckhohn had collected 156 (!) definitions of culture; today such a list would undoubtedly be much longer. In all these attempts at coming to grips with the notion of 'culture', two basic views of culture have emerged: the humanistic concept of culture and the anthropological concept of culture. The humanistic concept of culture captures the 'cultural heritage' as a model of refinement, an exclusive collection of a community's masterpieces in literature, fine arts, music, etc. The anthropological concept of culture refers to the overall way of life of a community or society, i.e., all those traditional, explicit and implicit designs for living which act as potential guides for the behaviour of members of the culture (see here Geertz 1973). Culture in the anthropological sense captures a group's dominant and learned set of habits, as the totality of its non-biological

DOI: 10.4324/9781003355823-5

inheritance involves presuppositions, preferences and values – all of which are, of course, neither easily accessible nor verifiable. In what follows, the broad anthropological sense of culture will be pursued.

Culture has often been linked with language. For instance, linguists in the Prague school of linguistics or inside **British Contextualism** looked at language as primarily a social phenomenon, which is inextricably intertwined with culture. So language is viewed as embedded in culture such that the meaning of any bit of language can only be understood with reference to the cultural context enveloping it.

Four analytical levels on which culture has been characterized can be differentiated (House 2005; and see House and Kadar 2021, Chapter 1): the first one is the general human level, at which human beings differ from animals. Human beings, unlike animals, are capable of reflection, and they are able to creatively shape and change their environment. The second level is the societal, national level, culture being the unifying, binding force which enables human beings to position themselves vis-à-vis systems of government, domains of activities, religious beliefs and values in which human thinking expresses itself. The third level corresponds to the second level but captures various societal and national subgroups according to geographical region, social class, age, sex, professional activity and topic. The fourth level is the personal, individual one relating to the individual's guidelines for thinking and acting. This is the level of cultural consciousness, which enables a human being to be aware of what characterizes his or her own culture and makes it distinct from others.

CULTURE AND NATIONAL CHARACTERS, MENTALITIES, STEREOTYPES

Culture has been defined most succinctly (if a bit flippantly) by Hofstede (1980) as a type of collective programming of the human mind. Other scholars, such as Goodenough, proposed a more elaborate formulation which however 'old' it may seem to some is still essentially valid today:

> Whatever it is one has to know or believe in order to operate in a manner acceptable to its [i.e., a society's, J. H.] members, and do so in any role

> that they accept for any one of themselves [...] culture is not a material phenomenon; it does not consist of things, people, behaviour, or emotions. It is rather an organization of these things. It is the forms of things that people have in mind, their model of perceiving, relating, and otherwise interpreting them.

(Goodenough 1964:36)

In these two definitions, the important and recurrent aspects of culture are emphasized: the cognitive one guiding and monitoring human actions and the social one emphasizing traditional features shared by members of a society.

In the past, cultures have often been associated with race, ethnicity, nation or region, lending themselves to cultural stereotypes, national mentalities and national characters. This line of thinking was boosted after the Second World War when US American scholars tried to establish the nature of the German 'national character' characterized as 'the Authoritarian Personality' (cf. Adorno et al. 1950). Other roots of such understanding of culture are to be found in wars, colonization and missionizing efforts, military and diplomatic incursions, global business campaigns, and also so-called peace-research – all these displaying a fascination with 'the other'. Often readers were urged to discover 'rich points', 'hotspots' or 'critical incidents' i.e., points where culture members differ critically. Here, we find simplified accounts of culture, oblivious of real socio-cultural diversity, complexity hybridity, individuality and constant fluidity, often instrumentalized for the continued expansion of neo-liberal capitalism, global business ventures and global tourism, 'humanitarian' interventions in the name of 'peace', 'security', 'democracy' and the 'fight against terror'. The personnel involved in these inroads into other cultures need to be alerted about 'clashes of civilization' inhibiting 'the remaking of the world order' (Huntingdon 1997). Today such ideas of setting up a wall between 'the West and the rest' and in particular fuelling beliefs of the progressive and democratic Western countries and the dangerously backward Islamic states have sadly gained new currency. The generalizations by Huntingdon and others come in handy for maintaining and spreading prejudice by today's populists in many countries. Particularly strong are such generalizations for the commercialization of so-called

'Intercultural Training', which has proved to be extremely lucrative in globalized companies, where managers are taught how to perceive and behave in a foreign cultural environment with the cultural 'other'.

Common to such views of culture is a trivialization and marginalization of language by prioritizing differences in behavioural etiquette, and by engaging in a (dangerous) discourse of exclusion. As pointed out by Edward Said (1993) in his description of how **Orientalist discourse** 'orientalizes' the Orient, cultures become sources of identity construction and of essentializing the Other whereby the – frequently – non-Western Other is described from the Western perspective: 'Culture comes to be associated, often aggressively, with the nation state; this differentiates "us" from "them", almost always with some degree of xenophobia' (1993:xiii).

Prominent propagators of what one may call 'the old thinking about culture' are for instance Hofstede (e.g. 1980), who has set up dimensions of cultural difference on the basis of the results of a questionnaire distributed to IBM employees in 40 different countries, among them: Power Distance, Uncertainty Avoidance, Individuality vs Collectivity, Masculinity vs Feminity. While such generalizations were heavily criticized in the literature, they have nevertheless been enormously popular in intercultural training programmes.

The Norwegian peace researcher Johan Galtung (1985) suggested different culture-conditioned so-called intellectual styles, which he called Saxonic, Nipponic, Teutonic and Gallic. Here again, we have far-reaching generalizations that lump together different groups, e.g. those speaking Romance languages or different Asian languages.

The American anthropologist Edward T. Hall (1976) classified cultures along assumed differences in the perception of time and space and came up with categories such as monochrome vs polychrome cultures, high vs low context cultures. Finally, the psychologist Alexander Thomas (1986) has set up what he called 'culture standards', which refer to phenomena such as interpersonal distance, rule orientation and authority-prone thinking – which entire nations are thought to share.

SMALL CULTURES, COMMUNITIES OF PRACTICE, SUPERDIVERSITY

Along with the recent rise of post-modernist thinking in the humanities, the whole notion of culture has for some time now also come under attack (cf. e.g. Holliday 1999). The critique formulated in post-modernist circles can be summarized as follows: the very idea of 'culture' is an unacceptable abstraction; there are never 'pure cultures' and there are no such things as 'social groups', because these groups are constantly destabilized by external influences, internal restructuring and individual idiosyncrasies and actions. Cultures themselves are, on this view, mere ideologies, idealized systems simply serving to diminish real differences that always exist between human beings in particular socially and geographically delimited areas. Is the very concept of a 'culture' therefore useless, in particular for an eminently practice-oriented field such as translation? Surely not. In the empirical social sciences, attempts to 'problematize' and 'relativize' the concept of 'culture' to the point of denying its usefulness altogether have as yet not prevented solid ethnographic descriptions. Moreover, if such criticism were taken to its logical conclusion by empirical social scientists, they would no longer exist.

One recent approach which seems to be particularly well-suited to resolve the hotly debated issue of generalization vs diversification and individualization of cultures is the one by Sperber (1996). Sperber views culture in terms of different types of 'representations' (which may be representations of ideas, behaviours, attitudes, etc.). Within any group, there exists a multitude of individual 'mental representations', most of which are fleeting and individual. A subset of these representations, however, can be overtly expressed in language and artefacts. They then become 'public representations', which are communicated to others in the social group. This communication gives rise to similar mental representations in others, which, in turn, may be communicated as public representations to others, which may again be communicated to different persons involving mental representations and so on. If a subset of public representations is communicated frequently enough within a particular social group, these representations may become firmly entrenched and turn into 'cultural representations'. The point at which a mental representation becomes sufficiently widespread to be called 'cultural' is, however, still a matter of degree and interpretation, as there is no clear division between mental, public and cultural representations, which may be taken as a rational argument against those facile and stereotypical statements that make up pre-judgments, or prejudice.

A conception of 'culture' as a 'mental category' is also reflected in the following statement by Baumann: 'Culture can thus not be regarded as "a real thing", but an abstract and purely analytical notion. It does not cause behaviour, but summarizes an abstraction from it, and is thus neither normative nor prescriptive' (Baumann 1996:11).

Members of a particular culture are constantly being influenced by their society's (and/or some of the society's cultural subgroups') public and cultural representations (with regard to values, norms, traditions, etc.). This influence is exerted most prominently through language used by members of the society in communication with other members of the same and different socio-cultural groups. Language as the most important means of communicating, of transmitting information and providing human bonding has therefore an overridingly important position inside any culture. Language is the prime means of an individual's acquiring knowledge of the world, of transmitting mental representations and making them public and intersubjectively accessible. Language is thus the prime instrument of a 'collective knowledge reservoir' to be passed on from generation to generation. But language also acts as a means of categorizing cultural experience, thought and behaviour for its speakers. Language and culture are therefore most intimately (and obviously) interrelated on the levels of semantics, where the vocabulary of a language reflects the culture shared by its speakers.

Given the recent widespread critique of the concept of 'culture' as an untenable generalization, we must ask whether it is possible to talk of the 'culture' of a speech community as though it were a static, monolithic, homogeneous entity. Has not the extension of 'culture' beyond the traditional ethnographic concern with 'the way of life' of indigenous peoples to complex modern societies brought about a widespread complexification and problematization of the concept of 'culture' which renders it useless as a methodological and conceptual entity? Obviously, there is no such thing as a stable social group uninfluenced by outside influences and personal idiosyncrasies, and obviously it is wrong to assume a unified culture in which all differences between people are idealized and cancelled out. There may be some justification in trying to describe culturally conditioned discourse phenomena from the dialectically linked etic (culturally distant) and an emic (culturally intrinsic) perspective. Further, linking 'culture' to concepts like 'discourse' clearly reduces the risk of ethnic and national stereotyping through prescribed difference because the focus in a pragmatic-discourse approach is on social groups displaying patterned, cohesive, varied, negotiable and changing verbal actions.

In view of the current doubts about the 'essentialist' concept of culture, it may be advisable to look at culture as a diversified entity that is dynamic, fluid and hybrid with cultural borders being increasingly difficult to determine in a globalized world (see here Piller 2013). Cultures are more and more interconnected and 'superdiverse' through multiple interactions and exchanges – not least through the increasing number of translations worldwide. So the assumption of a smaller unit than 'culture' such as **'small culture'** (Holliday 1999, 2012) and **'Communities of Practice'** (Wenger 1989) as well as considerations of cultures as being characterized by **'superdiversity'** (Blommaert 2013) may be eminently more practicable and useful for translation studies.

THE ROLE OF IDEOLOGY IN TRANSLATION

Since the 1990s and the so-called cultural turn in translation, discussions about translation and ideology have become popular, attracting many scholars from diverse disciplines (see for instance Tymoczko 2000, 2007; Munday 2007; Calzada-Pérez 2014). The idea that translations need to be seen as both embedded in their specific social contexts and envisaged through the lens of the translator's stance is, however, not new. It has been stressed early on, for instance by Catford (see Chapter 3, p. 26), and indeed by most functionally oriented translation scholars. What is new, however, is a recent focus on culture as a site of ideological struggle, a view of translators as stimulators of 'resistance' of hegemonic influence, and a focus on how 'meanings' in texts serve to set up and maintain relations of power and domination. Translation is here seen as an ideal site for unmasking and resisting hegemonic structures. These concerns, like many others before, follow the development of a particular brand of discourse analysis called **'critical discourse analysis' (CDA)** (see, for instance, Fairclough 1995; Wodak 2013). From the viewpoint of CDA, translation is regarded as a process that is inevitably influenced by the power differences between participants. CDA-inspired translation studies have dealt in particular with discourses of the media, news reporting, politics and institutions or advertising discourse (cf., e.g., Calzada-Pérez 2007). These discourse types seem to be particularly germane to the concept that discourse is both socially conditioned and shapes and changes social relationships. One of the criticisms of CDA in general and CDA-influenced translation studies refers to the methodology, which often appears to be impressionistic, focusing on selected examples of salient differences in power and status rather than exhibiting a serious systematic and all-encompassing linguistic analysis. Power relations are assumed to exist even before the analysis is undertaken and then projected onto the data, invariably proving the analyst's bias and preconceptions.

Similar to an interest in CDA in translation is the recent fascination with 'translation as ideology', with ideology as a crucial topic in translation studies, famously taken up by Hatim and Mason (1997) in their discussion of ideological mediation in translation and ways of revealing hidden, implicit ideology on translation. Mason has stated that for translation studies, it may be advisable to conceive of ideology not in the standard sense of a political doctrine but as a 'set of beliefs and values which inform an individual's or institution's view of the world and assist their interpretation of events, facts and other aspects of experience' (2010:86).

A fascinating topic for translation scholars who are interested in the role of ideology in translation is the genre of children's books. Here, scholars have looked at various linguistic and cultural aspects that undergo changes in translations of children's books (see e.g. House 2004), discourse and ideology in children's books (Kaniklidou and House 2018) and specific topics in children's books and their translation such as death (Ruzicka Kenfel and House 2020).

Looking for traces of implicit ideology in translation as CDA scholars do often reveals relations of (asymmetric) power, misuse of power and various manipulations in the interests of power – all these to be uncovered in the selection of texts for translation, the strategies used in the process of translation and the (intended) impact on the recipients of the translation. Ideology is also believed to be manifest in the ways translations are endowed with paratextual material that is used to frame the text, such as prefaces, afterwords and other interpretative 'aids'. It is also evident in the publication choices made by publishers and others in power. As I have shown in House (2008), a book by the British philosopher Ted Honderich (2002) which was heavily critical of Israel and its politics only briefly appeared in a German translation of his book by a well-known publishing house, but was swiftly removed from the market due to enormous ideological pressure by German politicians and the prevailing intellectual climate and public opinion in Germany. The text was later 'permitted' to be republished by a smaller, much less well-known publishing house equipped with an 'explanatory' preface guiding readers to the ideologically accepted interpretation of the work.

Revealing ideological biases as an agenda in translation studies is no longer a trend at the margins of the discipline but has come to inhabit a central space, to the point that some translation scholars maintain that the translator is invariably located in an ideological position within the target culture (see here the contributions in Almanna and House eds. 2023b). Others still speak of all work on translation being founded on the idea that there is a 'reality out there', that phenomena have an 'essential' inner structure, words have an inherent 'kernel of meaning' that can be more or less objectively grasped.

AUDIENCE DESIGN

In the previous section, we focused on translators and the types of cultural and ideological involvement they find themselves in. On the other side, so to speak, are the receivers or addressees of their translations, their audience. We can say that translators need to, and habitually do, adapt their translated texts to the (assumed) needs and expectations of an imagined audience. In other words, translators design their translations with a view of who the translated text is to reach, and what the intended readers expect of a particular translated text. Accommodating a translation to the intended addressees will, of course, strongly affect the style of the translation. One approach to translation, the so-called Skopos (purpose) theory of translation referred to in Chapter 3 strongly emphasizes the need of translators to make their translations 'relevant' to the recipients' expectations. Target culture norms are crucial here because it is in the target cultural environment that the translation will have to achieve its purpose. This means that the role and importance of the original text and its linguistic make-up is relegated to the background. The role of the individual translator, on the other hand, is of crucial importance since it is the translator who holds the key to fulfilling the translation's purpose and taking account of addressees' expectation norms. One critical issue here is whether the text to be translated can be assumed to have some kind of 'core meaning' which is independent of the meaning which the intended audience of the translation earmarked for a certain purpose ascribe to it. In the case of, for example, business correspondence, sales reports, tourist brochures, instructions for use, advertisements, etc., one may argue that they will have very little 'core meaning' worth maintaining in the translated text. Such texts can then be easily 'recast' for a different audience – especially since such texts tend to focus on recipients' immediate actions. So here, we have a situation where it is clearly not what the author talks about in the original text that matters most but rather the effect the translated text is to have on its recipients. However, does the focus on audience design and the effect of the translated text justify disregarding the original text in all text types? Certainly not! Many literary and scientific texts of historical importance may need to be translated in such a way that their meaning is translated faithfully, which means that they need to be given a degree of autonomy from recipients and that audience design clearly plays a negligible role. In translating such texts, their properties may need to exert some control over how they are to be translated.

PART 2

SOME MUCH-DISCUSSED CONCEPTS IN TRANSLATION THEORY

In this part we will look at several important issues in translation theory: translatability, translation universals, equivalence and evaluation of translation. Chapter 5 discusses possibilities and impossibilities of translation, Chapter 6 looks at universals in translation and Chapter 7 asks: How do we know when a translation is good?

DOI: 10.4324/9781003355823-6

5

POSSIBILITIES AND IMPOSSIBILITIES OF TRANSLATION

WHEN AND WHY IS TRANSLATION IMPOSSIBLE?

This chapter discusses the question of when and why translation is possible and when translation becomes impossible. We will first look at the philosophical, linguistic and socio-cultural underpinnings of translatability and its limits.

'LINGUISTIC RELATIVITY' AND TRANSLATION: AN HISTORICAL OVERVIEW

As opposed to the view that language 'reflects' the culture of a social group, the ideas that came to be known as **linguistic relativity** imply the very opposite: language in its lexicon and grammar has an influence on its speakers' thinking, their 'worldview' and on their behaviour (see here the overview in House 2000).

The idea that an individual's mother tongue is the primary source of socialization and cognitive conditioning goes back to German idealistic philosophy. Johann Georg Hamann handled the question of the influence of language on thinking, and Johann Gottfried Herder also regarded languages as embodying specific mental characteristics of their speakers, languages being but reflections of a certain 'national mentality'. But it was Wilhelm von Humboldt who became the first influential propagator of the idea that every language, as an a priori framework of cognition, determines the 'Weltanschauung' of its speakers. However, Humboldt

DOI: 10.4324/9781003355823-7

also looks upon language as a self-contained, creative, symbolic organization, as 'energeia' in a speaker – an idea later adopted in the twentieth century most prominently by Chomsky in his early work. Language, in this view, is conceived of as an active and dynamic force, which not only refers to experience and (what later came to be called) 'context' but also defines it for the speaker, because he unconsciously extrapolates from the language's implicit expectations. Any natural language is believed to have an 'inner form' peculiar to it, just as the 'external' (superficial) language structure varies widely among languages. This spiritual structure that languages possess corresponds to the thought processes of its users. In Humboldt's view, then, languages lie at the interface between objective reality and man's conceptualization of it. They act like coloured glasses, forcing speakers to perceive reality in language-specific ways.

Later in the twentieth century, the idea of 'linguistic relativity' was put forward by Edward Sapir and Benjamin Lee Whorf in the United States. Sapir (1921, 1949) expresses the crux of their ideas in the following manner:

> Human beings do not live in the objective world alone... but are very much at the mercy of the particular language which has become the medium of expression for their society... the real world is to a large extent unconsciously built upon the language habits of the group... the worlds in which different societies live are distinct worlds, not merely the same worlds with different labels attached.

> (Sapir 1949:162)

Sapir, and especially Whorf (1956), made some attempts to prove these ideas empirically. Whorf adduced a whole catalogue of impressive data illustrating the great differences between American Indian languages and what he called Standard Average European (SAE) languages, i.e., the undifferentiated collectivity of English, German, French, Italian, etc. Whorf also inferred mental and behavioural differences from differences between languages on the level of lexis. However, he particularly emphasized grammatical structure as the crucial feature in the connection between language, thought and the segmentation of reality.

While Whorf examined only such vastly different languages as SAE and American Indian languages, it is not difficult to list many other instances of grammatical diversity among the languages of the world. Languages differ strikingly in the grammatical categories that are obligatorily represented: for instance, the category of number is not obligatory in Chinese; Fijian has a four-way number system for personal pronouns (singular, dual, paucal, multiple) but no number at all for nouns. Gender is likewise not found in all languages and, in those in which it is found, the number of gender distinctions varies greatly. Many languages have an elaborate apparatus of aspects: momentaneous, continuative, incentive, cessative, durative, durative-incentive, iterative, momentaneous-iterative and so forth. Now, if languages display such striking grammatical differences, and if – as Whorf maintains – linguistic form has a truly 'tyrannical hold' upon our way of thinking and perceiving, one might conclude that the theoretical possibility of translating, not only from and into SAE and American Indian languages but also from and into many other languages, seems to be denied. If all our knowledge is mediated through our native language, it is not possible for human beings to rid themselves of that mediating influence.

Given Whorf's implicit view of meaning as concepts present in speaker-hearers' minds, it is logically impossible to know any foreign language, let alone translate, because the cognitive differences between members of different language communities will result in different and unknowable concepts or images of the same referents in their minds. One can never know the objective intellectual content of any foreign language, because this foreign language has to be learned in exactly the same way as any aspect of reality which is subject to, and shaped by, native-tongue conditioned ways of thinking.

Also, since in translation, grammatical form must necessarily change, the kind of grammatical meaning that Whorf imputed as being present in language users' minds, is, of course, routinely and necessarily lost in translation. On Whorf's view, then, a translation being thus formally different from its original, would no longer be a translation but a 'transfiguration'. Hence, we may conclude that linguistic relativity is the doctrine of untranslatability par excellence.

RECENT RESEARCH ON LINGUISTIC RELATIVITY AND ITS IMPACT ON TRANSLATION

While there have been very few early empirical studies testing the Whorfian assumptions in the past 40 years or so, interest in the question of how the language we speak influences the way we think and behave has recently stimulated empirical studies that examined how language, thought and reality are interconnected in clearly delimited areas. Examples are Lucy's (1992) study of how differences in grammatical number marking in English and Yucatec-Maya affect speakers' performance in tasks of remembering and sorting, or Slobin's (1997, 2009) finding that lexicalization patterns in different languages cause speakers to describe motions in distinct ways, leading to distinct narrative styles in the different languages (for a comprehensive overview see also Lucy 1997). And members of the Max Planck Institute for Psycholinguistics in Nijmegen looked at how space is handled in different languages using a variety of elicitation tasks. They found that speakers of different languages respond to these elicitation tasks in ways that correspond to their verbal practices. Finnish studies showed that higher rates of occupational accidents in Finnish-speaking contexts compared to Swedish-speaking contexts are explained by reference to structural differences and differences in orienting meanings between Indo-European languages, such as Swedish, and Ural-Altaic ones, such as Finnish.

Research such as the above supports the linguistic relativity postulate in specified ways. Structural differences are of central importance in any comparison of the meaning potential of two languages. Clearly, therefore, given that language structures necessarily change in translation, it is inevitable that any argument concerning the feasibility of translation has to be located at some other linguistic level, i.e., the level of discourse. Since discourse is realized inside the social and cultural traditions in the two linguacultures meeting in translation, and these can be analysed and compared, a basis for translatability may be guaranteed. Recent attempts at examining differences between languages at the discourse level (see, for example, Chafe 2000) have pointed to differences in the conceptualization of certain domains and to differences in speaker orientations to space, time, motion, to the reality of what is being said or the interaction between speaker and hearer themselves. But these differences are unlikely to amount to insuperable difficulties in translation, which would make translation ultimately impossible.

WHY TRANSLATION IS STILL POSSIBLE

As we saw above, the consequence of the strong linguistic relativity hypothesis for translation seems to be the denial of its theoretical possibility – 'theoretical' because the practice of translation flies in the face of this statement: translation practice has been with us from time immemorial! So why should we be faced with such an apparent contradiction? One answer might be: because of the nature of language and the nature of human beings. Arguing against the 'linguistically atomistic' nature of many early Whorfian studies, Longacre stated over 60 years ago: 'Language is not utterly at the mercy of its own distinctions and categories, but has within itself resources for outstripping and transcending these categories' (1956:304). This means that languages are not really that different from the viewpoint of the potential of the whole system: the differences between languages are not so much in kind as in the degree of explicitness and emphasis – what one language has built into the layers of its structure, another language expresses only very informally and sporadically, but all languages have the resources to express any experience or state of affairs in a comparable manner. Edward Sapir, who is often only quoted as a radical relativist, puts this very well: 'both Hottentot and Eskimos possess all the formal apparatus that is required to serve as matrix for the expression of Kant's thought' (1921:210).

Another argument relativizing the force of linguistic relativism on translation is language change. Languages change constantly; so does our experience and conception of the world around us. But the two do not change at the same pace or in direct parallel. Any language is full of fossils or anachronisms, and at any particular time much of language is conventionalized and automatic. The road from language forms to consciousness is still largely unknown and may be more complicated than is often assumed. Conclusions as to direct correlations between language thought and reality can therefore not be drawn.

Further, due to each individual language user's innate creativity and flexibility and simple cognitive competence, language can hardly ever have an overpowering influence on its users, i.e., we might supplement the axiom of expressibility with an axiom of conceivability. Langacker puts this nicely:

> We are perfectly competent of forming and mentally manipulating concepts for which no word is available. We can make up imaginary entities at will, and if we so choose, proceed to name them. For example, imagine a unicorn with a flower growing out of each nostril.
>
> (1967:40)

How well the influence of language on cognitive capacity, on the routes, rates and quality of human thinking can be counteracted is demonstrated by the (obvious) fact that different worldviews or philosophical positions have been expressed in the same language, and the same philosophical position has been expounded in structurally very different languages: Descartes, Comte and Bergson had the same grammatical structure at their disposal, and Aristotelian metaphysics has been developed by Arabic and Hebrew thinkers as well as by medieval Christian philosophers. Further, the very concept of one single monolithic and unchangeable mother tongue as an instrument of eclipsing powerful cognitive influence needs to be relativized.

There is little justification in arguing that all the speakers of a language community are affected by their language in the same way. Within each language community, contrasts in expressions and use of grammatical structure as well as discourse norms may be just as great as between different language communities. Certain subgroups, for instance professional or ethnic ones inside a language community, may have developed their own highly differentiated vocabularies and grammatical and discoursal norms that deviate from the norms of usage in other subgroups of complex societies. To posit habitual modes of thought of whole linguistic communities may thus turn out to be wildly unrealistic, not least because in any complex community a subgroup may be found that shares the cognitive and behavioural tendencies of members of another supposedly very different linguaculture. I use the term **linguaculture** to indicate an idea of culture as it is manifested through patterns of language use.

In a world which has always been multilingual, there can hardly be an overriding influence of 'the mother tongue' as a strongly thought- and behaviour-conditioning instrument. Foreign languages are acquired by individuals to admirable degrees of perfection, and the world is full of multilingual individuals, so the monolingual person is clearly an exception. John Macnamara's (1970) early *reductio ad absurdum* of the impossibility of both bilingualism and translation on account of linguistic relativism is still valid today. Macnamara had argued that, following a strong Whorfian hypothesis, a bilingual person would hardly manage to communicate with himself because, in switching to language B, he would never be able to understand or explain what he had just communicated in language A – a patent *reductio ad absurdum*.

In sum, then, linguistic relativity, though clearly affecting, in specified areas, some of our thinking and behaviour, can always be overcome. While it is undeniably true that differences in expression and obligatory structural distinctions in languages can have an effect on perception, thinking and behaviour, these effects do not amount to impenetrable differences in overall 'worldview' (whatever that may be) between different linguacultures. There is always an escape from the trap of one's language – through language itself, through the creativity, dynamism, flexibility, as well as the complexity and basic similarity of individuals and of languages. Translation is not in principle impossible.

CULTURE, CONTEXT AND TRANSLATABILITY

When we link linguistic diversity with external differences of historical, cultural and social background, rather than linking it with cognitive and linguistic differences, we can arrive at a more positive view of the possibility of translation. If languages are seen as structured in divergent ways because they embody different experiences, interests, conventions, priorities and values, then the importance of what may be called **linguistic-cultural relativity** emerges. Cultural knowledge, including knowledge of various sub-cultures, has long been recognized as indispensable for translation, as it is knowledge of the *application* that linguistic units have in particular situational and socio-cultural contexts which makes translation possible. 'Application' refers to the relation holding between an expression and the socio-cultural situation in which it is used: its pragmatic meaning. In establishing equivalences between linguistic units in translation, the notion of 'application' is crucial: if semantic meanings – sense and reference – differ for two linguistic units in two different languages (as they very frequently do), it is their *application* in particular, knowable cultural contexts that permits translatability. Linguistic units can never be fully understood in isolation from the particular cultural phenomena for which they are symbols. The Japanese key words *amae* and *enryo*, for instance, cannot be translated unless the relevant cultural features, to which these words are applied, are taken into account. Only knowledge of these renders translation – in the sense of reconstitution, not transfiguration of meaning – possible.

While differences in the worldviews of speakers of different languages resulting in different concepts in their minds may not be accessible to the translator, the intersubjectively experiencable application of linguistic units in a particular socio-cultural situation can. In other words, knowledge concerning when, why, by whom and to what effect language-specific units are employed can, in theory, be accessed. Linguists and ethnologists are capable of working with languages and cultures other than their own. Even if the cultural distance between languages is great, cultural gaps can always be bridged via ethnographic knowledge and insights or, stated negatively, untranslatability only occurs whenever such knowledge, such insights, such reflection is absent.

Conceptions of language within the broader context of culture, whereby meaning is seen as contextually determined and constructed, are not recent developments: they have long been considered inside Russian formalism, Prague School linguistics and British Contextualism. Scholars belonging to these traditions believed, as did the ethnographer Bronislaw Malinowski, that 'the main function of language is not to express thought, not to duplicate mental processes, but rather to play an active part in human behavior' (1935:7). Malinowski, whom we have already mentioned in Chapter 3 (p. 35) in connection with the notion of 'context of situation', thought that the meaning of a linguistic unit cannot be captured unless one takes account of the interrelationship between linguistic units and 'the context of the situation'. Such a view of meaning has important consequences for the possibility of translation: translation becomes 'rather the placing of linguistic symbols against the cultural background of a society than the rendering of words by their equivalents in another language' (Malinowski 1935:18). Similarly, scholars belonging to the School of British Contextualism view language as part of the social dynamic process, as observable and explicable 'language events', with meanings of utterances being defined in terms of their use and function in the context of a situation. Such social views of language have taken account of the fact that language is never a monolithic homogeneous whole but always reflects social, geographic, cultural and individual differences, and changes over time.

Given the importance of the 'context of situation', we can say that in translation, it is necessary to relate the original text to its cultural context, as it is only in this context that the text has meaning. As this meaning needs to be reconstituted in another linguaculture, the process of translation becomes a process of **re-contextualization**. In the process of re-contextualization, two types of translation, overt and covert translation, need to be differentiated. They differ fundamentally in their goals and procedures, and it is only in covert translation that linguistic-cultural relativity is built into the translation process itself. This may be achieved via the use of a cultural filter, whose basis should be a body of empirical cross-cultural studies. We will examine these different types of translation in Chapter 7.

Following up on Macnamara's refutation of linguistic relativity, recent empirical neurolinguistic studies of bilingualism and translation (see, for example, Paradis 2004) using modern technological means of neuro-imaging, such as fMRT, PET and ERP confirms his – at the time necessarily – more informal views. They suggest that in the bilingual's (and the translator's) brain a joint conceptual system can be accessed by different routes via different languages. Conceptual representations are language-independent, whereas lexico-semantic, morpho-syntactic and phonological representations are language-specific. The two languages are organized in two separate subsystems, and these subsystems can be activated simultaneously, with the possibility of a supervisory attentional system exercising inhibiting control for the comprehension of the source text and the production of a target text. The two languages involved in the process of translation are therefore conceptualized as both interconnected and separate. If they are used simultaneously, as in translation, speakers are in a 'bilingual mode', which enables them to understand, compare and transfer expressions in two different languages.

TRUE LIMITS OF TRANSLATABILITY

There are, however, a few exceptions to universal translatability, which I will now briefly discuss. All languages as creative dynamic systems are well-equipped to express ad hoc any aspect of human life whenever the need arises. In Roman Jakobson's much-quoted words: 'All cognitive experience and its classification is conveyable in any existing language. Whenever there is deficiency, terminology may be qualified and amplified by loan words, neologisms or semantic shifts, and finally by circumlocutions' (1959:234). Given this 'law of universal translatability', we should nevertheless not forget that there *do* exist certain real limits to translatability. First of all, and Jakobson recognizes this by explicitly referring to 'all cognitive experience', the possibility of translation is severely restricted if we take connotations into account. Connotations defy explicit definitions, and they vary even within one individual's mind, as her moods and experiences change. Also, connotations cannot be clearly delimited from denotative meanings. So connotative meanings are far too elusive to be captured in translation because of their inherently indefinable nature. And the enormous difficulties in literary translation derive, of course, mainly from the fact that literary texts abound in 'personal deviations' (i.e., connotations) from central denotative meanings. The second, and most formidable, limitation to translatability occurs in all cases in which language adopts a different function over and above its 'normal' communicative function.

Translatability is limited whenever the form of a linguistic unit takes on special importance. We can therefore qualify the dictum of universal translatability as Nida and Taber have done long ago: 'Anything that can be said in one language can be said in another, unless the form is an essential element of the message' (1969:4).

Form naturally plays an important role in literary texts, especially in poetry, which, according to Jakobson (1959:238), is by definition untranslatable. In poetry, only the creation of a new text is possible: **'creative transposition'** takes over where translation finds its limits. In literary texts, meaning and form operate together, and they are no longer arbitrarily connected. Therefore, the form cannot be changed without a corresponding change in meaning. Since the form cannot be detached from its meaning, this meaning can never be expressed in other ways: paraphrase, commentary, explanations of various kinds, coining or borrowing new words – all of which render pragmatic translation ultimately possible – are not sufficient in literary, especially poetic translation.

Another limit of translatability is due to the fact that each language is unique in its social and geographical diversification that is reflected in social and regional dialects of individuals and groups. Since each language is unique in its diversification, translation of this intralinguistic variation is severely curbed. Although, for instance, in the translation of dialectal passages, translators often try to achieve some sort of 'functional equivalence' by resorting to presumably corresponding dialects in the target language community (e.g. dialects in urban communities of supposedly equivalent prestige) this is more often than not unsatisfactory.

UNIVERSALS OF TRANSLATION?

This chapter sets out to answer the question: 'Are there universals in translation?' Before zeroing in on the issue of **translation universals**, we will first have a look at the long history of discussions of **language universals**

LANGUAGE UNIVERSALS AND UNIVERSALS OF TRANSLATION

Universals have a long and venerable tradition in the philosophy of language. Here, universals have been equated with those features of language that are part of a human being's genetic endowment. Medieval speculative grammarians and Renaissance Port Royal grammarians had already assumed that there exists only one grammar – the grammar of the human mind. This 'mental grammar' as part of human nature was then assumed to be fundamentally the same for all human beings despite the many different languages they spoke. In other words, underneath the bewilderingly varied 'surface structures' (i.e. the actual concrete organization of the physical signals into units of various complexity, size, sequence and arrangement) of all the languages of the world, all languages are alike in their 'deep structures', i.e., the underlying abstract stratum which determines the meaning of sentences and is represented in the human mind.

Early comparative language scholars and, of course, the followers of the linguistic relativity hypothesis ignored the quest for universals for a while, giving priority to the seemingly infinite diversity of

DOI: 10.4324/9781003355823-8

languages in their surface structures. Recent interest in universals was rekindled in the Western world in the early 1960s, culminating in the famous volume by Joseph Greenberg on 'universals of language' (1963), where linguists, anthropologists and psychologists mapped out generalizations about language, of a phonological, morpho-grammatical and semantic kind. On the basis of data from a 30-language sample and a 'basic-order typology' that involves basic facts of word order in declarative sentences, Greenberg proposed his famous 45 universals, which can be both absolute universals or universal tendencies, implicational ones (of the sort: 'If Language A has feature x, it will (tend to) have feature y') or non-implicational ones (of the type: 'All languages tend to have feature y'). Greenberg and others operating in the framework of what came to be known as the typological approach found out that an analysis of a substantial number of languages reveals not only the range of variation but also constraints on that variation, which show that languages do not vary infinitely and thus represent linguistic universals.

In this 'empiricist universalist tradition', where systematic surveys of as many languages as possible were conducted, different explanations have been offered, such as for instance by Hawkins (1994), who suggests that certain word orders prevail because they optimize language comprehension and production processes.

As regards semantic universals, Uriel Weinreich (1963 [1953]) – long before today's globalization and internationalization processes – proposed that through increasing contact and communication, languages consistently add to a corpus of common vocabulary (a common semantic stock), and particularly in the domain of natural science the lexica of different languages then come to share many references.

In one influential linguistic approach which – originally as a reaction against behaviouristic psychology – rose to fame in the middle of the twentieth century, namely generative grammar, a language acquisition device as a universal language faculty together with underlying principles were proposed, and are now widely taken for granted in cognitively oriented linguistics and language acquisition studies worldwide. As opposed to earlier attempts to 'discover' individual universal features ('bottom up') through wide-ranging analysis and comparison of as many languages as possible, linguists operating in the generative tradition posit ('top-down') linguistic universality as an a priori phenomenon, i.e. as the very basis for the general framework of their theory. Thus, Noam Chomsky (see for instance 1965) and his followers have suggested that it is the main task of any linguistic theory to develop an explanation of **linguistic universals**. The study of linguistic universals was seen as equivalent to the study of the properties of generative grammars for natural language. In the generative school, substantive and formal universals were distinguished, which were of a phonological, syntactic or semantic nature. Substantive universals are certain fixed items or categories specified in the vocabulary used to describe a language, i.e., noun, verb and so on. Traditional universal grammar was basically a theory of substantive universals since it assumed the existence of certain fixed categories. Formal universals, on the other hand, are much more abstract: they relate to the fact that a grammar must meet specific formal conditions. On the semantic level, for instance, such a formal universal might be that certain classes of lexical items meet specified conditions, such as for example: 'artefacts are defined in terms of certain human goals, needs, functions instead of solely physical qualities'.

More recently, Universal Grammar (UG) is used to explain more specifically what is universal in language, i.e., both the principles that constrain the forms of different languages – for instance the Locality Principle, according to which grammatical operations are local, such that, for example, auxiliary inversion preposes the closest auxiliary and wh-movement preposes the closest wh-expression, and certain Parameters, e.g. the wh-parameter which determines that a language either allows (Italian) or does not allow (German) finite verbs to have null subjects). These principles and parameters are innate. Given their abstract 'deep' nature, universals of language, as conceptualized in formal linguistic theorizing, can never imply a surface equivalence between different languages.

From a functional perspective, universals are viewed in a different, much less abstract way. They can be defined – for instance by Bernard Comrie – as 'those properties that are necessarily common to all human languages' (2003:195). Here, a claim is made about the human language potential, and universals are assumed to exist because of the way human beings are made, and the physical and cognitive limitations they are subjected to. Thus, for example, certain sounds may not be possible given the nature of the human body, and are thus universally absent from human language. The second major group of universals is related to the functions of language. The two essential functions of language – and thus of all the many human languages – are to convey information and to establish and maintain social relations between human beings.

The universals posited in the functional approach are used to represent bottom-up generalizations across languages. Their explanatory potential includes general cognitive, social-interactional, processing and perceptual as well as possibly other human faculties. However, one should not construe a non-compatibility between the two approaches to universals, both are also to a certain extent similar: they are after all both 'universalist', since both start from structural analyses, both consider abstractions from their data (across languages and within languages respectively) and both explain universals by pointing to universal, biologically given human faculties (the parent disciplines being genetics for the generativists, evolutionary theory for the functionalists). Thus, there remain only two major differences between the generative and the functional approach to linguistic universals: the emphasis in the latter on empirical cross-linguistic comparison and on the relationship between linguistic forms and language function.

In the following, I will look in some detail at one functional approach, the systemic-functional one, which has placed particular emphasis on the relationship between form and function, and which has proved to be most useful for the study of translation.

About the same time as Greenberg and Chomsky came up with their suggestions of linguistic universals, Michael Halliday (1961, 1973, 1994) also suggested that language as a system of 'meaning making' has a universal meaning potential, which evolved around three motifs, which he called '**metafunctions**': the ideational, the interpersonal and the textual metafunction. Ideationally, language reflects our human experience, our interpretation of all that goes on around us, outside and inside, mapping systems of meaning into language such that human beings as language learners and users can capture and construe their individual and collective experiences of the world. Interpersonally, language is a way of initiating and maintaining social relationships, and of construing human language learners and users as personal and collective beings. Textually, language involves the creation of information: it creates discourse, the patterned forms of wording that constitute meaningful semiotic contexts. We can see that – as opposed to the two basic universal functions, informing and socializing – the **textual function** clearly has an enabling, facilitative force, i.e. it allows the other two to operate.

The **ideational function** contains a general category of process: e.g. material, mental, relational, with processes happening to, or being enacted by, human agents in time and space, past or future, real or imaginary, here or there. The **interpersonal function** is a mode of enacting personal relationships of different kinds, exchanges of speech roles, realizing discourse functions, questions, commands, offers, etc. implying systems and resources of mood and modality.

Unlike the other two, the **textual function** does not originate in an extrinsic context, it is intrinsic to language itself and refers to the resources any language must have for creating discourse and ensuring that each instance of text makes contact with its environment. This 'environment' includes both the 'context of situation' (Malinowski 1935), of culture and other instances of text. The resources tapped here are potentially higher than clauses or clause complexes, setting up relationships which create not only semantic cohesion but also contributing to the overall grammar of the clause. A typical way of construing the clause as 'message' is as a combination of two perspectives: that of the speaker and that of the listener, which lead to different types of information flow. All languages display some form of textual organization of the clause. However, how far the tension between the speaker–listener perspectives are weighted one against the other in the languages of the world is far from clear. Here, an empirical survey of languages in the functional tradition is necessary. The textual metafunction also provides for the creation of 'cohesion' of four kinds: reference (or 'phora' [cf. anaphoric, cataphoric] to distinguish it from reference as defined in the philosophy of language), ellipsis, conjunction and lexical cohesion (Halliday and Hasan 1976). So in systemic-functional theorizing, it is at this 'deep' metafunctional level of language that we can say universality exists.

Given these two major types of proposals of universals in linguistics, the generative one and the functional one, let us now examine what universals – if they can be said to exist at all – might mean for translation.

TRANSLATION UNIVERSALS

Various so-called **translation universals** as universal tendencies of the translation process, laws of translation and norms of translation have been suggested in the literature by Blum-Kulka (1986), Baker (1993), Laviosa-Braithwaite (1998) and Toury (2001); see also the contributions to the volume on *Translation Universals – Do they exist?* (Mauranen and Kujamäki 2004). As prime candidates for translation universals the following processes, procedures or operations have been suggested: explicitation, simplification, disambiguation, conventionalization, standardization, 'levelling out', avoidance of repetition, over- or underrepresentation of source or target language elements as well as the general manifestation of a so-called third code, i.e. translation as translation in contradistinction to original non-translated texts. While Blum-Kulka and Toury largely relied on case studies and impressionistic qualitative work, involving informed intuition and richly contextualized pen and paper analysis, all the other researchers mentioned above have relied on, and copiously praised the methodological advantages of, corpus-based qualitative and quantitative work. I deliberatively said 'methodological' advantages: my point is that the more important theoretical question of how useful or indeed possible and thus justifiable the positing of translation universals such as the ones mentioned above are, has not been touched upon let alone recognized by all researchers in the field of translation studies. The unchallenged assumption has been simply that through the technical possibilities corpus methodology has recently afforded translation scholars, universals can be found – in the vein of the empiricist functional approach outlined above. However, there is a great difference in the two quests. Unlike the linguistically based quest for universals of language, the quest for translation universals is, in essence, futile, i.e. there can be no universals at the level of performance, i.e. no translation universals. This claim will be substantiated for the following four reasons:

1. Translation is undeniably an act that operates on language. Depending on one's preference of a formal or functional approach to explaining linguistic phenomena, one can state that universals proposed in these approaches must also apply to

translation. But these are then NOT universals of translation per se, or sui generis universals, but simply universals of language that also apply to translation.

2. Obviously, however, translation is not identical with language as such, let alone with the two linguistic systems involved in translation. Translation is no more and no less than a practical activity. It can be described as an act of performance, of parole, not of langue or competence. This is, of course, reflected in the nature of translation: it is inherently language-specific, and even if, as in some of the recent corpus studies, translations for instance from English into Finnish and Swedish, or from English into Arabic, French or Spanish are compared in the search for recurring regularities or 'universals', this language-pair specificity cannot really be offset, such that even corpus-based multi-pair comparisons remain agglomerations of different pairs. In the existing studies, this fact tends to be glossed over by a lack of careful and detailed comparative linguistic analysis. Terms like 'explicitness', 'explicitation', 'simplification', 'conventionalization' and so on are far too general, they should not be used unless one is perfectly clear about how they can be precisely defined and operationalized. There is recent research by Erich Steiner and his team in which, for instance, the concept of 'explicitation" is first subjected to solid and careful linguistic scrutiny. This is a promising approach (cf. Hansen-Schirra et al. 2007; Steiner 2008). There is also the work by Becher (2010, 2011), and the work by Fabricius-Hansen and her colleagues in Oslo (Behrens and Fabricius-Hansen 2009), all of whom have subjected the particular phenomena they investigate to a detailed linguistic analysis before making any claims to their universality in translation.

3. Closely related to the issue of language-pair specificity in translation is the issue of directionality in translation. In the context of our discussion of universals this means that candidates of universality suggested for one particular translation direction need not necessarily be candidates for universality in the opposite direction. My own work (House 2004) with a corpus of translations of children's books from English into German and German into English has clearly shown, for instance, that procedures of explicitation common in translations from English

into German are not traceable in the opposite translation direction. In fact, a body of earlier contrastive analyses of many different genres (House 2006b) suggest that explicitation holds for translations into German but NOT the other way round. But even this hypothesis can be disconfirmed, as was recently done in the Hamburg project 'Covert translation' (for details see Chapter 9). Baumgarten (2007), for instance, has shown that the use of German sentence initial coordinative conjunction *Und* (And) has significantly increased in German academic discourse under the influence of translations from English over a space of 25 years, and this can also be taken as indicating an increase of implicitness and vagueness, i.e. a decrease in explicitness regarding this particular functional category.

4. Another consideration, and one that clearly militates against an assumption of universals in translation, is genre-specificity and the dynamic development of genres over time. In the project 'Covert translation', we have compared English original texts, translations from English into German, French and Spanish, and comparable texts in these languages with a particular focus on how the phenomena 'subjectivity' and 'addressee-orientation' are realized linguistically and how they change over time under the influence of English as a lingua franca. While there is a tendency for explicitation (use of elaboration, extension and enhancement) in the German translations of popular science texts, this is not the case to the same degree for economic texts.

The sum of the findings of the project 'Covert translation' essentially disconfirms the claim of the universality of underrepresentation in translation of features unique to the target language. For example, when the source language simply does not encode a feature like a certain tense marking, it will be nearly impossible for the translator to reach a target language-conform frequency and distribution of this feature in translation. This suggests that underrepresentation is indeed a normal, maybe even necessary language-pair specific and thus translational phenomenon – albeit not a universal one.

HOW DO WE KNOW WHEN A TRANSLATION IS GOOD?

This chapter gives a brief overview of different approaches that tried to answer this question. Following a discussion of several well-known approaches, I will describe in some detail my own views of how to best answer the title question of this chapter. The reader might also refer to the brief and reader-friendly description given in House (2009).

One of the most intriguing questions asked in connection with translation is how to tell whether a translation is good or bad. This question cannot be answered in any simple way, because any statement about the quality of a translation implies a conception of the very nature of translation, in other words, it presupposes a theory of translation. And different theoretical stances will lead to different concepts of the quality of a translation and to different ways of assessing that quality. Theoretical stances can be grouped and subjected to a sort of 'meta-analysis' examining how they take account of the following three important issues:

1. the relationship between the original text and its translation;
2. the relationship between (features) of original and translated text(s) and how they are perceived by the human beings involved: the author, the translator and the recipient(s);
3. the consequences views about these relationships have when one wants or has to distinguish a translation from other types of multilingual text production.

DOI: 10.4324/9781003355823-9

In the following, we will first review various approaches that are explicitly or implicitly related to translation evaluation. Some of this review is reminiscent of what was discussed in Chapter 3, where we looked at different approaches to translation. In this chapter, however, we will specifically examine these approaches with a view to whether and how they are able to throw light on the three fundamental questions formulated above. More space will then be devoted to a discussion of my own model of translation quality assessment, which is still the only fully formulated one in existence.

DIFFERENT APPROACHES TO TRANSLATION QUALITY ASSESSMENT

PSYCHO-SOCIAL APPROACHES

ANECDOTAL AND SUBJECTIVE VIEWS

Anecdotal views are those age-old, spontaneous, intuitive and subjective judgements of 'how good or how bad somebody thinks a translation is'. In the vast majority of cases, these judgments rest entirely on impressions and feelings, and as such they lead to global, undifferentiated valuations like the following: 'This translation does not do justice to the original' or 'The tone of the original is somehow lost in the translation'. In recent times, this type of vague evaluation is replayed by neo-hermeneutic scholars, a philosophical school whose members believe in the legitimacy of subjective interpretations of the worth of a translation. Adherents of this approach (see e.g. Stolze 1992; Vermeer 1994) believe that the quality of a translated text predominantly depends on the reception and interpretation of the original leading to an 'optimal translation', which is rooted in intuition, empathy and interpretative experience. Translating is here regarded as an individual creative act where the 'meaning' of a text is also 'created' anew in an individual act of interpretation. There is no meaning in the text itself, the meaning being as it were in the 'eye of the beholder'.

To sum up, anecdotal and subjective approaches to translation quality emphasize the belief that the quality of a translation depends largely on the translator's subjective interpretation and transfer decisions, based on her intuition and experience. With respect to the three questions (relationship between original and translation; relationship between (features of) the texts and human agents; delimitation of translation from other text-processing operations), it is obvious that the subjective and neo-hermeneutic approach to translation evaluation can only shed light on what occurs between the translator and (features of) the original text. In concentrating on the individual translator's cognitive processes, the original text, the translation process proper, the relation between original and translation, the expectations of the target text readers are taken into account, and the problem of distinguishing between a translation and other types of text production is not recognized. Translation evaluation is here seen as an examination of a translation as an individual creative act.

RESPONSE-BASED APPROACHES

Proponents of response-based approaches believe it is necessary to have some external way of assessing translations. One can distinguish at least the following two types of such approaches: behaviourist views and functionalistic views.

BEHAVIOURIST VIEWS

This tradition, influenced by the psychological school of behaviourism, is associated with Eugene Nida's (1964) seminal work on translation which we looked at in Chapter 3 and his early suggestion of behavioural tests of the quality of a translation. These tests used such broad behavioural criteria as a translation's 'intelligibility' and 'informativeness'. They were based on the belief that a 'good' translation would have to lead to an 'equivalent response', a criterion linked to Nida's famous principle of 'dynamic equivalence', which holds that the manner in which the receptors of a translation respond to the translation is to be equivalent to the manner in which the source text's receptors respond to the source text. In the heyday of behaviourism, a number of imaginative tests were proposed: reading-aloud techniques, various cloze tests and rating tasks, all of which took observable responses to a translation as criteria of its quality. However, in hindsight, it is safe to say that these tests ultimately failed because they were critically unable to capture something as intricate and complex as the 'overall quality of a translation'. Even if one accepts the assumption that a translation of optimal quality should elicit an equivalent response, one is still faced with the awkward question of whether it is at all possible to capture what exactly such grand concepts as 'intelligibility' or 'informativeness' mean and how one can measure an 'equivalent response' in a valid and reliable manner. If one cannot do this, which turned out to be the case, then it is futile to propose such behavioural criteria in the first place. Further, and probably most critically, in the behavioural approach to translation quality assessment, the source text is largely ignored, which implies that nothing can be said about the relationship between the original and texts resulting from different textual operations.

FUNCTIONALISTIC VIEWS

Scholars in this approach (see, for instance, Nord 1997) think it is the **Skopos** or purpose of a translation, and the manner and degree to which target culture norms are heeded in a translation which are of overriding importance for translation evaluation. How a text's global Skopos is realized *linguistically*, and how one can determine whether a given translation is adequate vis-à-vis this Skopos, remains rather unclear. Given the crucial role assigned to a translation's 'purpose' and the concomitant reduction of the original text to a simple 'offer of information', which the translator is licensed to change, reject or 'improve upon', one can see the closeness of this approach to the hermeneutic approach, where it is also the case that the person of the translator is given enormous power in the translation process. What is ignored here is the fact that a translation is never an 'independent' text but always in principle a 'dependent' one. A translation is by its very nature simultaneously bound to its source text *and* to the presuppositions and conditions governing its reception in the target linguacultural environment. To stress only the latter factor, as is done in the functionalist(ic) approach to translation, is unwarranted. What is needed is a definition of what a translation is, when a text is no longer a translation but a text derived from different multilingual textual operations and an explicitation of the constraints governing the translation process. With regard to the three questions, we can say that it is particularly with reference to the issue of distinguishing a translation from other forms of texts that the functionalistic approach seems inadequate.

TEXT- AND DISCOURSE-ORIENTED VIEWS

Under this heading, I subsume descriptive-historical translation studies, post–modernist and deconstructionist views, as well as linguistically oriented approaches to translation quality assessment. I will discuss them in turn.

DESCRIPTIVE-HISTORICAL TRANSLATION STUDIES

In this approach, a translation is evaluated from the viewpoint of its potential recipients in terms of its forms and functions inside the system of the receiving culture and literature. The original is of subordinate importance. The procedure followed in this paradigm is thus essentially a retrospective one: from a translation to its original text the concept of equivalence is retained, but it does not refer to a one-to-one relationship between original and translation. Rather it is seen as sets of relationships found to characterize translations under specified circumstances. The characteristic features of a translation are 'neutrally described' according to whether these features are perceived on the basis of native culture members' tacit knowledge of comparable textual specimens in the genre into which the translation is inserted. They are not to be 'prescriptively pre-judged' in their correspondence to, or deviation from, features of the original text. However, if one wants to evaluate a particular translation, which is never an independent new text in a new culture alone, but is related to a pre-existing entity, then such a view of translation (quality assessment) seems strangely skewed. With respect to the three criteria, we can thus state that this theory is deficient with regard to illuminating the relationship between source and translation texts.

POST-MODERNIST, POST-STRUCTURALIST AND DECONSTRUCTIONIST APPROACHES

Proponents of these approaches try to critically examine original and translated texts from a psycho-philosophical, socio-political and ideological stance in order to reveal unequal power relations and manipulations in the textual material. In a plea for making translations and translators more 'visible', adherents of this approach try to make a point of focusing on the 'hidden persuaders' in texts whose potentially ulterior, often power-related motives are to be brought into the open. One may hold against such a predominant interest in 'external pressures' on translation the argument that translation is after all first and foremost a *linguistic* procedure – however conditioned this procedure may be through ideological positions and shifts. Before adopting a critical stance vis-à-vis translations emphasizing the importance of a macro-perspective, one needs to engage in a more modest micro-perspective, i.e., conduct detailed, theoretically informed analyses of the choices of linguistic forms in original texts and their translations as well as the consequences of these choices. However, it is also true that one does not exclude the other. In fact, many scholars would argue that both are necessary. With respect to the three questions posed above, post-modern approaches are most relevant in their attempts to find answers to the first question and also to the second one. However, no answers are sought to the question of when a text is a translation and when the translation results from a different multilingual textual operation.

LINGUISTICALLY ORIENTED APPROACHES

A pioneering approach to evaluating a translation in this paradigm is Reiss' (1971) attempt to set up a text typology relevant for translation evaluation. Following Bühler (1934/1965), she assumed that it is the text type (expressive, informative, operative) and the corresponding function of a text (see here also the classic typology by Jakobson 1960) to which the original belongs which, as the most important invariant for a translation, pre-determines all subsequent translational decisions. Unfortunately, Reiss failed to give precise indications as to how one might go about conducting an assessment of whether and how original and translation are equivalent in terms of textual type and otherwise.

Linguistic approaches to translation quality assessment take the relationship between original and translation seriously: they try to explicate the relationship between (features of) the text and how these are perceived by authors, translators and readers, but they differ in their capacity to provide detailed procedures of how to go about analysis and evaluation. Most promising are approaches that take account of the interconnectedness of context and text, because the inextricable link between language and the real world is definitive both in meaning making and in translation. Such a view of translation as re-contextualization is the line taken in House's model of translation criticism first developed in 1977, and revised in 1997 and 2015.

A LINGUISTIC MODEL OF TRANSLATION QUALITY ASSESSMENT

EQUIVALENCE AND 'MEANING' IN TRANSLATION

So far, we have considered different approaches to translation evaluation with a view to how they look upon the relationships between texts and human agents involved in translational action and between translations and other textual operations. These relationships implicitly touch upon the single most important concept in translation theory: that of 'equivalence', a concept briefly touched upon in Chapter 3. **Equivalence** is rooted in everyday folk linguistic understanding of translation as a 'reproduction' of something originally produced in another language – and it is this everyday view of what makes a translation a translation which legitimizes a view of translation as being in a kind of 'double-bind' relationship, i.e., one characterized by a relationship to both the source text and the translation text (see here especially the discussion in Koller 1995 and Krein-Kühle 2014). Over and above its role as a concept constitutive of translation, equivalence is also a fundamental notion for translation quality assessment. The linguistic, **functional-pragmatic model of translation criticism** which the author of this book has proposed is therefore firmly based on equivalence. Translations are here conceived as texts that are doubly constrained: by their originals and by the new recipient's communicative conditions. This is the basis of the 'equivalence relation', i.e., the relation between a source text and its translation text. Equivalence is the fundamental criterion of translation quality. One of the aims of an adequate assessment is to specify the equivalence relation by differentiating between different equivalence frameworks, e.g., extra-linguistic circumstances, connotative and aesthetic values, audience design and last but not least textual norms of usage that have emerged from empirical investigations of parallel texts and contrastive-pragmatic analyses.

While any translator sets up a hierarchy of demands on equivalence which she wants to follow, it stands to reason that functional-pragmatic equivalence is most relevant for translation. This is reflected in the functional-pragmatic model, where equivalence is related to the preservation of 'meaning' across two different languages and cultures. Three aspects of that 'meaning' are particularly important for translation: a semantic, a pragmatic and a textual aspect. Translation can then be defined as the replacement of a text in the source language by a semantically and pragmatically equivalent text in the target language, and an adequate translation is a pragmatically semantically equivalent one. As a first requirement for this equivalence, it is posited that a translation text should have a function equivalent to that of its original. However, this requirement needs to be differentiated given the existence of an empirically derived distinction into **overt and covert translation**, concepts which will be discussed in detail below.

The use of 'function' presupposes that there are elements in a text which, given appropriate tools, *can* reveal a function. The use of the concept of function is here not to be equated with functions of language – different language functions clearly always co-exist inside any text, and a simple equation of language function with textual function/textual type is overly simplistic. Rather, a text's function is defined pragmatically as the application of the text in a particular context (see here also House 2006a, where the relationship between text and context is explored in detail). Text and 'context of situation' should thus not be viewed as separate entities, rather the context of situation in which the text unfolds is encapsulated in the text through a systematic relationship between the social environment and the functional organization of language. So a text is to be referred to the particular situation enveloping it, and for this, a way must be found to break down the broad notion of context of situation into manageable parts, i.e., particular features of the context of situation or 'situational dimensions'. Within systemic-functionalist linguistics, different systems have been suggested featuring situational dimensions as abstract components of the context of situation. The original model of translation quality assessment developed by House (1977) used three dimensions characterizing the text's author according to her temporal, geographical and social provenance and five pragmatic dimensions of language use elaborating on the text's topic and on the interaction of, and relationship between, author and recipients in terms of their social role relationship, the social attitude or style level obtaining, the degree of participant involvement and the degree of writtenness or spokenness of the text. The operation of the model involved initially an analysis of the original text according to this set of situational dimensions, for which linguistic correlates were established. The linguistic correlates of the situational dimensions are the means with which the textual function is realized, and the textual function is the result of a linguistic-pragmatic analysis along the dimensions with each dimension contributing to the **two functional components**, the **ideational and the interpersonal**. Opening up the text with these dimensions yields a specific textual profile that characterizes its function, which is then taken as the individual textual norm against which the translated text is measured. The degree to which the textual profile and function of the translation (as derived from an analogous analysis) match the profile and function of the original is then the degree to which the translation is adequate in quality. The set of situational dimensions is thus a kind of 'tertium comparationis'. In evaluating the relative match between original and translation, a distinction is made between 'dimensional mismatches' and 'non-dimensional mismatches'. Dimensional mismatches are pragmatic errors, and non-dimensional mismatches are errors with regard to denotative meanings in the translation as well as breaches of target language norms. The final qualitative judgment of the translation consists then of both types of errors and of a statement of the relative match of the two functional components.

In the revised model, the classic Hallidayan **Register dimensions** of '**Field**', '**Mode**' and '**Tenor**' (see Halliday 1973, 1994; Halliday and Matthiessen 2011) are used. Field captures the topic and content of the text, its subject matter, with differentiations of degrees of generality, specificity or granularity in lexical items according to rubrics of specialized, general and popular. It also captures different so-called 'processes', such as material processes (verbs of doing), mental processes (verbs of thinking, believing, opining) or relational ones (of being and having). Tenor refers to the nature of the participants, the addresser and the addressees, and the relationship between them in terms of social power and social distance, as well as degree of 'emotional charge'. Included here are the text producer's temporal, geographical and social provenance and his intellectual, emotional or affective stance (his 'personal viewpoint') vis-à-vis the content he is portraying and the communicative task he is engaged in. Further, Tenor captures 'social attitude', i.e., different styles (formal, consultative and informal). Linguistic indices realized along the dimension of Tenor are those of Mood and Modality. Mode refers to both the channel – spoken or written (which can be 'simple', i.e., 'written to be read' or 'complex', e.g. 'written to be spoken as if not written'), and the degree to which potential or real participation is allowed for between writer and reader. Participation can also be 'simple', i.e., be a monologue with no addressee participation built into the text, or 'complex' with various addressee-involving mechanisms characterizing the text. In taking account of (linguistically documentable) differences in texts between the spoken and written medium (see Halliday and Hasan 1989), reference is also made to the empirically established corpus-based oral-literate dimensions (cf. Biber 1988; Biber et al. 1999) along which linguistic choices may reflect medium, i.e., involved vs informational text production; explicit vs situation-dependent reference; abstract vs non-abstract presentation of information.

The type of textual analysis in which linguistic features discovered in the original and the translation are correlated with the categories Field, Tenor, Mode does not, however, lead directly to a statement of the individual textual function (and its interpersonal and ideational components). Rather, the concept of 'Genre' is incorporated into the analytic scheme, 'in between', as it were, the register categories of Field, Tenor, Mode. Genre enables one to refer any single textual exemplar to the class of texts with which it shares a common purpose or function. Genre is a category superordinate to Register. While Register captures the connection between texts and their 'microcontext', Genre connects texts with the 'macrocontext' of the linguaculture community in which a text is embedded, for example the type of institution in which a text conventionally appears (for instance a sermon that traditionally occurs in a place of worship).

The resultant scheme for textual analysis, comparison and assessment is shown in Figure 7.1.

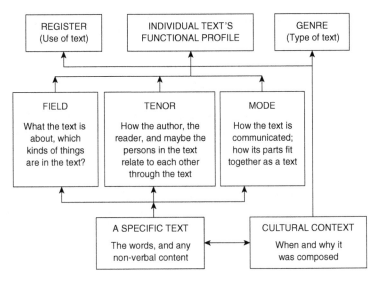

Figure 7.1 A system for analysing and comparing texts for translation purposes

Taken together, the analysis provided in this assessment model along the levels of the individual text, Register and Genre building one on the other in a systematic way yields a textual profile that characterizes the individual textual function. But, as mentioned above, whether and how this textual function can in fact be maintained depends on the type of translation sought for the original.

In the following section, the nature of these two fundamental types of translation is discussed.

OVERT AND COVERT TRANSLATION

The distinction between two fundamentally different types of translation: the terms overt and covert translation go back to Friedrich Schleiermacher's (1813) famous distinction between **'verfremdende' (alienating) and 'einbürgernde' (integrating) translations**, which has had many imitators using different terms. What sets the overt–covert distinction made in the assessment model apart from other similar distinctions is the fact that it is part of a coherent theory of translation quality assessment inside which the origin and function of the two types of translation are theoretically motivated and consistently explicated. The distinction is as follows: in an **overt translation**, the receptors of the translation are quite 'overtly' not being addressed; an overt translation is thus one which must overtly be a translation, not a 'second original'. The source text is tied in a specific manner to the source linguaculture. The original is specifically directed at source culture addressees but at the same time points beyond the source culture because it is also of general human interest. Source texts that call for an overt translation have an established worth in the source language community. They are either overt historical source texts tied to a specific occasion where a precisely specified source language audience is/was being addressed, or they may be timeless source texts transcending as works of art and aesthetic creations a distinct historical meaning.

A **covert translation** is a translation which enjoys the status of an original source text in the target culture. The translation is covert because it is not marked pragmatically as a translation text of a source text but may, conceivably, have been created in its own right as an independent text. A covert translation is thus a translation whose source text is not specifically addressed to a particular source culture audience, i.e., it is not firmly tied to the source linguaculture. A source text and its covert translation are pragmatically of comparable interest for source and target language addressees. Both are, as it were, equally directly addressed. A source text and its covert translation have equivalent purposes. They are based on contemporary equivalent needs of a comparable audience in the source and target language communities. In the case of covert translation texts, it is thus both possible and desirable to keep the function of the source text equivalent in the translation text. This can be done by inserting a 'cultural filter' between original and translation with which to account for cultural differences between the two linguistic communities.

Applying the concepts to overt and covert translation, we can propose the following: in overt translation, the translation text is embedded in a new speech event, which gives it also a new frame. An overt translation is a case of 'language mention', similar to a quotation. Relating the concept of 'overt translation' to the four-tiered analytical model (Function – Genre – Register – Language/Text), we can state that an original and its overt translation can be equivalent at the level of Language/Text and Register as well as Genre. At the level of the individual textual function, however, functional equivalence, while still possible, is of a different nature: it can be described as merely enabling access to the function the original has in its discourse world or frame. An example would be a speech by Winston Churchill during the Second World War at a particular time and in a particular location. A translation of this speech from English into any other language can obviously not 'mean the same' to the new addressees. So a switch in discourse world and frame becomes necessary, i.e., the translation will have to be differently framed, it will operate in its own frame and discourse world, and can thus reach at best 'second-level functional equivalence'. As this type of equivalence is, however, achieved though equivalence at the levels of Language, Text, Register and Genre, the original's frame and discourse world will be co-activated, such that members of the target culture may eavesdrop, as it were, i.e., be enabled to appreciate the original textual function, albeit at a distance. Coming back to the example of Churchill's speech, this distance can be explained not only by the fact that the speech happened in the past but also by the fact that the translation's addressees belong to a different linguacultural community. In overt translation, the work of the translator is important and clearly visible. Since it is the translator's task to permit target culture members to access the original text and its cultural impact on source culture members, the translator puts target culture members in a position to observe this text 'from outside', so to speak.

In covert translation, the translator will attempt to re-create an equivalent speech event. Consequently, the function of a covert translation is to reproduce in the target text the function the original has in its frame and discourse world. A covert translation operates quite 'overtly' in the frame and discourse world provided by the target culture. No attempt is made to co-activate the discourse world in which the original unfolded (see below for an explanation). Covert translation is both psycholinguistically less complex than overt translation and more deceptive. The translator's task is to betray the origin, to hide behind the transformation of the original, necessary due to the adaptation to the needs and knowledge levels of the new target audience. The translator in covert translation is clearly less visible, if not totally absent. Since true functional equivalence is aimed at, the original may be legitimately manipulated at the levels of Language/Text and Register using a so-called cultural filter (see below). The result may be a very real distance from the original. While an original and its covert translation need thus not be equivalent at the levels of Language/Text and Register, they will be equivalent at the level of genre and the individual textual function.

In assessing the quality of a translation, it is essential that the fundamental differences between these two types of translation be taken into account. Overt and covert translation make very different demands on translation quality assessment. The difficulty of evaluating an overt translation is reduced in that considerations of cultural filtering can be omitted. Overt translations are 'more straightforward', the originals being taken over 'unfiltered' and 'simply' transposed from the source to the target culture in the medium of a new language. The major difficulty in translating overtly is, of course, finding **linguistic–cultural 'equivalents'**, particularly along the dimension of Tenor and its characterizations of the author's temporal, social and geographical provenience. However, here we deal with **overt** manifestations of cultural phenomena that are transferred only because they happen to be manifest linguistically in the original. A judgment regarding whether, for example, a 'translation' of a dialect is adequate in overt translation can ultimately not be objectively given: the degree of correspondence in terms of social prestige and status cannot be measured in the absence of complete contrastive ethnographic studies – if, indeed, there will ever be such studies. In other words, such an evaluation will necessarily remain to a certain degree a subjective matter. However, as opposed to the difficulty in covert translation of evaluating differences in cultural presuppositions and communicative preferences between text production in the source and target cultures, the explicit overt transference in an overt translation is still easier to judge.

In assessing the quality of covert translations, we need to consider how the 'cultural filter' was applied.

THE CULTURAL FILTER

The **'cultural filter'** is a means of capturing socio-cultural differences in expectation norms and stylistic conventions between the source and target linguacultural communities. The concept was used to emphasize the need for an empirical basis for 'manipulations' of the original undertaken by the translator. Whether or not there is an empirical basis for changes of the original text would need to be reflected in the assessment of the translation. Further, given the goal of achieving functional equivalence in a covert translation, assumptions of cultural difference should be carefully examined before any change in the source text is undertaken. In cases of unproven assumptions of cultural difference, the translator might apply a cultural filter whose application – resulting in possibly deliberate mismatches between original and translation along several situational parameters – may be unjustified. The unmarked assumption is one of cultural compatibility. In the case of, for example, the German and Anglophone linguistic and cultural communities, such evidence seems now to be available, with important consequences for cultural filtering in the case of this language pair. Since its first proposal, the concept of cultural filter has gained substance through contrastive-pragmatic studies, in which Anglophone and German communicative preferences were hypothesized. Converging evidence from these studies conducted with many different data, subjects and methodologies suggest that there are German communicative preferences which differ from Anglophone ones along a set of dimensions, among them directness, content-focus, explicitness and a preference for using verbal routines over ad hoc formulation. For the comparative analysis of source and target texts and the evaluation of a covert translation, one needs to take account of whatever knowledge exists about linguacultural differences between source and target linguacultures.

In discussing different types of translations, we implicitly assume that a particular text may be adequately translated in only one particular way. The assumption that a particular text necessitates either a covert or an overt translation does, however, not hold in any simple way. Thus, any text may, for a specific purpose, require an overt translation. The text may be viewed as a document which 'has an independent value' existing in its own right, e.g., when its author has become, in the course of time, a distinguished figure, and then the translation may need to be an overt one. Further, there may well be source texts for which the choice between overt and covert translations is necessarily a subjective one, e.g., fairy tales may be viewed as products of a particular culture, which would predispose the translator to opt for an overt translation, or as non-culture specific texts, anonymously produced, with the general function of entertaining and educating the young, which would suggest a covert translation.

Returning to the three questions we asked at the beginning of this chapter: relationship between original and translation, between texts and human agents and a distinction between translations and other secondary textual operations – the assessment model presented here is firmly based on a view of translation as a double-linkage operation. It posits a cline along which the nature of the double-linkage can be revealed for any particular translation case – the two endpoints of the cline being overt translation and covert translation. The relationship between (features) of the text(s) and the human agents involved (as author, translator, recipient) is explicitly accounted for through the provision of an elaborate system of pragmatic-functional analysis of original and translation, with the overt–covert cline on which a translation is to be placed determining the type of reception sought and likely to be achieved. Finally, explicit means are provided for distinguishing a translation from other types of textual operation by specifying the conditions holding for a translation to turn into a version.

Integrating **empirically verified cultural filters** into the assessment process makes for greater certainty regarding when a translation is no longer a translation but a version. However, given the dynamic nature of communicative norms and the way research tends to lag behind practice, translation critics will still have to struggle to remain abreast of new developments that will enable them to judge the appropriateness of changes through the application of a cultural filter in any given language pair.

LINGUISTIC ANALYSIS VERSUS SOCIAL EVALUATION

In translation quality assessment, it is important to be maximally aware of the difference between (scientifically based) analysis and (social) judgment in evaluating a translation. In other words, there is a difference between comparing textual profiles, describing and explaining differences established in linguistic-textual analysis and evaluating the quality of a translation. What a linguistic model of translation quality assessment can do is provide a basis for systematic comparison, making explicit the factors that may theoretically have influenced the translator in making certain decisions and rejecting others, thus providing the basis for evaluating a particular case.

Instead of taking the complex socio-psychological categories of translation receptors' intuitions, feelings, reactions or beliefs as a cornerstone for translation quality assessment, a linguistic, functional-pragmatic approach, which takes account of language in its socio-cultural context, focuses on texts which are the products of (often unfathomable) human decision processes and as such are most tangible and least ambiguously analysable entities. Such an approach, however, does not enable the evaluator to pass judgments on what is a 'good' or a 'bad' translation. A linguistic approach can prepare the ground for the analysis of a large number of evaluation cases that would, in each individual case, not be totally predictable. In the last analysis, then, any evaluation depends on a variety of factors that necessarily enter into a social evaluative judgment. Such a judgment emanates from the analytic, comparative process of translation criticism, i.e., the linguistic analysis provides grounds for arguing an evaluative judgment. As suggested above, the choice of an overt or a covert translation depends not on the translator, on the source text, or on her subjective interpretation of the text but also on the reasons for the translation, the instructions given to the translator, the implied readers, publishing and marketing policies, all of which implies that there are many factors which have nothing to do with translation as a linguistic procedure. Such factors are social and socio-psychological ones, which concern human agents and are therefore subject to socio-cultural, political or ideological constraints. Linguistic description and explanation must not be confused with evaluative assertions made on the basis of social, political, ethical or individual grounds alone. It seems imperative to emphasize the distinction between linguistic analysis and social socio-psychological evaluation given the current climate where the criteria of scientific validity and reliability are often usurped by criteria such as social acceptability, political correctness, vague emotional commitment or fleeting 'Zeitgeist'. Translation as a phenomenon in its own right, as a linguistic-textual operation, should not be confused with issues such as what the translation is for, what it should, might or must be for. One of the drawbacks of an overriding concern with the covert end of the translation cline is that the borders between a translation and other multilingual textual operations become blurred. In view of this confusion, some conceptual clarity can be reached by theoretically distinguishing between translations and versions and by positing functional equivalence ('real' or second-level) as a sine qua non in translation.

The core concept of translation quality assessment is **translation quality**. This is a problematical concept if it is taken to involve individual value judgments alone. It is difficult to pass any 'final judgment' on the quality of a translation that fulfils the demands of scientific objectivity. This should not, however, be taken to mean that translation quality assessment as a field of inquiry is worthless. But one should be aware that in translation quality assessment, one will always be forced to move from a macro-analytical focus to a micro-analytical one, from considerations of ideology, function, Genre, Register to the communicative value of collocations and individual linguistic items and back again! In taking this dual, complementary perspective, the translation critic is enabled to approximate the reconstruction of the translator's choices and to throw light on her decision processes. That this is an extremely complex undertaking which, in the end, yields but probabilistic outcomes, should not detract from its usefulness. In translation quality assessment, one should aim at revealing exactly where and with which consequences and (possibly) for which reasons, a translation is what it is in relation to its original. Such a procedure, evolving from attempts to make explicit the grounds of one's (preliminary) judgments on the basis of an argued set of procedures, might guard against making prescriptive, apodictic and global judgments (of the 'good' vs 'bad' type), which can never be verifiable.

Translation quality assessment, like language itself, has two functional components, an ideational and an interpersonal one, that lead to two separable steps: the first and primary one referring to linguistic analysis, description and explanation based on knowledge and research; the second and secondary one referring to value judgments, social and ethical questions of relevance and personal taste.

In the study of translation, we need both. Judging without analysing is irresponsible, and analysing without judging is pointless. To judge is easy, to understand less so. If we can make explicit the grounds of our judgment on the basis of an argued set of procedures, such as the one developed in the assessment model presented above, we can discuss and refine them; if we do not, we can merely disagree.

MOST RECENT VERSION OF HOUSE'S QUALITY ASSESSMENT MODEL

This newly revised model (House 2015a) integrates findings from contrastive pragmatics, intercultural communication and from corpus studies.

Contrastive pragmatics and intercultural communication are of increasing importance for substantiating the notion of the cultural filter in the model, but the possibility of variation and change in an age of increasing mobility needs to be constantly watched. This throws an extra burden on the translation quality assessors. There are no easy, all-purpose and eternally valid generalizations that can be employed, but individual cases must be considered to determine whether and how cultural filtering is to be applied.

Corpus studies, discussed in detail in Chapter 9, are naturally important for extending an evaluator's view of the individual text as a single exemplar to a collectivity of similar texts in the same genre. This means that the notion of Genre in the assessment model can now be made more concrete. Corpus studies provide the evaluator with information about whether and how far features of a single text are in line with the norms and conventions of the Genre in the target culture. There is also an obvious link here with the notion of the cultural filter such that the two notions supplement one another.

Over and above these modifications of the model which originated in taking cognizance of new research in selected areas, the model was also revised 'internally' in the dimensions of Field, Tenor and Mode. Thus, within Field, the analysis now focuses exclusively on lexis, granularity of lexis, lexical fields and Hallidayan processes (Material, Mental, Relational). Within Tenor, lexical and syntactic choices are examined along the subcategories of Stance, Social Role Relationship, Social Attitude and also Participation. And along Mode, the analysis looks at textual matters featuring as before Medium (spokenness versus writtenness), Theme–Rheme, Connectivity (Coherence and Cohesion).

The resulting newly revised model is displayed in Figure 7.2.

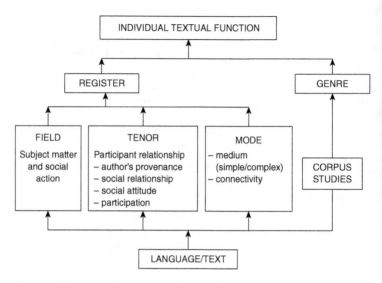

Figure 7.2 A revised scheme for analysing and comparing originals and translation texts

SOME RECENT DEVELOPMENTS IN TESTING TRANSLATION QUALITY

Since the early proposals of tests of translation quality in the 1960s followed by response-based tests in the form of comprehension, readability and naturalness checks, more recent progress in computer and communication technology, coupled with an ever-increasing demand in a globalized world for fast and inexpensive translations has led to the development of formalized approaches to translation quality assurance including quality assurance software such as TRADOS, WF or QAD. These programs are mainly used to verify terminology, compare source and target text segments and to detect (mostly formal and terminology related) errors. Such software does not replace human editors, it assists them. However, it cannot at the present time detect stylistic and Register infelicities resulting from faulty understanding of the source text.

In addition to translation quality assurance software and metrics following the demand for measures that are repeatable, reproducible and objective, the availability of large multilingual parallel corpora adds important knowledge sources for tests of both automatic and human translation quality. Many automatic evaluation methods using translation quality metrics such as BLEU (Bilingual Evaluation Understudy) now compare machine translation output with reference translations trying to correlate automatic translations with judgments by expert human translators or quality panels for validation and the generation of similar scores.

PART 3

SOME IMPORTANT NEW TRENDS IN TRANSLATION STUDIES

This part looks at several newer trends in translation studies. Chapter 8 describes studies of what goes on in a translator's mind while she is translating, Chapter 9 discusses a new and influential methodology in translation studies: corpus studies, and Chapter 10 looks at the impact that contemporary, worldwide political, social and technological trends are having on translation.

DOI: 10.4324/9781003355823-10

WHAT GOES ON IN TRANSLATORS' HEADS WHEN THEY ARE TRANSLATING?

This chapter discusses some methods and results of research into the process of translation. We will look at methods by which one tries to tap into what goes on while a translator is translating and at methods that ask translators after they have been translating. We will also examine some new experimental methods of researching the process of translating, such as keylogging or eye-tracking, as well as neuro-linguistic studies for translation and, finally, we will examine a new combination of a translation theory and a neuro-functional theory of bilingualism.

TRANSLATION PROCESS STUDIES USING INTROSPECTION AND VERBAL REPORTING

Introspective and **verbal report data** are oral productions by translators elicited while they are in the process of translation (i.e., concurrently) or immediately afterwards (retrospectively). They frequently involve monologic, sometimes also dialogic tasks, as well as rating and other decision-eliciting tasks, such as interviews with translators, questionnaires or surveys, and they have been an immensely popular research paradigm since their inception in the 1980s. The theoretical and methodological framework of cognitive explorations of translation comes mainly from cognitive psychology and in particular from Ericsson and Simon's (1984) framework which is based on the assumption that human cognition resembles information processing and that human beings are in a position to accurately report on what is being processed in working memory at

DOI: 10.4324/9781003355823-11

any point of time. **Thinking aloud** is supposed to give insight into translators' cognitive processes if they involve consciously processed information. In the case of retrospective translation process research, the participants' working memory constraints may be a critical factor, and some researchers (for instance Muñoz Martín 2010) have questioned whether translators can retrospectively access the same cognitive processes that occurred during the act of translation. Muñoz Martín suggested that it is more likely that during retrospection translators tend to construct knowledge about what they *think* has happened during the process of translation.

The validity and reliability of the verbal report data elicited in such process studies, however, have more often than not been taken for granted, although they are in fact far from clear. Despite many attempts over the past decades to improve the quality of **thinking-aloud protocol (TAP)** data – offering intensive preparatory training sessions to better enable subjects to provide insights into their strategy-using behaviour – the general assumption behind this type of research has not really been questioned. The fundamental question underlying all verbal report studies is that persons involved in the act of translating have substantial control over their mental processes, that these processes are to a large extent accessible to them, i.e., open to their conscious inspection, and that they can be reliably talked about. It is, however, far from clear that this assumption is valid. Even more important is the fact that at present it is not at all clear that this assumption *can* be confirmed or falsified.

There seem to be at least five important but still unresolved questions with regard to translation-related introspective and retrospective research methodology:

1. Is what ends up being verbally expressed in thinking-aloud sessions really identical to underlying cognitive processes?
2. Exactly which cognitive processes are accessible to verbalization and which are not, i.e., how can one differentiate between metacognitive monitoring and reflective (declarative) behaviour on the one hand and routinized (procedural) behaviour on the other hand?
3. Does the fact that translators are asked to verbalize their thoughts while they are engaged in translating, change those cognitive processes that are (normally) involved in translation?

In other words, are translators engaged in introspection sessions subject to the so-called observer's paradox?

4. What happens to those parts of (often expert) translators' activity that are highly, if not entirely, routinized and automatized and are thus *per definitionem* not open to reflection?

5. With regard to retrospective translation-related research: how can data from *ex post facto* interviews or questionnaires access translation processes given working memory constraints and given the pressure felt by subjects to provide data that will satisfy the researcher? Is it not likely that subjects will make meta-statements about what they think they had thought?

Over and above these five queries, **translation process research** needs to take into account one of the most controversial issues in cognitive science today: the nature of consciousness. Much recent neuroscience literature in fact stresses the importance of the non-conscious – indeed, a depressing finding for translation process research. We first need a comprehensive theory of consciousness that goes beyond an exclusive focus on (inaccessible) representations and that attempts to explain how those representations are experienced and accessed by multiple functions in the human brain.

Fortunately, there is an increasing awareness of the critical methodological issues in translation process research mentioned above. Thus, in a paper with the promising title – 'Back to Basics: Designing a Study to Determine the Validity and Reliability of Verbal Report Data on Translation Processes' – Riitta *Jääskeläinen* (2011), an eminent translation process researcher, has sensibly pointed out that there is a need for a systematic methodological study on the use of verbal report data, a study that would take into account the specific nature of translation tasks and incorporate contrastive analyses of the language pairs involved in the translation on hand.

TRANSLATION PROCESS RESEARCH USING BEHAVIOURAL EXPERIMENTS

Given the type of disappointment with attempts to look into the translator's 'black box' in introspective and **retrospective translation process research** described above, translation scholars have now tried to remedy the situation. They came up with more controlled behavioural experiments designed to avoid examining and making claims about the 'black box' and instead directly trace linear and non-linear translational steps and phases in translational behaviour, measuring the temporal progress or delay, the types and numbers of revisions undertaken by the translator, the (measurable) effort expended, the nature and number of attention foci and attention shifts as well as the frequency and kind of emotional stress responses shown by the translator while translating. This ambitious agenda was made possible through recent, mostly computer-related technological progress such that experiments using keystroke logging (or keylogging), screen recording, eye-tracking and various other physiological measures could now be undertaken.

Physiological measures directly record stress, frustration, arousal and other types of emotion that might occur during the translation process. Skin responses, blood volume pressure and EEGs (electroencephalography) are among the most frequently used physiological measures. The skin response test measures the flow of electricity through the skin, which increases when an individual sweats more when she is under stress. EEGs use electrodes to measure the activity in the brain in response to emotions, stress, etc.

Keystroke logging involves the use of computer software to log every key pressed down on the keyboard including deletions, up and down scrolling, cutting and pasting, switches between mouse and keyboard as well as pauses. Originally developed for human-computer research and especially for research into the writing process, keystroke logging was also adapted for translation process research. A keystroke logging tool called Translog was designed (see here Jakobsen and Schou 1999, and for a newer overview Carl et al. 2015). **Translog** records the keys pressed down during the activity of translation and it produces a log file, which can then be analysed in a systematic way. Keystroke logging has been employed to examine a number of different questions concerning the translation process such as, for instance, is there evidence for the existence of 'units of translation'? What is the difference between expert and novice translators? Do expert translators use the keyboard differently from novice translators? With Translog one also gets a 'screen recording', which can be used to play back and then see what actually happens on the translator's monitor during the translation. Such 'screen recording' is often used to supplement thinking-aloud protocols and keylogging data as well as data gained through other means, such as interviews, questionnaires or surveys. Screen recordings can also be used to help participants in retrospective activities. Here, the translator watches the screen recording and uses it to help him construct a representation of what he was thinking during the translation process.

In the **eye-tracking method**, cameras are used to track the position of the translator's eyes on a user interface. Infrared light is reflected off parts of the eye and specialized software records the eye movement data. When we are processing information, our eyes make either rapid movements, known as 'saccades', or longer, sweeping movements. The latter provides evidence of attention shifts. Forward and backward saccades are normal in reading and writing tasks. Longer sweeps of the eye, however, can provide evidence of attention shifts between original and translation texts. This, in turn, can be used to detect difficulties with parts of the original text or can throw light on differences between normal monolingual reading and 'reading for translation' (see here Jensen 2008).

Eye-tracking equipment can also be used to record measures that have been shown to be indicative of cognitive effort. These measures include fixations and pupil dilation. (Fixations are eye movements that stabilize the retina over a stationary object of interest.) In translation process, research measuring fixations can, for instance, be used to examine differences between expert and novice translators in terms of handling translation problems.

Another strand of research into the process of translation concerns the quest for the '**translation unit**' associated with cognitive effort expended during a translation task (see for instance Alves et al. 2010). From a traditional, cognitive-oriented view, a translation unit was defined as the segment actually processed and identified on the basis of cognitive processes observable (indirectly) in a set of data. Alternatively, Alves et al. (2010) suggest combining a product perspective with a process perspective for defining translation units, and they suggest that time and the translator's momentary focus of attention are crucial for a definition of a translation unit and for establishing what type of unit is being processed at any given moment in the ongoing translation activity. So translation units are source text segments, of whatever extension or nature, which attract the translator's focus of attention at a given time in the translation process. Although translation units are source text segments, by analysing ongoing target text production, one can also momentarily capture a translation unit as a target text production segment located between pauses that can then be mapped onto a source text segment.

Overviews of **behavioural translation-related research** that often neatly combines various tools (e.g. keystroke logging and eye-tracking) (see, for instance, Shreve and Angelone 2010; O'Brien 2011) make the important general point that much of this type of translation process research regularly displays great individual variation, which, Sharon O'Brien claims, is only to be expected given the fact that we are here dealing with individual human beings. It might be advisable to go beyond those predominantly quantitative data elicited via keystroke logging, eye-tracking and so on by attempting a more integrative take on the translation process involving a translator's personal 'life story'. Still, there remain at least two critical points:

- Can measurements of observable behaviour (as provided in keylogging, eye-tracking, etc.) inform us about cognitive processes that occur in a translator's mind?
- Can measurements of observable behaviour explain the nature of cognitive representations of the two languages, can they throw light on a translator's metalinguistic and linguistic-contrastive knowledge, and illuminate comprehension, transfer and reconstitution processes emerging in translation procedures?

What such experiments *can* and *do* measure is exactly what they set out to measure: observable behaviour, no more and no less. This is not to belittle their worth – far from it. However, the results of such behavioural experiments cannot be taken as indications of processes in the minds of translators. Rather, they should be seen as interesting hypotheses. If such experiments are combined with theoretical models that incorporate features of semantic representation and of processing, they may pave the way towards abandoning any clear-cut distinction between product and process in favour of more a holistic and unitary perspective on product and process. It is necessary, however, to always clearly differentiate between cognitive-psychological processes and the underlying neural correlates. The number of gaze fixations, pause length, incidence of self-corrections examined in keylogging and eye-tracking experiments cannot point to the involvement of certain neurological substrates. Rather, they are likely to point to certain translation difficulties and the necessary decision processes, and these may involve certain neural networks more than others. Still, the crux is that the involvement of neural networks cannot tell us exactly *which* processes are connected with these networks. This problem led many to look at a new research strand: bilingual neuro-imaging studies have emerged, only recently made possible by technological progress.

BILINGUAL NEURO-IMAGING STUDIES

Can **neuro-imaging studies** give us 'a direct window' on the translator's 'black box', on what goes on in a translator's mind, finally providing us with a solution to Krings' question in 1986: 'What happens in translators' heads?' First of all, we may well doubt the accuracy of the findings of such studies, not least because they crucially depend on the type of task used. With the exception of some rare recent use of isolated sentences, **functional magnetic resonance imaging (fMRI), positron emission tomography (PET) and event-related potential (ERP)** studies are word based. However, translation is, as we have discussed above, essentially text based. Any application of neuro-imaging experimental research to translation thus faces the dilemma that translation research is essentially interested in less controllable, larger and more 'messy' units.

The neurolinguistics researcher Michel Paradis commented on the lack of ecological validity of neuro-imaging research:

> The use of any task other than the natural use of language (including natural switching and mixing) has the same consequence as using single words: the task does not tap the normal automatic processes that sustain the natural use of language including the contribution of pragmatics and its neural underpinnings.
>
> (2009:157–158)

Over two-thirds of neuro-imaging studies on laterality and language switching and mixing use single words as stimuli, for instance in picture-naming experiments where subjects are asked to switch on command. However, as Paradis has pointed out, brain activity crucially differs for language use in natural situations and in language use 'on cue', and, most importantly, these situations correspond to opposite types of processes. Indeed, single words are very different from the rest of language. They are part of the (conscious) vocabulary of a language, not part of the lexicon. The latter includes morpho-syntactic properties and is integrated into each language subsystem's neural network in the bilingual brain. Single word stimuli are explicitly known form-meaning associations subserved by declarative memory, while procedural memory underlies normal, natural language use. Each memory system relies on distinct neuro-functional structures. And normal, natural language use also critically involves cortical areas of the brain's right hemisphere to process the pragmatic aspects of utterances – this, however, is irrelevant in processing single words that are used out of context.

Another problem with neuro-imaging data that needs to be addressed relates to the nature of the evidence from neuro-imaging data: blood flow and other hemo-dynamic responses routinely provided in such data cannot be taken to be direct measures of neuronal activity. Most neuro-imaging studies have not been replicated. Many reported neurological activations are strongly task-dependent and rely on a particular technique employed, so that replication is difficult. And it is this task and technique dependence which suggests that the reported activations in the brain are indicative of the particular task and technique employed rather than being indicative of language representation, processing and switching per se.

Given these shortcomings, it is advisable to first look for a theory with enough descriptive and explanatory potential before expecting enlightenment from experimental neuro-imaging studies, whose usefulness for translation studies is, at the present time, not clear at all.

A NEURO-LINGUISTIC THEORY OF THE FUNCTIONING OF TWO LANGUAGES IN THE BRAIN

Paradis (2004:227) has proposed the **neuro-linguistic theory** illustrated in Figure 8.1– the neuro-functional and linguistic-cognitive system of the bilingual mind.

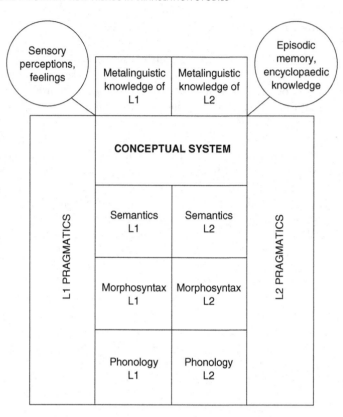

Figure 8.1 A schematic representation of the components of verbal communication (taken from Paradis 2004:227. Reprinted with the kind
permission of John Benjamins Publishing Company)

The model features different levels for explicit metalinguistic
knowledge of a bilingual's two languages L1 and L2, sensory perceptions, feelings, episodic memory and encyclopaedic knowledge, a joint conceptual system and different language-specific
levels of semantics, morphosyntax and phonology. Conceptual
mental representations are independent of language. In translational L1 and L2 contact situations, the degree of overlap depends
on their relative typological closeness. Paradis' model emphasizes
the need

to distinguish between representation and control, between what is represented and how it is represented, between what is represented and how it is accessed, and between what is represented in each language and how these language representations are organized in the brain into systems or subsystems.

(2004:230–231)

In **Paradis' model,** the pragmatics of the two languages involved in both bilingualism and translation encompasses and feeds into both the conceptual system and the different language levels. Implicit linguistic competence and metalinguistic knowledge are independent systems. Only the use of metalinguistic knowledge is consciously controlled. The use of implicit competence is automatic, devoid of conscious effort, awareness of the process involved or attention focused on the task on hand. Languages are represented as neuro-functional subsystems of the language system (the implicit linguistic competence), which is a component of the verbal communication system that, in addition to the language system, contains metalinguistic knowledge, pragmatic ability and motivation. This verbal communication system is connected to the cognitive system where intentions to communicate a message are formulated or messages are received and interpreted according to the lexicogrammatical constraints of the two languages that activate the relevant concepts and depend on pragmatic context-dependent inferences. The intention to communicate triggers how the message formulated in the cognitive conceptual system is actually expressed. The implicit linguistic competence ('the grammar') constrains the encoding of the message and the pragmatics component makes selections in terms of styles, registers, discourse norms, speech act directness, politeness, etc.

Paradis suggests that bilinguals (including translators) have two subsets of neuronal connections, one for each language, and these are activated or inhibited (for instance in the process of translation) independently. But there is also one larger set from which they can draw items of either language at any one time. All selections are automatic – i.e., unconsciously driven by activation levels. With specific reference to translation, Paradis proposes the operation of two distinct translation strategies:

1. A strategy of translating via the conceptual system involving processes of linguistic decoding (i.e., comprehension) of source text material plus encoding (production) of target text material.
2. Direct transcoding by automatic application of rules, which involves moving directly from linguistic items in the source language to equivalent items in the target language. In other words, source language forms immediately trigger target language forms, thus bypassing conceptual-semantic processing.

Paradis' theory is relevant for translation in that he presents an explanation for the representation modi of two languages as keys to essential translation processes of decoding, comprehending, transferring, re-assembling and re-verbalizing. Of particular importance in his model is the role he assigns to the two pragmatics components which impact on the conceptual system and on the other linguistic levels. With regard to the joint separate conceptual system, the model can explain that expert translators often do not need to access the conceptual system as they tend to move directly from the source language to the target language. This has also been proved in an experiment by Tirkkonen-Condit (2004).

The importance accorded by Paradis to the pragmatics component suggests the possibility of combining his model of the bilingual (translator's) brain with my own functional-pragmatic translation theory of linguistic text analysis, translation and translation evaluation detailed above in Chapter 7. Paradis' theory clearly supports the concept of the cultural filter in covert translation with its hypothesized complete switch to the target language pragmatic norms and the hypothesized co-activation of the two pragmatics components in overt translation. Paradis' theory supports in particular the claim that overt translation is psycholinguistically more complex due to an activation of a wider range of neuronal networks – across two pragmatics-cum-linguistics representational networks (see Figure 8.1) in the translation process, as well as the claim that covert translation is psycholinguistically simple since only one pragmatics-cum-linguistics representational network – the one for the target language – is being activated in translation.

For a new linguistic-cognitive orientation in translation studies that may emanate from a critical look at current research into translation process research and neuro-imaging studies, a fresh attempt at theorizing might be a good start. For this, an appropriate neuro-linguistic theory of bilingualism that is compatible with a theory of translation is clearly needed.

USING CORPORA IN TRANSLATION STUDIES

This chapter looks at how corpora (plural of corpus) have changed translation studies and translation practice over the past decades. Translation scholars and practising translators can now greatly benefit from the rapid technological progress that enables large quantities of data to be stored and manipulated. We will examine different types of corpus work and consider some practical examples.

THE USE AND FUNCTION OF CORPORA IN TRANSLATION

What is a **corpus?** For the purpose of translation studies, a corpus can be defined as a body of computer-readable texts analysable (semi-) automatically and sampled in a principled and transparent way.

Mona Baker (1993, 1995), a pioneer in applying **corpus studies** to translation, has identified three corpus types for translation studies:

1. Comparable corpora consisting of two collections of texts in the same language: one corpus consists of original texts in the language in question and the other consists of translations in that language from a given source language or languages;
2. Parallel corpora consisting of original source language texts in one language and their translated texts in another language;
3. Multilingual corpora consisting of sets of two or more monolingual corpora in different languages built up either in the same or different institutions on the basis of similar design criteria.

DOI: 10.4324/9781003355823-12

This tripartite division was, however, not successful and was soon collapsed into two main types, comparable and parallel corpora, which are now widely accepted in the scientific community.

Corpora are today fruitfully used to help make the concept of equivalence through empirical work less subjective, especially if the corpus represents a variety of translators (see, for instance, Krein-Kühle 2014). In order to be optimally useful, corpora need to be carefully designed and they need to be provided with appropriately contextualized data (for a good example of such a corpus see Krein-Kühle 2013 and the Cologne Specialized Translation Corpus (CSTC)). Corpora such as this one are useful for going beyond individual exemplar-based translation evaluation such as the analyses of individual texts provided by the House model. Corpora can lift the results of the analyses of individual texts on a more general level. In short, they can make results more intersubjectively reliable and valid (see here Kruger et al. 2011).

Translation corpora provide a reliable tool for clarifying hypothesized equivalences and for establishing reliable patterns of translation regularities (see here Zanettin 2014). An optimal use of corpora needs to be based on a theoretical and methodological framework which gives pride of place to the concept of equivalence. Put differently, equivalence in translation can be made open to generalization and intersubjective verification through the use of parallel corpora and comparable corpora.

The use of **corpora in translation** studies has a useful function as *one* of many tools of scientific inquiry. Regardless of frequency and representativeness, corpus data are useful because they are often better data than those derived from accidental introspections, and for the study of certain problems, such as overall development of the use of modal verbs, corpus data are indeed the only available data. But if the use of corpora is to maximally fulfil its potential, it should be used in conjunction with other tools, namely, introspection, observation, textual and ethnographic analysis. In translation studies, as in other disciplines, we must assess the relative value of the analytical-nomological paradigm on the one hand, where already existing hypotheses (and categories) are to be confirmed or rejected, and where variables are explicated and operationalized, and the explorative-interpretative paradigm on the other hand, where in-depth case studies are conducted to develop categories for capturing newly emerging phenomena. It is important that these two lines of inquiry, the qualitative and the quantitative, are not considered to be mutually exclusive, rather they should be regarded as supplementing each other.

Corpus evidence, and in particular seemingly impressive statistics, should never be seen as an end in itself, but as a starting point for continuing richly (re)contextualized qualitative work with values one finds interesting – and these must not necessarily be the most frequent phenomena, for the least frequent values can also catch one's attention. In the last analysis, the object of corpus translation studies should not be the explanation of what is present in the corpus, but the understanding of translation. The aim of a corpus is not to limit the data to an allegedly representative sample but to provide a framework for finding out what sort of questions should be asked about translation and about language used in different ways. The value of corpus translation studies lies in how it is used. The field of corpus studies is not a new branch of translation studies, it is simply a methodological basis for pursuing translation research. In principle, it should be easy to combine corpus translation studies with many other traditional ways of looking at translation. If this is done, corpus translation studies can greatly enrich our vision of translation.

AN EXAMPLE OF A CORPUS-BASED TRANSLATION PROJECT

Not only can corpora provide an extension and validation of qualitative work based on a single text exemplar, but they can also be used as a link between qualitative and quantitative research. In the following, we will look at an example of a longitudinal corpus-based project that effectively links qualitative and quantitative work: the **diachronic project 'Verdecktes Übersetzen – Covert translation'** conducted in the framework of the German Science Foundation's Research Centre on Multilingualism in Hamburg from 1999 to 2011 (Principal Investigator: Juliane House, see summaries of the project in Becher et al. 2009 and Kranich et al. 2012). The general assumption underlying this corpus-driven project is that the dominance of the English language in many domains of everyday life will eventually lead to variation and change of indigenous communicative norms in

German (and other languages) in both covert translations from English and in non-translated original texts such that a gradual adaptation to Anglophone norms results. More concretely, it was hypothesized that adaptations to Anglophone communicative norms can be located along dimensions of empirically established communicative preferences, such as the ones established for English and German (see the description in Chapter 7). An influence of English texts on German texts would manifest itself in quantitative and qualitative changes over time in the use of certain lexical items and structures in German translations and in German original texts (comparable texts) in genres where Anglophone dominance is particularly noticeable, such as, it was assumed, popular science texts and business texts.

To test this project hypothesis, a multilingual corpus was put together holding about 650 texts of English–German originals and translations, as well as a few French and Spanish control texts. The selected sources reflect a sphere of text production and reception that was assumed to be of pervasive socio-cultural influence. The texts in the genre 'popular science' comprise for the time frames 1978–1982 and 1999–2002 articles on topics of general socio-political relevance. These texts, totalling about 700,000 words, have been selected from popular science publications (e.g. *Scientific American*, *New Scientist* and their satellite journals produced in other languages such as German, French and Spanish). The genre 'business texts' comprises about 300,000 words of annual reports by globally operating companies, as well as letters to shareholders, missions, visions, corporate statements and product presentations. An investigation into the reverse translation relation – German–English, French/Spanish–English – is also of interest in reference to this genre.

Figure 9.1 presents the structure of the project corpus showing the functions of, and the interrelations between, the various subcorpora: English Original Texts (E-ORI), German Translations (G-TRA) and German Original Texts (G-ORI).

The research was divided into three phases: qualitative analyses, quantification and re-contextualized qualitative analyses following from the results of the quantitative analyses. In the qualitative analyses, House's translation quality assessment model (described above in Chapter 7) was used as a controlled procedure to avoid the creation or perpetuation of 'scientifically manufactured stereotypes'. In

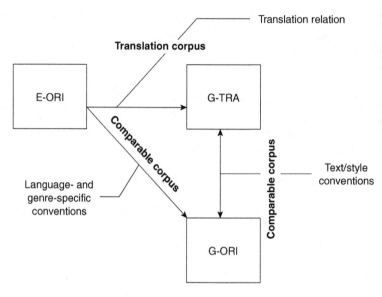

Figure 9.1 Translation and comparable corpora (example: English–German)

an early study within the framework of this project, Nicole Baumgarten et al. (2004) found that in English popular scientific articles, a consistent effort is made to simulate interaction with assumed readers. This means that readers are often addressed directly and as it were 'drawn into' the scenes described in the text. Consider the following telling example taken from the popular science journal *Scientific American*:

Example 1

(1a) E-ORI: Suppose YOU are a doctor in an emergency room and a patient tells YOU she was raped two hours earlier. She is afraid she may have been exposed to HIV, the virus that causes AIDS, but has heard that there is a 'morning-after pill'.... Can YOU in fact...

This opening passage of an article on HIV-infections is translated into German for the German daughter publication *Spektrum der Wissenschaft* as follows:

(1b) G-TRA: In der Notfallaufnahme eines Krankenhauses berichtet eine Patientin, sie sei vor zwei Stunden vergewaltigt worden und nun in Sorge, AIDS-Erregern ausgesetzt zu sein, sie habe gehört, es gebe eine 'Pille danach'.... Kann der Arzt überhaupt... (Back translation into English: In the emergency room of a hospital a patient reports that she had been raped two hours ago and was now worrying that she had been exposed to the AIDS virus. She said she had heard that there was an 'After-Pill'. Can THE DOCTOR in fact...?)

The German translation shown above seems to be aimed at adapting the American English original to the reading habits of the German target audience. Note that changes have been made in particular concerning the degree of addressee-involvement: the German reader is no longer asked to imagine herself to be one of the agents of the scene presented. Instead, the scene in the hospital is presented in the German version 'from the outside'. The addressee is not asked to actively engage with what is presented.

The **qualitative project analyses** revealed that, in the English popular science texts, readers are often 'invited' to identify with the persons depicted in the text through the employment of the following linguistic devices: mental processes (i.e., verbs of thinking and believing) that serve to establish a personal relationship with the reader; simulated dialogues drawing readers into the text; repetitions that help engage readers emotionally; 'framing' and other narrative devices are used to personalize and dramatize science. Now, as opposed to the English originals, the German popular science texts in the first time frame (1978–1982) tend to avoid all these devices. Consequently, the German texts are much less person-oriented, and they are less persuasive and tend to be more technical and 'seriously scientific'. In addition, no framing or other narrative devices are present in these German texts. A certain 'didactic tenor' is also often noticeable, i.e., the translator may have assumed a lack of knowledge on the part of the reader, a situation in need of being remedied by the text producer. Interviews which project members conducted with translators of these texts that appeared in the German journal *Spektrum der Wissenschaft* as well as journalists working for the journal *Scientific American* confirmed these results and interpretations.

The ensuing **quantitative project work** was conducted, first, to test the results of the qualitative analyses and show up how frequencies of occurrence of those linguistic devices which were particularly vulnerable to variation and change developed over time under Anglophone influence in translation. Second, the quantitative work was designed to reveal preferred usage of those vulnerable linguistic devices that were found to express 'subjectivity' and 'addressee orientation' in various co-occurrence and collocation patterns. The linguistic devices found in our qualitative analysis to express 'subjectivity' and 'addressee orientation' in English and German include the following: modal verbs, modal particles, mental processes, personal pronouns, connective particles, sentence adverbials, progressive aspect, sentential mood and commenting parentheses.

The frequency of the occurrence of these linguistic devices was then examined, such as, for instance, the use of personal pronouns and connectives as prime means for producing more interactionality in a written text and indicating author–reader dialogue, as well as the use of modal verbs as a means for presenting opinions brought forward in a text as less definite, thus leaving more room for addressees to exercise their own judgment.

It was expected that English–German translations in the field of popular science would allow more and more importations of conventions and norms from the English source text, which would then also gradually find their way into German comparable, monolingually produced (non-translated) texts. However, the evidence to support this view was not strong. While findings suggest that the German originals become more interactional overall over time, an influence attributable to translation could not be established. An indirect type of Anglophone influence might be a more plausible explanation. Over the past decades, a general trend is that texts become more informal and more colloquial, and hence more interactional can be observed. This trend can be linked to general cultural processes, such as the democratization of knowledge and a growing taste for informality in interaction. These processes may well be operative in Germany as well. And this shift towards more reader–author dialogue in the German original texts in our corpus may well have been caused by the presence of the prestigious Anglophone model in a rather indirect way. As far as the impact of

English–German translations on changes in German genre conventions is concerned, it was therefore concluded that its role is marginal, as this corpus-based project has shown.

AN EXAMPLE OF A CORPUS-BASED CASE STUDY OF TRANSLATION

A small case study (House 2015b) conducted within the framework of the above project investigated the linguistic behaviour of two linking constructions: *for example* and *for instance* in the project's popular science corpus.

'**Linking constructions**' are multi-word discourse markers usually in the form of lexico-grammatical patterns with which the relationship between some portion of prior and ensuing bits of a text are indicated. So linking constructions are inherently relational in nature, and they often share with discourse markers the positions of the left periphery of a text that earmarks them as connective elements.

Apart from providing cohesion and coherence in a text, linking constructions also function interpersonally to support audience design (see Chapter 4) and improve addressees' text comprehension by signalling how one idea leads to another. The use of linking constructions also helps to gain and maintain addressees' attention, ensuring that the writer's assumptions match those of his or her envisaged addressees in the ongoing discourse.

The two linking constructions *for example* and *for instance* are prepositional phrases which, broadly speaking, function to specify what has been said before, and are rather typical of the popular science genre. They focus on what will follow in ensuing text segments, where information will be added, concretized or explained via exemplification. They are thus cohesion-producing elements, overtly marking the way text stretches are meant to hang together. *For example* and *for instance* are also formulaic expressions, 'frozen' in meaning and resembling idiomatic and routinized expressions.

The hypothesis underlying this case study mirrors the overall project hypothesis, i.e., that English discourse norms and conventions have an impact on German norms, with German translations from English paving the way for an eventual adaptation of original German texts to English norms, and with perceived interlingual formal and functional equivalence playing an important part in blocking cultural filtering and initiating English influence. This influence would manifest itself in changes in the use of certain linguistic items and structures both in German translations and comparable German texts. In this study, it was hypothesized that the English preference for routine expressions such as *for example* and *for instance* would be reflected in both the German translations and the original German texts.

The database is the popular science part of the 'Covert translation' corpus of texts in the two time frames 1978–1982 and 1999–2002. All occurrences of ***for example*** and ***for instance*** in a co-text of five preceding and five ensuing sentences were extracted from the English originals and their translational German structures as well as equivalent occurrences in the comparable original German texts. Manual annotation followed this extraction process with a view to establishing co-occurrences with other linking constructions, as well as any further significant phenomena.

While the two constructions *for example* and *for instance* are often used interchangeably in many English text types, the analysis of the newer original English texts in the popular science corpus reveals that the occurrence of *for instance* has more than doubled over time. Further, *for instance* was found to be preferred in 82% of its occurrences in non-abstract descriptions of events and states of affairs. In order to explain this remarkable increase in frequency, a detailed analysis of the linguistic environment of all its occurrences was undertaken. The results show that *for instance* tends in fact to co-occur with descriptions of concrete events and states of affairs. Such descriptions in written discourse are commonly associated with simulated interactions in colloquial and oral style. The following is an example of this particular use of *for instance* in the English original texts.

Example 2

E-ORI: An influenza strain can produce a local or global epidemic only if the people exposed to the virus lack immediate immunity to it. *For instance when someone has the flu, the immune system produces molecules known as antibodies.*

Here, we see a description of a concrete state of affairs and how it affects a human being.

While constructions featuring complex grammatical processes of nominalization and abstraction are usually associated with written language, concrete descriptions of events and states of affairs characterize spoken varieties of a language. We may therefore put forward the hypothesis that the increase in the use of *for instance* over time reflects a move towards greater spokenness in the English original popular science texts. Such an interpretation would be in line with the general trend towards greater informality, orality and colloquiality in many contemporary written English genres, a trend that has been established in work with many larger English language corpora (see here e.g. Mair and Leech 2006).

A second result relates to the way the linking constructions *for example* and *for instance* are translated into German.

In contrasting occurrences of *for example* and *for instance* in the original English texts with their German translations in both time frames, an amazing variety of translation-equivalent forms was found, such as: *zum Beispiel, beispielsweise, nehmen wir ein Beispiel, das Beispiel... zeigt, Das Beispiel... mag das illustrieren, man denke beispielsweise an..., nämlich, etwa, nehmen wir zum Beispiel..., nehmen wir einmalan..., angenommen, ob... ob, so* and zero realization (omission).

The tendency in the German translations of *for example/for instance* to employ a wide variety of different tokens as translation equivalents can be taken to confirm a general trend in preferred choices of expression in English and German discourse: whereas a fixed set of all-purpose routine formulas is often preferred in English genres, comparable German genres show a preference for situation-anchored, ad hoc formulations with a concurrent display of a wide variety of expressions adapted in situ to the respective contexts (see here House 2006b). As revealed in this corpus-based case study, this difference in preferring a closed versus an open choice option also holds for the selection of routinized linking constructions in the English texts and a very broad repertoire of linking constructions in their German translations. And the fact that this choice is upheld in the German translations may also be interpreted as a sign of continued cultural filtering, i.e., a non-adoption of, or a resistance to, Anglophone discourse conventions.

Another difference in the use of *for example/for instance* in the English original texts and their German translations is a frequent addition of another connector, *so*, to the German translation equivalents of *for example/for instance* – a phenomenon that led to further investigation, namely a corpus search for all occurrences of *so* in its function as an adverbial connector.

Here is an example illustrating the co-occurrence of the German adverbial connector *so* and *zum Beispiel* as one translation equivalent of *for example*.

Example 3

E-ORI: The composition of sea water and the needs of the phyto-plankton seem to be intimately related. *For example*, the essential nutrients nitrogen and phosphorus tend to be found...

G-TRA: Zwischen der Zusammensetzung des Meerwassers und den Lebensbedingungen des Phytoplanktons scheint nun ein enger Zusammenhang zu bestehen. *So* ist *zum Beispiel* das Verhältnis zwischen den wichtigen Nährstoffen Stickstoff und Phosphor im Phytoplankton... (Back translation: Between the composition of sea-water and the life conditions of the phytoplankton there now seems to be a close connection. So there is for example the relation between the important nutrients nitrogen and phosphorus...)

The next question in this study was therefore a corpus-based investigation of the effect of the addition of *so* in the German translation corpus. The results suggested, first, that the addition of *so* further promotes syntactic integration of the various linking constructions employed as translation equivalents of *for example/for instance*. And second, the deictic quality of the connector *so* renders local cohesive linkage more global and coherence-based. *So* is a powerful backwards- and forwards-directed 'hinge' directing or re-focusing readers' attention onto what came before and what will follow, and forcing addressees to cognitively integrate the two perspectives. German *so* in its connective use has no direct equivalent in English, and that despite the fact that English *so* and German *so* may be described as fulfilling broadly similar functions in discourse in that both establish semantic relations within and across clauses.

So this small corpus-based case study leads to the tentative result that the closest German equivalent of *for example/for instance* is in fact *so*, and NOT the more immediately obvious *zum Beispiel*. It would then be *zum Beispiel* that could be said to have been added (redundantly) to *so*. This hypothesis gains support from the observation that the expression *zum Beispiel* on its own was found to be rather rare in the German part of the corpus.

In the English originals, the connective *so* was found to function much more locally than the German connective *so*, and it was also found to occur exclusively in 'oralized' discourse stretches where writer–reader interaction is simulated. And in this use, *so* is left untranslated in the German part of the corpus. While the English discourse marker *so* is used with great frequency in English conversation and everyday informal talk, it was found to be highly infrequent in academic prose such as popular science texts. Here is an example to illustrate the distinctly oral nature of the use of *so* in the English original popular science texts.

Example 4

> E-ORI: In short, the weather was clear and dry. *So* what had gone wrong with the prediction?
>
> G-TRA: Kurz gesagt, das Wetter war klar und trocken. Was war also bei der Voraussage schiefgelaufen? (Back translation: Briefly put, the weather was clear and dry. What had then gone wrong with the prediction?)

In the comparable German texts in both time frames, the marker *so* was found to be much more frequently used on its own than co-occurring with *zum Beispiel*, *beispielsweise*, etc. The remarkably frequent absence of a co-occurrence of German *so* with *zum Beispiel/beispielsweise*, etc. in the German comparable texts is in stark contrast to the behaviour of the connective *so* in the German translated texts, where greater pragmatic explicitness is achieved via the double use of linking mechanisms such as e.g. *so* plus *zum Beispiel*, etc. What we see in the comparable German corpus is that conventional German clausal linkage using linking constructions appears to operate quite differently from the English norm, i.e., leaving the achievement of textual linkage to the discourse marker *so* and *only* to it.

When used on its own, *so* can effectively take on the functions of exemplifying, elaborating and enhancing previous utterances in the comparable German corpus, thus assuming the full connective potential of such linking constructions as *zum Beispiel/beispielsweise*, etc. *So* is here placed at a point of transition where a first segment can be interpreted as being preliminary to an ensuing segment which follows the marker *so*. *So* connects two discourse stretches in which the second stretch often appears as a logical or natural sequence of the first one. In signalling the relationship between two discourse segments, German *so* functions differently from its English pseudo-equivalent *so*. Despite the fact that both operate at transitional points, English *so* seems to be less potent as a cohesion and coherence-enhancing, bi-directional hinge: like *for example/for instance*, it is primarily used as a more 'forward-directed' specifier, while German *so* makes the text stretch in which it appears relevant all round. These differences may also explain why the English connective *so* never readily translates into German *so*.

To summarize the findings of this small corpus-based case study: the frequency with which *for instance* is used in English popular science texts has more than doubled over time. This may be a sign of oralization and colloquialization of written English discourse, and it confirms findings from larger native English corpora.

English preference of the routinized linking constructions *for example/for instance* was established in the corpus examined and found to be in stark opposition to the occurrence in the German translations of a wide variety of different ad hoc formulations contextualized and locally anchored in the discourse. The hypothesis formulated for this study was thus NOT confirmed.

In the German translations, the use of *so* in combination with *zum Beispiel/beispielsweise*, etc. leads to greater textual-pragmatic explicitness in the German translations because the marker *so* acts as an explicit 'hinge'.

The surprisingly frequent co-occurrence of German translation equivalents of *for example/for instance* and the connector *so* revealed in the corpus analysis stimulated a contrastive follow-up analysis of the behaviour of *so* in the English originals and the German comparable (non-translated) texts, suggesting the following hypotheses:

- *So* as an English connective particle occurs mainly in 'oralized' discourse stretches in which writer–reader interaction is simulated as part of the writer's attempt to 'involve' readers.
- In the German comparable texts, *so* is used surprisingly often on its own. In this stand-alone use, *so* is a device for initiating explanation, elaboration and exemplification, thus effectively assuming the connective potential of *zum Beispiel/beispielsweise*.
- German *so* and English *so* behave very differently: English *so* is used to 'oralize' written discourse and is, in this function, not directly translatable into German. German *so* is a powerful 'hinge' aligning writer and reader knowledge states at particular points in the discourse.
- The tendency towards greater textual explicitness in the German translations is documented again in this study via the systematic addition of *so* which suggests the continued use of a cultural filter. The addition of *so* in the German translations may have been occasioned by deep-seated grammatical differences between English and German.

On a different line of argumentation, one may query whether the German linking construction *zum Beispiel* can actually be regarded as a true functional equivalent of *for example*, given the findings from the comparable corpus in this project. It may thus be the case that the 'primary' strategy for exemplification in German is simply using *so*, whereas in English, it is *for example/for instance*.

Perceived formal and functional differences in the use of the linking constructions *for example/for instance* and their German translation equivalents may have acted against any English impact on German text norms, leaving cultural filtering intact, thus disconfirming the main project hypothesis that English norms impact on other languages via translation. The project question whether and how translation leads to language variation and change can therefore – again – not be answered in any simple way.

Much more longitudinal corpus-based research is needed in future, taking account of a host of different factors that influence language variation and change through language contact in translation. In particular, there is a need to assess the statistical significance of theoretical claims that are based on quantitative corpus data alone. Further, it is necessary to combine corpus techniques and the computational techniques used to investigate them with other data sources, in particular translation process data of the kind described in the previous Chapter 8 of this book. Such data could be stored and analysed using corpus techniques (see here Alves and Vale 2011), thus effectively breaking down the traditional boundary between product-oriented and cognitively oriented process research in translation studies. Another important future research avenue for corpus-based research in translation studies relates to the inclusion of popular, wide-spread new forms of translation activities including various types of non-professional translation such as community translation, volunteer translation of different kinds, and **translanguaging** (see here the journal '*Translation and Translanguaging in Multilingual Contexts*') as well as post-editing procedures.

As we have also seen in the description of the methods used in the research project 'Covert Translation' above, it is important to triangulate one's data sources and methods so as to be able to capture the complexity of translation in its various forms (Malamatidou 2018).

TRANSLATION IN THE AGE OF GLOBALIZATION AND DIGITALIZATION

In this chapter, we will look into the current processes of **globalization** and their social, political, economic and linguistic consequences on contemporary life, institutions and the workplace. We will examine what these developments mean for translation. We will also discuss the role of the English language in its function as a **global lingua franca** and the way English might affect the nature, frequency and indeed further existence of translation worldwide. The conclusion drawn in this chapter will be that, far from damaging the demand for translation, processes of globalization and internationalization are also responsible for a drastic increase in the demand for translations. One such demand involves contexts that can be characterized by unequal power relations between individuals, groups, languages and literatures. Translators are here asked to play a critical role in questioning and/or resisting existing power structures. Here, translation does not function only as a conflict mediating and resolving action but rather as a space where tensions are signalled and power struggles are played out. An extreme case of such tensions is the positioning of translators in war zones of war. In such a context, translation scholars have looked at the impact that the performance of translators has had on the different parties in a war zone, whether and how translators align themselves with their employers or refuse to do so, and how personally involved they become in situations of conflict, war and violence.

DOI: 10.4324/9781003355823-13

WHAT IS GLOBALIZATION?

Globalization is a process that makes national borders more transparent or even eliminates them completely, with restrictions on many kinds of exchanges becoming rapidly obsolete. Globalization can produce interconnectedness and interdependence among different people and nations. It involves a variety of processes – economic, technological, social, cultural and political – which have for some time now denationalized policies, capital, urban spaces and temporal frames, and it relates countries through their shared political and economic activities. From a more critical perspective, globalization processes increase undesirable homogenization and worldwide assimilation to leading elitist groups, groups that benefit most from globalization.

Globalization coincides with increasing international mobility and transnational residency, the acceleration of global media and what Jan Blommaert and Ben Rampton (2011) have called 'superdiversity'. They characterize this phenomenon as

> a tremendous increase in the categories of migrants, not only in terms of nationality, ethnicity, language and religion, but also in terms of motives, patterns and itineraries of migration, processes of insertion onto the labour and housing markets of the host societies, and so on.

> (2011:1)

Globalization has today turned into a buzz-word used to describe the flow of goods, people, capital, symbols and images around the world, facilitated by modern technological advances in the media and in information and communication technology that have led to global mobility in business and culture, and to large-scale economic de-localization, mass migration and phenomena like 'global terrorism'. Globalization and translation are closely intertwined: linguistic superdiversity across the globe is part of globalization and of the growing necessity to translate (see here, for instance, Cronin 2003).

In the field of globalized discourse, computer-mediated linguistic aspects play an increasingly important role. Linguistic aspects of globalized discourse can be located at various linguistic levels, e.g. lexical, semantic, pragmatic-discourse and socio-semiotic ones. At the lexical level, globalized discourse has often been characterized as featuring a large amount of so-called internationalisms, and here especially Anglicisms. Such borrowings have been either categorically condemned for damaging local languages in their expressive potential, or they have been welcomed as facilitating intercultural communication processes by creating common lexical reservoirs.

GLOBALIZATION AT DIFFERENT LEVELS OF LANGUAGE

At the semantic level, globalized trends have been identified in the semantic development of routine formulae and illocutionary force indicating devices (IFIDS), such as *please, sorry* or *thank you* (see here Terkourafi 2011). The semantic flexibility of such seemingly fixed items has often been underrated in intercultural contexts. Such borrowings tend to be put to the service of functions that already exist in the receiving languages, while at the same time contributing to the development of new, additional functions from their original functions in English.

At the pragmatic and discourse level, globalized norms of written discourse in various genres seem to 'drift' towards English-based rhetorical structures. English-based forms of rhetorical patterns have been observed to filter into academic, scientific and economic discourse in many other languages. Since cultures are in principle hybrid and dynamic, negotiation and accommodation processes tend to be set in motion in any text production in a globalized world. Globalized discourse has also recently been described as an assemblage of 'globalized linguistic signs' that lead to the creation of new globalized multilingual landscapes, and indeed linguistic landscapes are an important new research strand in intercultural pragmatics. It looks at how written language is made visible in public, often urban, spaces in hitherto unexplored ways. Much research has been done on East Asian megacities, but recently also in large conurbations in the West, where the increased usage of multilingual and multicultural signs in a globalized urban world has been documented.

An important area in studies of globalized intercultural discourse is concerned with the use of modern technology. Computer-mediated communication and Internet domains as influential new communities of practice have thus become increasingly popular research foci. Many studies in this paradigm look at the steady influx of English words into blogs or television commercials in many other languages. Such imports are remarkable, because they do not fill a lexical gap in the receiving language, rather perfectly simple words are more often than not easily available in the receiving language, but they are strategically replaced by English words in order to achieve certain effects. For instance, the use of the English word 'car' in a blog is chosen to add a certain pragmatic function like advertising one's 'global identity', modernity or rebellion in computer-mediated communication. Clearly, the English language is here instrumentalized as a resource for 'interculturalizing' a native language. It remains an open question, however, whether the Internet is on its way to becoming an 'equalizing' force, an all-embracing 'global language' in a 'virtual universe' able to create an egalitarian ubiquitous society without political, social or linguistic borders – a type of universal intercultural communication, or whether it is an elitist tool for promoting more inequality between the haves and the have-nots.

In discussions about globalization, Jan Blommaert has introduced the important notion of '**orders of indexicality**' (2005:73), by which he means that indexical meanings, i.e., connections between linguistic signs and contexts, are ordered and closely related to other social and cultural features of social groups. This should help us to focus both on concrete empirically observable semiotic means as micro-processes and on wider socio-cultural, political and historical phenomena. Globalization leads to an increasingly intensified flow of movements of images, symbols and objects causing forms of contact and difference. This means that classic sociolinguistic notions like 'speech community' can today no longer be legitimately held to be true. The focus needs to be on langue in motion, with various spatiotemporal frames simultaneously interacting. Increasingly problematic is also the idea of a maintenance of functions: when linguistic items travel across time, space and indexical order, as they always do in translation, in transnational flows, they may well take on different locally valid functions. When basic cultural values and orientations are transmitted and expressed in and through language in globalized discourse, they need to be problematized and relativized. And in order to investigate what globalization does to discourse, we need to examine how language functions in different societies, and discourse needs to be broken down in richly contextualized forms that occur in society. These forms are complex and variable, emanating from language users' linguistic repertoires. But these repertoires no longer isolatedly belong to a single national society, rather they are a sort of *world system*. An important feature of the phenomenon of globalized discourse in the modern world is its 'layered simultaneity', propelled by modern technological means and revealing a growing interconnectedness. If we want to grasp the type of globalized discourse we are confronted with today, we need to engage in close analysis of situated social events which reveal how multiple orders of indexicality are at play simultaneously. Such an analysis is today also often conducted in the new research paradigm translanguaging (see for instance Li 2018, and with relevance to translation see Baynham and Lee 2019). Translanguaging is a natural phenomenon which occurs in multilingual societies and is one of the most pervasive realities in 21st globalized societies. Translanguaging can be characterized as those fluid and dynamic practices engaged in by multilingual individuals who manage to go beyond the boundaries of discrete, named languages, language varieties as well as other semiotic systems.

ECO-TRANSLATOLOGY

A new approach originating in China, **eco-translatology**, needs to be mentioned. Eco-translatology has its own journal, the *Journal of Eco-Translatology* founded in 2011, and its ideas have been disseminated in annual international symposia starting in 2009.

Eco-translatology looks at the phenomenon of translation as a very broadly conceived eco-system in which the ideas of 'translation as adaptation and selection', of translation as a 'textual transplant' promoting an 'eco-balance' are integrated into an all-encompassing vision. Such a broad vision is today particularly important as globalization and internationalization tend to increasingly blur the lines between the particularity and culture specificity of eco-contexts leading to a very new, not undangerous global similarity. Eco-translatology upholds contextual uniqueness, emphasizing the deep entrenchment of texts, translations and the human agents involved in their production and reception in their very own habitus. Proponents of eco-translatology (cf. Hu 2013) try to include all the factors of the surrounding environments that impact on the work of the translator.

The translator's choices may indeed be determined by her being immersed in the richness of the cognitive, social, situational and socio-cultural environment, but still she remains at the centre of it all.

With its cross-cultural and cross-disciplinary nature, the ecological approach to translation is both old and new. It is old because the notion of situational and cultural context which is all-important in the eco-translatology approach has been part and parcel of translation theory for a long time – at least in the Western world – witness Eugene Nida's context-sensitive conceptualization of translation in the 1960s and 1970s and, of course, J. C. Catford's introduction of Malinowski's concept of the 'context of situation' in the 1960s and 1970s. The eco-translatological approach is new because the notion of 'context' propagated here is broader than in the earlier theories, and time will tell whether such an extensive conception of context can pass the test of translational practice.

THE ROLE OF ENGLISH AS A GLOBAL LINGUA FRANCA FOR TRANSLATION

Globalization also affects the role of globalized languages such as English, the use of which in different locales results in the employment of different, particular forms of discourse. To understand this, socio-cultural, intrinsically historical macro-processes need to be examined in order to see what is going on at the micro-process level.

One of the most influential developments in the worldwide use of languages today is the spread of English as a global language and the ever-growing importance of the English language in many domains of use, contexts and genres worldwide. This situation also has important consequences for the practice of translation. Translations both into English and from English have increased astronomically (see here the distinction by Bellos 2011, who calls translations into a language with a superior status e.g. English 'Translations UP' and translations from a language with a superior status e.g. English 'Translations DOWN').

A recent breakdown by source languages presented by the European Commission's Directorate-General for Translation (DGT)

(2009) shows that as many as 72.5% of source texts translated by the DGT (including those originating outside the Commission) were drafted in English (for comparison: 11.8% were drafted in French, 2.7% in German!). The English texts were frequently written not by native speakers of English but by speakers of English as a lingua franca (ELF). What this surge in ELF texts may mean for translation and for translators is a field of inquiry that is as yet largely uncharted.

Since the primary aim of any lingua franca communication is intelligibility in efficient and easy processes of communication, correctness tends not to be an important criterion. Equally non-important in ELF use is what generations of learners of English have both dreaded and unsuccessfully imitated: culturally embedded, typically English forms such as idioms or other routinized phrases full of insider cultural-historical and national references, invariably based on national tradition, convention or class.

The most important features of the use of **English as a lingua franca** today are its enormous functional flexibility, its immense variability and its spread across many different linguistic, geographical and cultural areas, as well as the readiness with which linguistic items from different languages can be, and in fact are, integrated into the English language. Internationally and intra-nationally, ELF can also be regarded as a special type of intercultural communication. Since the number of non-native speakers of English, i.e., speakers of ELF, is now substantially larger than the number of native speakers of English (the ratio is about four to one, tendency rising), English in its role as a global lingua franca can be said to be no longer 'owned' by its native English speakers.

Global English in its function as a lingua franca is also definitely not a language for specific purposes, or some sort of pidgin or creole. Nor is it some species of 'foreigner talk' or learner language. And it is not BSE – Bad Simple English. The Interlanguage paradigm with its focus on the linguistic deficits of learners of a foreign or second language measured against an – in principle – unattainable native norm is also no longer valid here. ELF speakers are not to be regarded as learners of English but as multilingual individuals with linguistic-cultural 'multicompetence'. And it is this multicompetence which needs to be taken as a norm for describing and explaining what ELF speakers do in communicative acts of speaking, writing or translating. ELF speakers are per se multilingual and multicultural speakers, for whom ELF is a 'language for communication' (House 2003), a medium which can be given substance with different national, regional, local and individual cultural identities. As a 'language for communication', ELF does not offer itself as a language for emotional identification: users of ELF tend to prefer their own mother tongue for such an affective purpose.

As a scientific and commercial lingua franca, ELF is spread across the globe. In globalized enterprises, the use of one language is becoming increasingly indispensable. Speakers of other languages have to learn English in order to become known in domains such as science, technology, engineering, medicine and others. But the steady advance of English did not go without protest and opposition against a monolingual English-only science that dominates the world at the expense of other languages and local knowledge. It is probably too late for a counter-current, and the solution would not be to replace English. What needs to be done, however, is to encourage foreign language learning and replace monolingualism – particularly in the English-speaking world – by multilingualism. This would be especially useful in domains involving non-specialists, such as participants in fieldwork by anthropologists or patients in the domain of medicine. Multilingualism is important to counteract a world in which all significant work is done in English, and other languages would consequently fail to develop the necessary technical terms essential for progress in science. The result would be a situation of diglossia; i.e., local languages would be used in informal, domestic affairs, and the 'important' affairs in science and business would be done in English. This is not what we would wish our future to look like!

But what about translation? Does the increasing use of ELF constitute a threat to translation? Not at all! The very same phenomena that have caused the use of ELF to grow have also influenced translation, i.e., globalization processes that boosted ELF use have also led to a continuing massive increase in translations worldwide. Alongside the impact of globalization on the world economy, international communication and politics, translation has also become much more important than ever before (see here e.g. the discussion in MacKenzie 2018; Mauranen 2021, as well as a special issue of the *Journal of English as a Lingua Franca* (2020, volume 9, Issue 2) edited by Michaela Albl-Mikasa and Juliane House entitled:

English as a Lingua Franca and Interpreting and Translation, which presents current views of the intersection of translation and English as a lingua franca by researchers and practitioners.

Information distribution via translation today relies heavily on new technologies that promote a worldwide translation industry. Translation plays a crucial and ever-growing role in multilingual news writing for international press networks, television channels, the Internet, the World Wide Web, social media, blogs, Wikis, etc. Today, CNN, the BBC, Al Jazeera International, Russia Today, Deutsche Welle, Press TV and many other globally and multilingually operating TV channels rely heavily on translations of messages into many different languages. Whenever information input needs to be quickly disseminated across the world in different languages, translations are indispensable. Translation is also essential for tourist information worldwide and information flow in globalized companies, where – supported by translation processes – ELF is now often replaced by native languages to improve sales potentials.

Further, there is a growing demand for translation in localization industries. **Software localization** covers diverse industrial, commercial and scientific activities ranging from CD productions, engineering, testing software applications to managing complex team projects simultaneously in many countries and languages. Translations are needed in all of these. Indeed, translation is part and parcel of all worldwide localization and glocalization processes. In order to make a product available in many different languages, it must be localized via translation. This process is of course similar to 'cultural filtering', an essential practice in covert translation. Producing a localized, i.e., culturally filtered and translated, version of a product is essential for opening up new markets, since immediate access to information about a product in a local language increases its demand. An important offshoot is the design of localized advertising, again involving massive translation activity. Translation can thus be said to lie at the very heart of the global economy today: it tailors products to meet the needs of local markets everywhere in processes of glocalization.

Translation is also increasingly propelled by the World Wide Web, whose development has spread the need for translation into e-commerce globalization. And the steady increase of non-English-speaking Web users naturally also boosts translation. Another factor contributing to the growing importance of translation is e-learning. The expansion of digital industries centred around e-learning and other education forms spread over the Web in many different languages again shows the intimate link between translation and today's global economy.

In sum, globalization has led to a veritable explosion of demand for translation. Translation is therefore not simply a by-product of globalization, but an integral part of it. Without translation, the global capitalist consumer-oriented and growth-fixated economy would not be possible. Therefore, we cannot really say that ELF has threatened, or diminished the importance of, translation. Not everybody, however, shares this essentially positive assessment of the relation between ELF and translation.

In an article for *The Linguist*, Snell-Hornby deplores 'the hazards of translation studies adopting a global language' (2010:18). To support her argument, Snell-Hornby presents examples of defective translations into English reputedly taken from millions of texts that look like English but are not really English. Snell-Hornby employs the terms 'Globish/American/British' (GAB), 'Eurospeak', 'McLanguage' or even 'Global English' (used here, idiosyncratically, with a negative connotation) to refer to an inferior system of verbal communication based on a low common denominator of English). While the use of ELF for simple communicative acts (e.g. SMS, chats, blogs etc.) is innocuous in Snell-Hornby's opinion, it is useless in more complex and sophisticated forms of communication – including those involved in the publication and dissemination of scientific knowledge. As English has increasingly asserted itself in academic circles over the past decades, a need has arisen for scholarly publications and academic conference presentations to be either written in English in the first place or translated into English by non-native ELF speakers. In Snell-Hornby's opinion, differences in communicative conventions between English and other languages are likely to be routinely overlooked by academics forced to write in ELF and by translators translating from and into ELF. As a result, written and oral texts written and/or delivered by non-native ELF speakers often fail to comply with standard lexicon-grammatical choices or widely held rhetorical conventions in English, thus making ELF communication less effective and more difficult to follow.

Many people today are wary of, and criticize, the role which the continued dominance of English in conferences and publications plays in shaping disciplinary agendas across different academic fields. Foremost among the effects of this dominance is the exclusion of many scholars who lack sufficient knowledge of English from the academic discourse, and the deficient type of English that many academics speak and write.

However, we might bear in mind that ELF is not a defective, but a fully functional communication tool, and that the arguments put forward against ELF come close to an appeal for an out-dated prescriptive English native norm (see here House 2010). More importantly, the claim that ELF speakers' written and oral contributions to journals and conferences, etc. are 'exceedingly difficult' to follow is not based on empirical research. Snell-Hornby's claim that the use of ELF is detrimental to intellectual progress – on the grounds that it is more difficult for the contributions of non-native users of English to be acknowledged by mainstream disciplinary discourses – has also been discussed by scholars in the field of translation studies. Today many translation academics from developing nations are active in the discipline professionally, and they publish articles and contribute to conferences because of the common medium of ELF.

While recent scholarly work on ELF has gone some way towards challenging and often reducing negative perceptions of communicative practices involving the use of English as a vehicular language, translator trainers and translation industry players continue to perceive ELF translation as a dubious form of mediation. At the centre of this stance are two assumptions, i.e., the traditionalist view that non-native speakers of English cannot match the output of an English-native professional translator, either in terms of quality or of productivity; and, by extension, the commonly held position across European universities that translator training programmes should focus on fostering students' direct translation skills, i.e., their ability to translate into their mother tongue. Ultimately, the debate on the professional and academic recognition of ELF translation has been framed in terms of directionality, i.e., into and out of the translator's mother tongue.

Traditional attitudes towards translation into a non-native tongue have been affected in recent decades by a set of new factors pertaining to the impact of globalization and the ubiquity of new communication technologies, and of course the growing use of English as an international language and as a language of administration within certain multilingual countries (such as India, Brazil or South Africa), higher education and business. This new scenario has brought about a range of developments that are fostering the generalization of translation into English by speakers of other languages.

One such development is 'internationalization' – understood as the generalization of a product such that it can handle multiple languages and cultural conventions without the need for costly redesign – as well as processes of economic and cultural globalization. In today's global economy, companies seeking to market their goods and services globally will often begin by translating their brochures and websites into English. Insofar as these texts translated into English are normally intended for international consumption, the fact that translators may not have a native-speaker competence in the target lingua-culture is often found to be less significant.

Another factor is the continual increase in translation projects in the digital economy, which are carried out by teams of professionals under the supervision of a project manager. Within these teams, translation into English as a non-mother tongue is increasingly common, as the fact that some individual translators may lack native-speaker competence in the target language can be addressed at the final stage of the project. The involvement of non-native English translators in collective translations into English is particularly frequent in cases where quality testing involves either a 'pragmatic revision' of the translated text, usually performed by an English-native reviser or by a 'fresh look', where the native English reviser approaches the translation as an independent text and evaluates it with a view to target readers' expectations. In collective translations involving competent non-native professionals and qualified native-speaker advisers, translations into a non-mother tongue can be just as successful as those produced by native speakers of the target language.

Another important point is that growing translation costs incurred by corporate organizations and public institutions alike have prompted some clients to commission new types of translation that do not require native-speaker competence in the target language. This is the case, for example, of the European Commission, where translation requesters are encouraged to state explicitly the purpose that the translation is meant to serve. Among the five types of translation that requesters can choose from (i.e., 'basic understanding', 'for information', 'for publication', 'for EU image' and 'legislation'), at least the first two can be competently translated by professionals working out of their native language into English. This idea could be extended to other professional contexts and also placed at the centre of translator training activities.

While translation into English as a non-mother tongue has consolidated its presence in professional settings, the assumption underpinning the debate on this type of translation is that translators should adhere to the expectations of native English readers, rather than those of readers using English as a lingua franca. Such an attitude may well change as we can now see a veritable explosion of demand for translation from and into English as a lingua franca, translation being at the heart of the global economy. Globalization, which characterizes much of contemporary life, has brought about a concomitant rise in the demand for texts that are simultaneously meant for recipients in many different languages and cultures. Until recently, translators and text producers routinely applied a cultural filter to localize texts in the process of translation. However, due to the impact of English as a global lingua franca, this situation may now change, leading to a conflict between culture specificity and universality in textual norms and conventions, with 'universality' really standing for Anglo-Saxon norms. While the influence of English on other languages in the area of lexis has long been acknowledged, its impact on the levels of syntax, pragmatics and discourse has barely been researched. Rules of discourse and textualization conventions often operate stealthily at deeper levels of consciousness and thus present a particular challenge for translation studies (see here, for instance, House 2013).

Globalization has had an enormous impact on translation (see e.g. Wu 2021) and there is now an ever-increasing demand for both professional and non-professional translations in many more domains of everyday life than ever before. Globalization and translation are closely intertwined, and it is through translation that languages and cultures are more intimately brought together. The use of English as a global language and the use of translation can and will exist – now and in future – side by side, supplementing and benefiting from each other.

PART 4

TRANSLATION IN THE REAL WORLD

This final part discusses the role of translation and translators in different contemporary domains of practice. Chapter 11 looks at how translation is managed in a global business context and Chapter 12 discusses the important question whether culturally-embedded concepts can really be appropriately translated. Chapter 13 examines the role of translation in contexts of language learning and teaching, and the final chapter of this book, Chapter 14, looks at translation as a social practice in contemporary real world situations.

DOI: 10.4324/9781003355823-14

11

TRANSLATION AS COMMUNICATIVE PRACTICE IN A GLOBALIZED BUSINESS CONTEXT

This chapter examines how a particular linguistic phenomenon is translated in the context of a globally operating company. Concretely, the chapter looks at how the second person pronominal T form is translated in IKEA catalogues into many different languages.

It is well-known that IKEA uses the T form as a brand: IKEA promotes this form even in countries where it may not be perceived favourably. IKEA's choice of the 'T policy' as its brand is often said to relate to the fact that the T form is associated with positive and egalitarian values in Scandinavian cultures. However, IKEA is a globally operating company, and such values may not appeal to many other countries. So, an examination of translational choices in IKEA catalogues reveals interesting deviations from the company's stereotypical T policy: the translated IKEA catalogues do not unanimously use the T form. The examination of the translations of the T form in IKEA catalogues is a good example of using pragmatics in translation studies. This chapter will consider how examining translations of such seemingly 'simple' expressions as second person pronominal forms into many different languages can provide insight into a cluster of cross-cultural pragmatic differences. We will also learn about perceptions of the (in)appropriacy of the translational choices studied.

Let us now first look at previous studies on T/V pronouns. Many languages feature a formal V (from the French *vous*) and an informal T (from the French *tu*) pronominal form, and in various languages, there are more than two second person pronouns. Even in languages such as Japanese and Korean – which do not operate with narrow-sense pronominal forms – pragmatic norms still

DOI: 10.4324/9781003355823-15

regulate the use of quasi-2nd person pronominal forms, and these norms are centred on in/formality. Previous work on T/V pronouns owes much to the classical work of Brown and Gilman (1960), who coined the terms **'pronouns of power and solidarity'**. They argued that social relationships are defined in a particular way by using either the T or the V form: the T form indicates solidarity and familiarity between speakers, and the V form indicates power, authority and seniority between them. Later studies on address terms – in particular, the T form – stressed the fact that it "enables the speaker to generalize and personalize at the same time" (Bolinger 1979:207). In particular, Bolinger's distinction between 'impersonal' and 'personal' uses of the T form is relevant here. Bolinger notes that the pragmatic relationship between personal and impersonal T uses can be intricate: "The deeper we go into impersonal you, the more personal it seems. If the reference is to a stage on which the speaker has trouble imagining himself, you is proportionately difficult – which is to say that you adopts the viewpoint of the speaker" (Bolinger 1979:205). One may assume that impersonal pronominal use in IKEA catalogues in different languages is likely to occur, given the nature of these texts.

The study presented in this chapter used a bottom–up, corpus-based contrastive pragmatic approach to translational choices in global communication in a two-fold way:

1. Examining the ways in which T/V pronominal forms and their linguacultural equivalents are deployed in a corpus of translated IKEA catalogue. The goal here was to find out whether the use of second person pronominal forms in the IKEA catalogues examined reflects IKEA's aforementioned T policy.
2. Examining how language users evaluate the appropriacy of the use of second person pronominal forms in the translated versions of the catalogues, by conducting interviews with native speakers of the languages of the catalogues studied.

As regards the first approach, the T/V uses in IKEA catalogues are compared with the English version of the catalogue, which serves as the 'basic text' (as IKEA terms it) for all covert translations (see Chapter 7) into the 38 languages in which IKEA markets its products. It is the Swedish IKEA headquarters that produces this 'basic' English text. In the English text, only the T form 'you' is of course used. The T/V choices studied may include both languages with 'proper' T/V forms and other languages such as Japanese, where one needs to focus on the way in which the Japanese IKEA catalogue handles the personal–impersonal pronominal distinction. For personal use, the Japanese catalogue deploys the honorific form of address *okyakusama* お客様 ([hon.] visitor, i.e. 'honoured customer') together with other honorific forms, whereas for impersonal use they apply *anata* あなた ('you'), which is a quasi-pronoun with an honorific origin. Note that *anata* is not frequently used in service encounters but may occur in public announcements and other written genres.

All IKEA catalogues comprise two main sections:

1. 'product descriptions'
2. 'instructions for customers'.

We may assume that the 'product description' is impersonal in tone, i.e. if a T form is used in this section in accordance with IKEA's policy, it assumes a more general pragmatic meaning. By contrast, the second section – in which IKEA instructs the customer how to proceed with the purchase – is personal, i.e. it addresses the customer as an individual.

As regards the second analytic approach, 40 interviews were conducted with 8 native speakers of the following linguacultures represented in the corpus: Mainland Chinese, Hong Kong, Japanese, Hungarian and German. These interviews revealed the perceived appropriacy of the pronominal choice of the translations in the IKEA catalogues. In each group of interviewees, we involved two age groups (four interviewees each):

1. Age group 1: 18–35 years
2. Age group 2: 36–65 years

This grouping was used to find out whether there is a generational difference between the perception of the appropriacy of the translational choices studied. Interviewees were first shown excerpts of the catalogues in their own language, and then asked four questions not only about their perceived appropriacy of the T/V choice but also about local norms of T/V usage in the interviewees' own linguacultures.

The corpus of IKEA catalogues consists of IKEA catalogues of the year 2019 published in:

- Hong Kong (in Mandarin)
- Belgium (Belgian Dutch and Belgian French)
- Mainland China
- Japan
- The Netherlands
- Germany
- Hungary

The data analysis consists of three parts: (1) an examination of the translational choices of the pronominal forms in the catalogue corpus, (2) a focus on two different translational strategies in selected IKEA catalogues and (3) the results of the interviews.

AN EXAMINATION OF THE TRANSLATIONAL CHOICES OF THE PRONOMINAL FORMS IN THE CATALOGUE CORPUS

In some IKEA catalogues, only the V form is used, i.e. these catalogues openly defy the original IKEA T policy. This is the case in the Hong Kong Mandarin and Belgian French catalogues, as the following excerpts from the 'product description' sections of these catalogues will show. (Unfortunately, the French catalogue could not be analysed because it is structured very differently from the others and thus defies comparison.) Excerpts of any text in languages other than English will be provided with a 'back translation' (BT).

EXCERPT 1

渴望远离繁嚣的城市，深呼吸一下，让脑袋好好休息，哪怕只是短暂的悠闲？您并不孤单。要打造如此恬静的空间看似不难，但其实不然。(*Hong Kong Mandarin*)

BT: Want to break away from the bustling city, take a deep breath, get the brain to have a good rest, even if for a fleeting moment? You (*nin*) are not alone. It is not difficult to create a tranquil space with careful planning.

EXCERPT 2

Vous avez déjà eu cette envie irrépressible de laisser l'agitation du monde derrière vous, de souffler et de respirer, même pour un moment? Vous n'êtes pas seul. Pas simple d'y parvenir? Vous seriez peut-être étonné … (*Belgian French*)

BT: Have you (*vous*) ever had this irresistible urge to leave the world behind you (*vous*) and to have a breath, even for a moment? You (*vous*) are not alone. Not easy to achieve this? You (*vous*) might be surprised…

The Hong Kong catalogue excerpt (1) uses the V form *nin* 您, and the Belgian French excerpt (2) the V form *vous* consistently both in the product description and the instructions to customers. The V choice in the catalogues shows that the choice of T/V forms is anchored in translational choices and is motivated by a cluster of sociocultural preferences. The overriding role of sociopragmatic rather than linguistic factors in such pronominal choices becomes particularly evident when we compare the Hong Kong Mandarin catalogue with the Mainland Chinese version; the latter uses the T form *ni* 你 only in the standard situation 'product description', as the following extract illustrates:

EXCERPT 3

你是否有过那样的瞬间?急切地想要将这个纷乱的　世界甩在身后，关掉对外的开关，深呼吸，哪怕只是一会儿？大概每个人都有吧!想实现却不太容易，也不尽然。 (*Mainland Chinese*)

> BT: You (*ni*) had that kind of moment, didn't you? When you really want to leave the bustling external world, close out the world outside, have a deep breath, even for a moment. Probably all people have these moments. You would think it is not easy to achieve, but it is not necessarily like that.

In the case of the Mainland Chinese and Hong Kong catalogues, it is clear that it is not language that dictates the choice of a pronominal form. Similarly, in the case of the Belgian French versus Dutch/Belgian Dutch versions, it is more likely that the choice of V and T forms represents an alignment to the Dutch or the Francophone linguaculture, respectively. It is worth mentioning that the French catalogue consistently deploys the V form, a translational choice which in our view reflects pragmatic preferences in the Francophone world. The following are excerpts from the Dutch, Belgian Dutch and Belgian French IKEA catalogues, featuring the product descriptions.

EXCERPT 4

> Heb je wel eens zin om de drukte te ontvluchten – uitloggen en op adem komen – al is het maar voor even? Je bent niet de enige. En het hoeft ook helemaal niet moeilijk te zijn om dit te realiseren. (*Dutch*)
>
> BT: Have you (*je*) ever felt the need to escape the crowds – logging out and catching your breath – if only for a moment? You (*je*) are not the only one. And it does not have to be difficult at all to realise this.

EXCERPT 5

> Voel jij ook soms die nood om alle drukte achter je te laten, de knop om te draaien en even op adem te komen? Je bent niet alleen. Het lijkt misschien moeilijk, maar dat hoeft het niet te zijn. (*Belgian Dutch*)

BT: Do you (*je*) sometimes feel the need to leave all the hustle and bustle behind, turn the knob and catch your breath? You (*je*) are not alone. It may seem difficult, but it does not have to be.

EXCERPT 6

Vous avez déjà eu cette envie irrépressible de laisser l'agitation du monde derrière vous, de souffler et de respirer, même pour un moment? Vous n'êtes pas seul. Pas simple d'y parvenir? Vous seriez peut-être étonné … (*Belgian French*)

BT: Have you (*vous*) ever had this irresistible urge to leave the world behind you (*vous*), to breathe and breathe, even for a moment? You (*vous*) are not alone. Not easy to achieve this? You (*vous*) might be surprised…

Excerpts (4) and (5) from the Dutch and Belgian Dutch catalogues are using the T form *je*. Excerpt (6) – from the Belgian French catalogue – deploys the form *vous*.

If we look at those catalogues that use only the T form – i.e. Dutch, Belgian Dutch, German and Hungarian in our corpus – we discover a sense of unresolved ambiguity in their use of the T form: In the product descriptions (the main part of the IKEA catalogue), it is impossible to decide whether the T form is used in a personal or an impersonal way. A 'product description' may never be completely impersonal because it is still basically a persuasive advertisement implicitly addressed to the customer. However, given Bolinger's above paradox, the impersonal nature of these forms makes them perlocutionarily even more personal. Consider the following excerpts (of the same 'product description' featured in the previous excerpts) from the German and Hungarian catalogues, respectively:

EXCERPT 7

Verspürst du auch manchmal den Wunsch, innezuhalten, durchzuatmen und die Welt draußen zu lassen – und wenn es nur für einen Augenblick ist? Damit bist du nicht alleine. Und es geht einfacher, als du vielleicht denkst. (*German*)

BT: Do you (*du*) sometimes feel the desire to pause, breathe, and lock the world out – if only for a moment? You (*du*) are not alone in that. And it is easier to do this than you (*du*) might think.

Note that the Hungarian version in Excerpt (8) does not include a single use of the T form. This is because, in Hungarian, T/V use can adroitly be expressed by inflection. The entire Hungarian catalogue is translated with T inflection. From the reader's perspective, there is no pragmatic demarcation between the impersonal address form used in the 'product description', and the personal address form used in the 'instructions for customers' section.

Now, this ambiguity is cleverly resolved in the Mainland Chinese and Japanese catalogues, as Excerpts (9) and (10) below from the 'product description' and the 'instructions to customers' respectively show.

EXCERPT 8

Érezted már valaha, milyen jó volna legalább egy rövid időre magad mögött hagyni a nyüzsgő külvilágot, és végre kikapcsolni egy kicsit? Ezzel nem vagy egyedül. A megvalósítás bonyolultnak tűnhet, de nem feltétlenül az. (*Hungarian*)

BT: Have you ever felt how good it would be to leave the bustling world behind, even for a short time, and to switch off a little bit? You are not alone. It may look difficult to realise this, but it is not necessarily so.

EXCERPT 9

你是否有过那样的瞬间?急切地想要将这个纷乱的世界甩在身后，关掉对外的开关，深呼吸，哪怕只是一会儿? 大概每个人都有吧!想实现却不太容易，也不尽然。 (*Mainland Chinese*)

BT: You (*ni*) had that kind of moment, didn't you? When you really want to leave the bustling external world, close out the world outside, have a deep breath, even for a moment. Probably all people have these moments. You would think it is not easy to achieve, but it is not necessarily like that.

送货服务

在宜家，运费从未被加进您购买家具的售价中。只要您需要，我们就会提供有偿服务。与宜家合作的第三方服务商为您送货上门，只收取合理费用。 (*Mainland Chinese*)

Delivery service

BT: At IKEA, the delivery fee is never included in the price of the product you (*nin*) purchase. Only if you (*nin*) want that we will offer a beneficial delivery service. IKEA will collaborate with a third party service provider to deliver your (*nin*) purchased goods to your door, for a reasonable fee.

EXCERPT 10

ほんのわずかない時間でいいから、忙し現実を忘れ、頭と心を空っぽにしてひと息つきたい。そんな思いに駆られたことがあるのは、あなただけではありません。 (*Japanese*)

BT: Only a few precious moments are great, when the busy realities are to be forgotten, when the head and heart are to be cleared and want to breathe. It is not only you (*anata*) would have such a feeling.

おまかせ配送サーヒス

お客さまに代わり、イケアがご希望の商品をすべてそろえて、ご自宅までお届けします。 どんなにたくさん送っても3,990円一律(メインエリア内) (*Japanese*)

BT: Voluntary home delivery

If our honoured customer ([hon.] customer, *okyaku-sama*) wishes so, IKEA will follow their high wish ([hon.] wish, *go-kibou*) and will deliver the product to their noble dwelling ([hon.] accommodation, *go-jitaku*). All deliveries will be made within the 3,990-yen price range.

Customers reading the Mainland Chinese or the Japanese catalogue do not have the opportunity to interpret the T form as personal. This is because in the 'instructions for customers', in which the customer is addressed in a personalized way, the T form is systematically replaced with either the V form in Mainland Chinese Mandarin, or with the quasi-V form and other honorific forms in Japanese. In the Mainland Chinese version, the catalogue consistently deploys the V form *nin* in the 'instructions for customers' section. The above-mentioned pragmatic ambiguity created by the T form in a number of catalogues is thus disambiguated in the Mainland Chinese version. There is even less ambiguity in the Japanese version. The 'product description' uses *anata*, which is approximately equivalent to the T form. However, the Japanese catalogue deploys a translational strategy attempting to use this T form as little as possible. In the 'instructions for customers' section, the Japanese catalogue not only stops using this T form but also suddenly switches to an honorific communication style. For instance, in Excerpt 10 above, the text uses the quasi-V form *okyakusama* in its reference to the customer and also deploys two other honorific forms *go-kibou* ご希望 ([hon.] wish, 'high (respected) wish') and *go-jitaku* ご自宅 ([hon.] accommodation, 'noble dwelling').

The analysis so far has shown that in some IKEA catalogues the two sections 'product descriptions' and 'instructions for customers' may be clearly demarcated if both the T and the V forms are deployed. Certain catalogues – the Mainland Chinese and the Japanese – appear to be particularly skilfully translated so as to downtone and thus neutralize the effect of IKEA's T policy in instances where this policy may go against local linguacultural norms. In other words, translational choices are made in order to culturally filter the covertly translated text and make it potentially more acceptable to local customs. This case study will devote particular attention to the translational strategies deployed in the Mainland Chinese and Japanese IKEA catalogues, in order to model the translational complexities that surround cultural filtering of IKEA's policy in these linguacultures. One may argue that the Mainland Chinese and the Japanese IKEA catalogues represent a 'third way' to avoid both the strict renunciation of the T form and the complete adoption of the (in this context) culturally alien T form.

STRATEGIES OF TRANSLATING THE T FORM IN THE MAINLAND CHINESE AND JAPANESE IKEA CATALOGUES

The Mainland Chinese IKEA catalogue and, to a greater extent, the Japanese catalogue deploy two types of translational strategy in an attempt to avoid using the T form in the 'product descriptions'. The Mainland Chinese catalogue adopts various diversions from how the English 'basic' text deploys 'you', so as make the use of the T form *ni* more localized for native readers. While in the Chinese linguaculture the T form *ni* is preferred in certain contexts, in marketing, it may appear to be rather too intimate, as the Mainland Chinese IKEA catalogue reveals. The Japanese translation shows even more drastic translational solutions. Few Japanese companies use the quasi–T form *anata* for their customers: this form would not be acceptable in marketing practices.

TRANSLATIONAL STRATEGY NO. 1: AVOIDING THE T FORM

Avoiding the T form is a straightforward option when it comes to decreasing the pragmatic ambiguity that the use of the T form may cause. However, this translational strategy is not an option for many languages. For instance, the following English, German and Hungarian equivalents of an excerpt from the 'product description' section of the English catalogue illustrate that neither of these catalogues avoid using the T form or related inflection (in spite of the fact that they would be able to deploy general pronouns):

EXCERPT 11

> With floor-to-ceiling curtains, you decide when to let the world in. (*Basic English*)
>
> Mit Gardinen entscheidest du selbst, wie viel (oder wenig) du von der Welt hereinlässt. (*German*)
>
> BT: With curtains you (*du*) decide yourself how much or how little you let in from the world.

> Válassz földig érő függönyöket, így te döntheted el, mennyit engedsz be a külvilágból. (*Hungarian*)
> BT: Choose curtains that reach the floor, so you (T form) can decide how much you let in from the external world.

The Hungarian translation is even more heavily T-loaded than its English and German counterparts, due to the aforementioned fact that, in Hungarian, inflection (e.g. *válassz* – BT: 'you choose [T]') is bound to T/V use. Mandarin Chinese is different in that in Mandarin, clauses can be adeptly formed without the use of pronouns. It is interesting to compare the Hong Kong and Mainland Chinese equivalents of the excerpt analysed in Excerpt (11) above:

EXCERPT 12

裝上落地窗簾，由您決定何時讓光線照進屋內。(*Hong Kong Mandarin*)
BT: Fitting in curtains that reach the floor, you (*nin*) decide when you allow the light to shine into the room.
有了落地窗帘，享受私密还是拥抱世界，随心掌握。(*Mainland Chinese*)
BT: Having curtains that reach the floor, closing in or embracing the world, follow your heart how you wish to have your room.

The Hong Kong Mandarin is close to the English, German and Hungarian texts as it uses a pronominal form, even though this form is the V *nin*. However, in the Mainland Chinese text the T form *ni* is *not* used at all. There are altogether 17 out of 95 product descriptions where such a discrepancy exists between the Mainland Chinese and Hong Kong catalogues. When the Mainland Chinese catalogue uses this strategy of avoiding the second person pronominal form, the translation does not become 'vague' because the text clearly addresses the reader, even if it does not explicitly use the T form. For instance, the phrase *suixin-changwo* 随心掌握 lit. 'follow your heart to decide on the pattern' in the Chinese translation above clearly represents a personalized instance of language use. However, the removal of the T form often coincides with a sense of ambiguity, as the analysis of the second translational strategy below will illustrate.

The Japanese text also follows the translational strategy of T avoidance. The quasi-T form *anata* tends to be avoided in the Japanese catalogue: it is used only six times in the entire 'product description' section. This means that a major discrepancy exists between the Japanese translation and the (original) basic English text where the form *you* is used 299 times in the 'product description' section. Even the quasi-V form *okyakusama* is used more frequently – 16 times – than the quasi-T form *anata*, in the 'instructions for customers' section of the Japanese catalogue.

Excerpt 13 – the Japanese translation of excerpt (12) above – illustrates this translational strategy:

EXCERPT 13

天井から床までのカーテンで自分だけの空間をつくりましょう。ひとりの時間が欲　しいときはカーテンを閉めて。
(*Japanese*)

BT: Let us make our own private space by fitting in floor-to-ceiling curtains. When we want our own time only, let's close the curtain.

Here, the Japanese translation prefers the plural imperative *mashou* ましょう, which makes the text more impersonal in style.

TRANSLATIONAL STRATEGY NO. 2: MAKING THE PRODUCT DESCRIPTIONS VAGUE

The Mainland Chinese and the Japanese translations of the IKEA catalogue do not only tend to remove the T form but also often make the product description vague by not mentioning the customer at all as a person targeted for choosing a particular product.

While in the strategy of removing the T form, the reader is addressed indirectly, in 8 cases in the Mainland Chinese catalogue and 19 cases in its Japanese counterpart, the strategy of making the 'product description' vague means that the translation becomes completely 'reader free'. The contrastive analysis of the same passage in the English, German, Hungarian, Hong Kong, Mainland Chinese and Japanese versions illustrates this point:

EXCERPT 14

Upsize without moving. Go for a loft bed, place a sofa underneath, and – hey presto – you've got a living room and a bedroom. (*Basic English*)

Ruck-zuck mehr Platz: Nimm ein Hochbett und stell ein Sofa drunter – schon hast du Wohnzimmer und Schlafzimmer in einem. (*German*)

BT: More space very quickly: take a loft bed and put a sofa underneath-and immediately you (*du*) have a living room and a bedroom in one.

Nem kell költöznöd ahhoz, hogy több helyed legyen. Válassz galériaágyat, tedd alá a kanapét, így kész is a nappalid, amely egyben hálószoba is. (*Hungarian*)

BT: You don't have to move to have more space. Choose a gallery bed, put the sofa below, and lo! your living room is ready, and it is a bedroom at the same time.

不用搬家，也能創造更大的生活空間！選用高架床，床下再放一張梳化，讓您瞬間同時擁有客廳和睡房！(*Hong Kong Mandarin*)

BT: Don't have to move, it is possible to create a larger living space! Choose a larger bedframe, place a sofa below, let you (V form) have both a living room and a bedroom in an instant!

合理規劃，不搬家也能擁有更多空間。选择高架床，床下的空间摆沙发，卧室、客厅瞬间都搞定。(*Mainland Chinese*)

BT: Reasonable plan, it is possible to gain lots of space without moving. By choosing a loft bed and with a sofa beneath it, bedroom and living room will be arranged in an instant.

ロフトベッドの下にソファを置けば、　リビングルーム
とベッドルームのできあがり。　引っ越さずに部屋を広く
するアイデアです。(*Japanese*)
BT: If a sofa is placed below a loft bed, the living room and the
bedroom will be there. The room will be larger without moving.

The Hungarian, German and Hong Kong Mandarin texts follow what we have previously observed: the Hungarian translation uses the T inflection and its German and Hong Kong counterparts consistently use the T *du* and V *nin*. By contrast, the Mainland Chinese version of this excerpt is void of any personal references. For instance, while the Hong Kong translation formulates the initial part of the message as *Buyong banjia, ye neng chuangzao da-de shenghuo kongjian!* 不用搬家，也能創造更大的生活空間! (BT: 'There is no need [for you] to relocate, it is also possible to create a larger living space'), the Mainland Chinese translation uses the words *Heli-guihua, bu banjia ye neng yongyou gengduo kongjian.* 合理规划，不搬家也能拥有更多空间。(BT 'It is a reasonable plan to create more living space without moving home'.). The Japanese translation is equally impersonal, and – as a recurrent pattern in the translated catalogue – it even changes the information structure by foregrounding information on the product that IKEA is proposing to the customer. This foregrounding makes the promotion activity even less personal, as it changes the standard logic 'the customer wants *x*' → 'product *y* fulfils this wish' of the narrative.

In this section, I have discussed the translational strategies by means of which the Mainland Chinese and Japanese catalogues creatively cope with IKEA's T policy – a policy that might be at odds with the pragmatic norms of these linguacultures. By applying a cultural filter (see Chapter 7), the translations make the text more palatable to local readers while at the same time managing to maintain a certain 'IKEA style'. For instance, while there are few *anata* forms in the Japanese IKEA catalogue, these few uses are different from the default style of Japanese marketing practices as the interviews below have revealed. So the few *anata* forms in the Japanese translations can be taken to display IKEA's global T policy. The analysis has shown that certain catalogues do not simply refuse using `the T form – such as the Hong Kong Mandarin and Belgian French translations do – but rather absorb the T form by employing a cultural filter. The relationship between global communication and localized language use seems to be more complex than what is often assumed. In what follows, I will examine language users' evaluations of the (in)appropriacy of T/V translational choices in the translated KEA catalogues studied.

LANGUAGE USERS' EVALUATIONS OF THE USE OF THE T/V FORMS IN TRANSLATED IKEA CATALOGUE

For the interview study, cohorts of native speakers – eight speakers in each cohort – were recruited belonging to two different age groups in the following linguacultures: Mainland Chinese, Hong Kong, Japanese, Hungarian and German. In the 40 interviews conducted, 3 excerpts of pronominal translation choices from both catalogue parts were shown to participants. Following this, the interviewees were asked the following 4 questions:

1. Do you find the choice of pronouns in this catalogue appropriate?
2. If yes, why, and if not, what is the problem with this use?
3. Is this use of second person pronoun common in marketing materials in your culture?
4. Can you elaborate on this?

Questions 1 and 3 are 'yes/no' questions, which provided this research with quantitative evidence, and Questions 2 and 4 are open questions that provided data for the ensuing qualitative analysis. The language of the interviews was English, and sensitive information about the identity of the interviewees was removed from the data. The responses to Questions 1 and 3 showed that there seems to be a major gap between the ways in which the German and Hungarian respondents and their Hong Kong, Mainland Chinese and Japanese counterparts answered Question 1. Many Germans and Hungarians – five out of eight Germans and seven out of eight Hungarians – felt that the T pronoun in the catalogue was inappropriate. This is in stark contrast to the three other cohorts in the interview corpus. In response to Question 3, six out of eight Germans and five out of eight Hungarians felt that the pronominal use in the translations in the respective catalogues does not accord with the general marketing conventions they are familiar with in their countries. While the small size of the interview corpus obviously cannot 'represent' the entire population of the linguacultures investigated, the contrastive differences between the evaluation tendencies in the dataset are still noteworthy: these tendencies indicate that the translational T choice in the respective IKEA catalogues is problematic for Germans and Hungarians, while the translational choices in the East Asian catalogues seem to be less controversial for the East Asian interviewees.

The interview responses to Question 2 reveal that the reason for the negative evaluations of the T form by Germans and Hungarians is that these interviewees felt that IKEA's T use is too intrusive. Excerpt 15 shows how one of the German interviewees responded:

EXCERPT 15

> Anna (German, 32 years old): I am not particularly happy with IKEA's style, although I wouldn't have sleepless nights over it either. I never understood why this company insists of duzing [using the T form] its customers.

In response to Question 4, several German and Hungarian interviewees explained their negative evaluations by arguing that IKEA's T style is somehow 'jarring' and very 'foreign'. In excerpt (16), the same German respondent expresses the following view:

EXCERPT 16

> Anna (German, 32 years old): Some companies may duz [use the T form] you, but they are in the minority and they are usually American chains. It is not how German-owned companies usually talk to their customers.

The reasons behind such negative evaluative tendencies may be that in Germany, the traditional pronominal style of the service sector has been V in the past, and even IKEA used the V form when it first opened its stores in Germany in 1974. IKEA only changed its translational choice of V in 2005 (personal communication with IKEA's German PR Manager, Anja Staehler, on 13/05/2019). In Hungary, IKEA opened its stores in 1990, straight after the downfall of Communism, and the company used the T form right from the beginning. However, this policy has met with resistance, as the following Hungarian newspaper extract illustrates:

EXCERPT 17

Sok fogyasztó kifogásolja, hogy a Magyarországon tevékenykedő multinacionális vállalatok közül többen tegezik őket – áll a Magyar Nemzet mai számában. A lap szerint van olyan vásárló, aki a tegeződés miatt a lábát sem hajlandó betenni az IKEA-áruházba.

[BT: Many customers have complained about the fact that various multinational companies in Hungary use the T-pronominal form towards them – stated the newspaper Magyar Nemzet today. The newspaper quoted customers who do not ever want to cross the threshold of an IKEA store precisely because of this language behaviour.]

(https://www.penzcentrum.hu/vasarlas/ezert-tegez-le-minket-az-ikea.1029858.html)

Even after 29 years, strong feelings continue to surround IKEA's T policy, as Ildikó's response to Question 2 below illustrates:

EXCERPT 18

Ildikó (Hungarian, 59): I just find it revolting that a foreign company ignores basic civility in a country. It is so typical to IKEA, although McDonalds and many other companies just do the same. I could never get used to this.

In response to Question 4, another Hungarian interviewee, Enikő, explained her evaluation in Excerpt 19 by arguing that the spread of the T form in the business sector is part of a worldwide colloquialization and personalization of language use.

EXCERPT 19

Enikő (Hungarian, 63): This impolite custom seems to me to be part of something broader. In Socialist times, however bad they were, advertisements used Ön [respectful V form]. The adverts themselves were stupid, as were services, and I'm not saying that those were more polite times, but still there was a sense of distance, and sometimes I am missing that.

The East Asian respondents were much more satisfied with the translational choices in their respective IKEA catalogues than their European counterparts. Question 1 triggered an unanimously positive evaluation. In response to Question 3, only one out of eight Hong Kong and two out of eight Mainland Chinese interviewees felt that the translational choice of the catalogues is different from what they are accustomed to in their linguacultures. For instance, Linglang from Mainland China said the following:

EXCERPT 20

Linglang (Mainland Chinese, 29): There is basically nothing wrong with using ni in this catalogue. However, service style in China has become very polite, and I feel that the style of the catalogue is a foreign way of marketing.

A surprising number of Japanese respondents, seven out of eight, felt that the pronominal choices of the Japanese catalogue deviate from the general style of Japanese marketing. These evaluations are centred on the infelicity of the quasi-pronoun *anata*, as Noriko's response below illustrates:

EXCERPT 21

Noriko (62, Japanese): Clearly, IKEA pursues a foreign advertisement style. Japanese companies don't use anata towards customers even when they describe a product.

In addition to linguacultural variation in evaluations of translational choices, there appears to be also generational variation. In both the German and the Hungarian cohorts, it is members of the older generation who are much more dissatisfied with the use of the T form in the translated IKEA catalogues. That is, younger interviewees seem to be much more tolerant, as Judit's response to Question 2 below illustrates:

EXCERPT 22

Judit (Hungarian, 27 years old): Honestly, I don't think that IKEA is alone in behaving in this way. Everyone is doing that nowadays. Also, on social media and everywhere my generation stopped magázódás [using the V form]. Actually, it would be pretty dumb for IKEA not to follow this trend.

All the older generation German respondents evaluated the T use as different from general German marketing conventions, while their younger peers were divided on this point.

The above-discussed difference between the German and Hungarian translations of the IKEA catalogues on the one hand, and their Hong Kong, Mainland Chinese, and Japanese counterparts, on the other hand, also holds for evaluations by respondents from different generations. However, a noteworthy phenomenon can be noticed in the Mainland Chinese interview corpus. Interestingly, in this cohort, it was members of the *older* generation who felt that the catalogue's T-style fits into the norms of Chinese marketing, whereas younger people were more divided on this question. An excerpt from Meifang's response to Question 4 illustrates this point:

EXCERPT 23

> Meifang (Mainland Chinese, 59 years old): Ni is the standard style of advertising in China, although some companies nowadays use nin. I think even those companies that are for older people tend to use ni because the owners know that older people like me were young in the 80s when [...] ni was standard even in the North of China [Meifang here refers to the fact that in spoken Mainland Mandarin the V form is more frequented in the North].

Meifang's response provides a sociopragmatic insight into a generational issue in Mainland China where the V form spread in services seems to follow the rapid economic advancement of the country.

SUMMARY OF THE RESULTS OF THE CASE STUDY PRESENTED IN THIS CHAPTER

Several catalogues – including the German, Hungarian, Dutch and Belgian Dutch ones – simply adopt IKEA's T policy. Another simple translational solution is to openly defy IKEA's T policy, as we could see in the case of the V-only catalogues (Hong Kong Mandarin and Belgian French). A 'third way' is the one followed by the Mainland Chinese and the Japanese catalogues that adopt two different translational strategies. The contrastive study of translated IKEA catalogues in different languages has thus shown that seemingly 'simple' expressions can be difficult to translate, provided they are 'pragmatically loaded' as is the case with T/V pronoun.

In order to test the acceptability of the T/V translational choices in the IKEA catalogues studied, groups of respondents were asked to look at excerpts from the catalogues. The responses showed that the translational strategies of (a) resisting IKEA's rather aggressive T policy and (b) resolving it strategically were received more favourably than the translational choice of straightforwardly accepting this policy. The use of the T form is IKEA's globalizing brand, and it would be easy to condemn it as attempts to 'colonize'. Interviewees' evaluations have shown that such a negative description of the effect of globalization would be an overgeneralization. While indeed the T form tends to be received critically by many in those cultures where this form is externally 'forced' on local customs, there seems to be an important generational difference between evaluations of this translational choice. While many German and Hungarian respondents evaluated the T form negatively, in lingua–cultures where the translated catalogues handle the T/V distinction in a more differentiated way, the evaluations revolved more around the 'foreignness' rather than the unacceptability of the T use.

The study presented in this chapter only looked at the global marketing practices of one particular multinational company. Many other global players such as McDonalds, Lidl, Zara and H&M follow a similar practice, and so while the 'T policy' is often associated with IKEA, it is in fact a policy followed by many other multinational companies worldwide. The research presented in this chapter may thus be easily replicable with other global firms.

CAN CULTURALLY EMBEDDED CONCEPTS REALLY BE APPROPRIATELY TRANSLATED?

In this chapter, I ask whether concepts that are deeply culturally embedded can really be translated in a satisfactory manner. To investigate this question, this chapter presents a case study examining the Chinese policy-related expression **wenming** 文明. While *wenming* has a cluster of complex meanings and uses in Chinese, it often ends up being translated into English simply as 'civilised'. Such a translation narrows down the manifold uses of *wenming*, occurring in a variety of collocations which are rather alien to non-Chinese audiences.

The case study follows a multimethod approach based on multiple corpora. The approach is bottom-up: when one examines expressions assumed to occur frequently in the communication of policies in a particular linguaculture, one first needs to examine whether this is in fact the case and, if so, exactly how? A contrastive approach is particularly useful for unearthing the relationship between expressions and policy communication because there is significant linguacultural variation in the salience of certain comparable expressions in the communication of policies. For instance, while *wenming* is a policy-related expression, the English *civilised* is generally not – with serious consequences for translation.

Policy-related expressions in Chinese are not only used by the media but also very often on public signs and notices. For example, *wenming-xiaoyuan* 文明校园 (lit. 'civilised campus') – describing a university's policy to maintain orderly traffic, cleanness, etc. on campus – not only appears in printed and online materials but may also be displayed in the form of public banners.

DOI: 10.4324/9781003355823-16

The study uses a multimethod approach to examine *wenming*. It is data-driven in nature which means that

a.   Instead of considering ready-made dictionary meanings of *wenming* and *civilised*, or relying on any other *a priori* assumptions, the study contrastively investigates exactly how *wenming* and *civilised* are used in the corpora.

b.   Instead of assuming that *wenming* is inherently related to policymaking, the study approaches *wenming* 'innocently', by investigating (1) how it collocates with other linguistic units and (2) which collocations indicate policies.

The study is based on a tripartite approach, involving the following three phases:

1.   First an individual corpus search of the adjectival uses of *wenming* and *civilised* is conducted, followed by a contrastive pragmatic analysis of these uses and relevant collocations. The corpora used in this phase permit one to consider the broader context of the uses and collocations of *civilised* and *wenming*: both corpora provide links to longer stretches of the texts in which these critical tokens occur. A representative set of 200 examples in each language was sampled via a manual exclusion of invalid examples (e.g. when *civilised* is used as a verb). Initially, no linguacultural differences between the uses and collocations of *wenming* and *civilised* were assumed given the bottom-up procedure used, so it was simply investigated how these tokens are used in the individual corpora. This investigation revealed that the uses of *civilised* and *wenming* can be differentiated according to the following criteria:

   a.   whether they relate to the behaviour of an individual or a group;

   b.   whether they describe a state already achieved or a state to be achieved.

   These two criteria acted as focal points in the corpus-based annotation of the uses and collocations of *civilised* and *wenming* with the objective of obtaining an empirically-grounded set of categories that would be useful and manageable in the ensuing contrastive analysis of the uses and collocations of *wenming* and *civilised*. For example, certain uses of *wenming* were first annotated as 'polite', but ultimately as 'well-mannered', simply because 'politeness' has a specific academic meaning. The number of categories was then harmonised, by keeping the number of use-type categories of *wenming* and *civilised* below the threshold of five in each linguaculture and by merging less frequent categories into more frequent ones. The ultimate goal of this contrastive research was to identify problem sources for translators.

2. Research in the second phase looked at how *wenming* is rendered in the English version of Chinese news outlets. First, *wenming* translations in the corpus of bilingual media texts were categorised according to the *wenming* annotation categories obtained during the first phase. Then, I examined on the basis of my model for translation quality assessment (see Chapter 7) whether *wenming* in the bilingual texts really turned out to be problematic to translate, i.e. by considering whether *wenming* is translated overtly or covertly in the corpus.

3. The third phase of the research consisted of a translation task and follow-up interviews, conducted with a panel of ten expert translators in China. The aim of this follow-up approach is to triangulate the research, i.e. to test whether the translational tendencies overt versus covert translation (see Chapter 7) in phase two can also be observed in the translational solutions provided by expert translators. This is an intriguing question because I expected that Chinese public media sources follow preset conventions when it comes to translating policy-related expressions due to the importance and general validity of such policies – i.e. one needed to find out whether translational tendencies can be interconnected with the Mode involved (see Chapter 7). The task for the participants consisted of short examples drawn from the Chinese corpus (phase one), reflecting the uses of *wenming* according to the outcomes of phase one. Following the test, the participants were interviewed regarding the reasons for their translational choices.

The corpora used during the first phase of the study include the Balanced Chinese Corpus (BCC; http://corpus.zhonghuayuwen.org/

Table 12.1 Our corpus of media texts (Chinese texts only)

wenming	*Number of tokens*	*Number of news featuring wenming*	*Size of the Chinese corpus (Chinese characters)*
China Daily (in Chinese)	140	124	50,375
Huanqiu shibao	49	41	16,665
Total	189	165	67,040

CnCindex.aspx) and the British National Corpus (BNC). The results of the Chinese and English corpus search amounted to 200 valid examples per linguaculture.

The second phase of the research involves Chinese–English bilingual news outlets that feature the expression *wenming* in Chinese, and its English translations. Only reports on domestic Chinese events were included to ensure that bilingual news featured the 'native' uses of *wenming* and their English translations. The corpus was drawn from the following two news outlets:

China Daily: https://language.chinadaily.com.cn/
Global Times: https://www.huanqiu.com/; https://www.globaltimes.cn

These sources were selected because they are very well-known. The following Table 12.1 summarises the frequency of occurrence of the expression *wenming* in the corpus of source texts:

The third phase of the research, i.e. the translational task involved occurrences of *wenming* in utterances drawn from the BCC, and the consequent interviews with the participants. The overall length of these interviews was approximately 100 minutes.

PHASE ONE: CORPUS-BASED EXAMINATION OF CIVILIZED AND *WENMING*

First, the use of *civilised* and *wenming* in the English and Chinese corpora was examined, followed by a contrastive analysis.

USES OF CIVILIZED EXTRACTED FROM THE BNC

Table 12.2 provides a summary of our annotation categories for *civilised* and their frequency in our sample of 200 examples drawn from the BNC:

Table 12.2 Annotation categories for civilised and their frequency in a sample of 200 examples (BNC)

Annotation category	Frequency
1. Cultured and developed	97 (48.5%)
2. Governed by law and regulations	49 (24.5%)
3. Sophisticated and refined	23 (11.5%)
4. Well-mannered	21 (10.5%)
5. Well-looked-after and cared-for	10 (5%)

Here are some examples of the use of *civilised* to illustrate these five annotation categories.

Cultured and Developed

EXAMPLE 1

In these civilised times, husbands are no longer given the right to beat their wives.

EXAMPLE 2

It has often been noted that while barbarians fight with hatchets, civilised men fight with gossip.

Here, *civilised* indicates a sense of advancement, which distinguishes members of one society from those of another more 'primitive' one. In terms of the above listed focal points, this adjectival use refers to the behaviour of a group and a state which the given group has already achieved.

Governed by Law and Regulations

EXAMPLE 3

The Intifada, now two years old, has brought the first chance for a civilised end to the Arab-Israeli conflict.

In this category, *civilised* is used in reference to supra–individual norms to describe the characteristics of a group and an already achieved state.

Sophisticated and Refined

EXAMPLE 4

MR DAVID MELLOR, the Home Office minister handling the Broadcasting Bill, is a civilised chap, the sort of Government minister you will find on a Friday night addressing the Putney Music Club...

EXAMPLE 5

Where the Healey is a fairly civilised blend of high-speed tourer and sporting pedigree, comfortable enough for long-distance continental holidays as well as for Sunday afternoon thrashes through the countryside, the Cobra is just a beast.

As opposed to the previous categories, such use of *civilised* tends to refer to an individual entity and a state already achieved.

Well-mannered

EXAMPLE 6

Other plus-points are civilised lift queues ...

In this category, *civilised* refers to the characteristics of an individual's behaviour and a state already achieved.

Well-looked-after and Cared-for

> **EXAMPLE 7**
>
> Her civilised paw curves round a glass.

In this case, *civilised* denotes the very opposite of neglect, referring to the behaviour of an individual and a state already achieved.

Table 12.3 summarises the uses of *civilised* in the corpus through applying the two categories of 'Relation to individual versus group' and 'State achieved versus state to be achieved':

Table 12.3 Characteristics of the uses of civilised (in order of frequency)

Annotation category	Relation to individual versus group	State achieved versus state to be achieved
1. Cultured and developed	Group reference	State achieved
2. Governed by law and regulations	Group reference	State achieved
3. Sophisticated and refined	Individual reference	State achieved
4. Well-mannered	Individual reference	State achieved
5. Well-looked-after and cared-for	Individual reference	State achieved

Uses of wenming Extracted from the BCC

Table 12.4 provides a summary of our annotation categories for *wenming* and their frequency in the sample of 200 examples drawn from the BCC:

Table 12.4 Frequency and annotation categories for *wenming* in a sample of 200 examples (BCC)

Annotation category	Frequency
1. Cultured, developed and well-mannered	131 (65.5%)
2. Modernised	33 (16.5%)
3. Accountable, responsible and environmentally-friendly	28 (14%)
4. Civilised	8 (4%)

Table 12.4 shows that, in keeping with the English corpus, the most frequent use of *wenming* relates to 'cultured and developed'. However, this similarity does not imply translational equivalence (see more below), and not surprisingly the category of 'Cultured, developed and well-mannered' was labelled differently by the Chinese team than the English 'Cultured and developed' even after the harmonization process. This is because this use of *wenming* tends to be associated with good manners (see more below), unlike the comparable English category ('Well-mannered' is a different category for *civilised*, cf. Table 12.3).

Cultured, Developed and Well-mannered

EXAMPLE 8

这个县开展争创"十星级文明户"活动，以家庭为单位，通过"自我申报，群众评议，支部审定，三榜定星"的方式进行。

This county initiated the "Ten Star Wenming Household" Movement, taking households as units, by means of "individual applications, public evaluations, Party branch approval, and a three-fold approval system".

In this case, *wenming* not only refers to the public domain, but it also describes states which are to be achieved by members of the public. This highlights the fact that *wenming* has a policy-related characteristic here, and this is further reinforced by the fact that, in this category, *wenming* frequently appears in slogans as a modifying adjective. In such collocations, *wenming* is often used in four- and six-character combinations (*sizi/liuzi-shuyu* 四字、六字熟语) which is a typical Chinese layout for routine formulae (see also Coulmas 1979).

Such *wenming* uses are often interrelated with good manners, and in some cases in our corpus, *wenming* is used with the expression *limao* 礼貌 ('politeness'), as in the following example:

EXAMPLE 9

在今年全国文明礼貌月活动中，解放军某部干部战士奋战三天，才把垃圾清除

During this year's National Wenming Limao Month, it took three days for the soldiers of the PLA to remove the rubbish

Here, one can witness a near-tautology, in that it is very difficult to distinguish between the meanings of *wenming* and *limao* in the title 'National *Wenming Limao* Month'.

Not all uses of *wenming* in this category are found in titles, as the following example demonstrates:

EXAMPLE 10

同时，我也期盼广大市民"与文明同行，做文明乘客"，相互尊重，平等友善地对待出租车驾驶员，理解和支持我们的工作。

At the same time, I also expect most citizens to "proceed in a wenmingly way, and become a wenming passenger", respect each other mutually, be nice to taxi drivers and understand and support our work.

Modernised

This category is close to the previous category of 'Cultured, developed and well-mannered', but *wenming* is often used here in the context of governmental modernization policies, as the following example illustrates:

EXAMPLE 11

石狮市永宁镇山边村为推进新农村建设，构建和谐社会，树立文明乡风，建立了村读书室...

Shishi City Yongning Township Shanbian Village, to promote new countryside, well-structured and harmonious society and to encourage creating a wenming countryside atmosphere, created a village reading room ...

In this category, *wenming* is used in routine formulae that describe future states to be achieved by the public.

Accountable, Responsible and Environmentally-friendly

Since Deng Xiaoping's reforms in the 1980s, China has undergone significant modernization, particularly in the building and industrial sectors. As part of this modernization programme, governmental organizations often initiated policies to reduce the negative impact that modernization had on the public's welfare. As the following example illustrates, *wenming* is often used to communicate such policies:

EXAMPLE 12

企业要将文明生产、文明施工作为科技进步和技术创新的重要条件和内容，
The key condition and content for the enterprise is to operate according to wenming production and wenming construction to achieve scientific progress and innovation.

Here, *wenming* is used in routine formulae that refer to future states to be achieved by the public.

Civilised

The final category of *wenming* includes cases where it denotes 'civilised' in a historical sense:

EXAMPLE 13

胡锦涛说，中国和印度都是文明古国，也是发展中大国。
Hu Jintao said, both China and India are wenming ancient countries, and both are large countries in development.

It is only this use of *wenming* which does not refer to a state to be achieved.

Table 12.5 Characteristics of the uses of *wenming* (in order of frequency)

Annotation category	Relation to individual versus group	State achieved versus state to be achieved
1. Cultured, developed and well-mannered	Group reference	State to be achieved
2. Modernised	Group reference	State to be achieved
3. Accountable, responsible and environmentally-friendly	Group reference	State to be achieved
4. Civilised	Group reference	State achieved

Table 12.5 summarises the uses of *wenming* in the Chinese corpus through the two categories of 'Relation to individual versus group' and 'State achieved versus state to be achieved'.

CONTRASTIVE ANALYSIS

Table 12.6 summarises the differences and similarities between the uses of *civilised* and *wenming*:

Table 12.6 is divided into two different parts: Part 1 considers the uses that exist in both linguacultures, while Part 2 considers the uses which exist in only one of the two linguacultures.

Wenming and *civilised* have two comparable uses (Part 1 of Table 12.6), with the first one being the most frequently employed in both linguacultures. While in this use both *wenming* and *civilised* refer to the state of groups, it is only *wenming* which refers to a state to be achieved, a fact which stems from the policy-related nature of this expression. The second comparable use of *wenming* is the least frequently employed in the Chinese corpus (see Table 12.4). This use is listed second in Table 12.6 because, to a certain degree, it is comparable to that of *civilised*. While in this case *wenming* still refers to groups, whereas *civilised* refers to individuals, these uses are essentially comparable because both describe a state that has already been achieved. The examination of such uses of *wenming* has revealed that this category is the only non-policy-related one in Chinese, and this is why it does not relate to a future state of affairs.

Table 12.6 Similarities and differences between the uses of civilised and wenming

Civilised: Annotation category	Relation to individual versus group	State achieved versus state to be achieved	Wenming: Annotation category	
Cultured and developed	Group reference	*wenming*: state to be achieved *civilised*: state achieved	Cultured, developed and well-mannered	Part 1
Sophisticated and refined	*wenming*: group reference *civilised*: individual reference	State achieved	Civilised	
NIL: no equivalent use of *civilised*	Group reference	State to be achieved	Accountable, responsible and environmentally-friendly	Part 2
NIL: no equivalent use of *civilised*	Group reference	State to be achieved	Modernised	
Well-mannered	Individual reference	State achieved	NIL: no equivalent use of *wenming*	
Well-looked-after and cared-for	Individual reference	State achieved	NIL: no equivalent use of *wenming*	
Governed by law and regulations	Group reference	State achieved	NIL: no equivalent use of *wenming*	

In summary, Part 1 of Table 12.6 consists of two comparable uses of *wenming* and *civilised*, with the first of these uses being the most frequently employed in both linguacultures. However, these uses differ significantly and, as such, might lead to translational difficulties.

The uses detailed in Part 2 of Table 12.6 might imply different translational difficulties than those in Part 1 because they have no linguacultural equivalent. At this point, one can hypothesise that this lack of linguacultural equivalence might trigger a preference for covert translation and cultural filtering, in comparison to the first use in Part 1.

The following discussion will only consider the first use in Part 1 and those uses of *wenming* in Part 2 for which there are no equivalent uses of *civilised*, i.e. the first two rows in Part 2. These uses of *wenming* are all group-related and indicate states to be achieved, i.e. they are typically policy-related expressions.

THE ENGLISH TRANSLATIONS OF *WENMING*

Table 12.7 provides a summary of the *wenming* translations in our Chinese–English corpus of media texts:

Table 12.7 has been aligned with Table 12.6: the translational categories were divided into two parts, as outlined above. Those uses were highlighted that according to the research outcomes of phase one, may be particularly problematic for translators. As Table 12.7 shows, by far the most frequent translational solution in the present

Table 12.7 Translations of *wenming*

Wenming (Chinese original)	Category	Translation	Frequency	Percentage	
	Cultured, developed and well-mannered	*Civilised*	116	61.4%	
		Best	3	1.6%	
		Civility	2	1.1%	Part ⌉
		[Omission]	4	2.1%	
	Civilised	*Civilisation*	10	5.3%	
		[Omission]	5	2.6%	
	Accountable, responsible and	*Civilised*	11	5.8%	⌋
	environmentally-friendly	Appropriately	4	2.1%	⌉ Part 2
	Modernised	*Civilised*	31	16.4%	
		Positive	3	1.6%	⌋
Total			189	100%	

corpus of Chinese–English translations includes instances of overt translation and the related lack of cultural filtering: in 158 cases, representing 83.6% of the translations, *wenming* is translated according to its 'civilised' dictionary meaning. This tendency can be explained by referring to the category of Tenor in my translation model: since *wenming* tends to be used in communicating policies, both the source texts and translated texts are characterised by a social relationship between an authoritative power (the government) and its citizens who have to form alignment with the creator of the discourse in Goffman's (1981) sense.

Let us now first examine translations of the 'Cultured, developed and well-mannered' use of *wenming*, representing Part 1 in Table 12.7 followed by an examination of the other two uses of *wenming*.

Cultured, Developed and Well-mannered

Example (14) represents a typical overt translation of *wenming* in this category – here the translation relies on the dictionary meaning of 'civilised':

EXAMPLE 14

在仪式上，福州、西藏道路交叉口、黄皮公路、淮海路被列为"十大文明路口"，70条、49条公交线路被评为 "十大文明公交线路"。

At the ceremony, the intersections at Fuzhou and Xizang roads, and Huangpi and Huaihai roads were on the list of the Top 10 Civilised Intersections, and bus lines 70 and 49 were ranked among the Top 10 Civilised Bus Lines.

This is the standard translation when it comes to this most frequent use of *wenming*. As Table 12.7 shows, there are also a small number of covert translations in the corpus:

EXAMPLE 15

"星级文明户" 评选、寻找"最美家庭"等活动，社会主义核心价值观广泛传播，贫困地区文明程度显著提升。

> Activities, such as competition for best households and families, have been organised to carry forward cherished family traditions, spread core socialist values and enhance social etiquette and civility.

In the Chinese original, *wenming* occurs as a qualifying adjective in the proper noun expression *Xingji-wenming-hu* 星级文明户 (lit. '*Wenming* Household of Star-Award Level'). The translation resolves the difficulty of conveying the original message by using cultural filtering and converting the original proper noun into a common noun in English. This is clearly different from example (14), in which the translated text keeps intact the original Chinese proper noun.

Accountable, Responsible and Environmentally-friendly

When it comes to the categories 'Accountable, responsible and environmentally-friendly' and 'Modernised', one witnesses a similar preference for overt translation and the consequent lack of cultural filtering as in the case of the 'Cultured, developed and well-mannered' category. Thus, the hypothesis that the lack of equivalence of use between Chinese and English could translate into cultural filtering turned out to be invalid. The following examples illustrate overt and covert translations of these uses of *wenming*:

Overt translation:

EXAMPLE 16

铁道部要求，要引导风景名胜区、宾馆饭店等履行社会责任，加强自律，倡导文明旅游。

The ministry called for efforts to guide scenic spots, hotels and restaurants, among others, to fulfil their social responsibilities, strengthen self-discipline and advocate civilised tourism.

Covert translation:

EXAMPLE 17

办法要求寄递企业规范操作和文明作业，避免抛扔、踩踏等行为。

The guideline also requires companies to deliver parcels appropriately, banning behaviour such as tossing and stamping on parcels.

While the foreign reader of example (16) may find the *civilised*-collocation distinctly odd and culturally alien, this problem is resolved in example (17) by cultural filtering. However, once again such cultural filtering is rare in the data because of the Tenor of the texts, which appears to preclude the creative adaptation of the Chinese text for a foreign, English-speaking audience.

TRANSLATION TASK AND FOLLOW-UP INTERVIEWS

During the third phase of this study, ten professional Chinese translators were asked to translate eight utterances including *wenming* drawn from BCC. These eight examples were chosen because phase one had revealed that *wenming* affords four different uses, i.e. two examples for each use. The goal in this phase of the research was to test whether translational tendencies (in particular, overt versus covert translation) can also be observed in the expert translators' translations, and whether the fact that the task was unofficial – allowing for 'private' solutions – influences translational preferences. Table 12.8 shows translational choices:

Table 12.8 Translations of *wenming* by Chinese translators

Category	Translation	Number of translations	Frequency (%)
Cultured, developed and well-mannered	Civilised	14	70
	Model	3	15
	Harmonious	1	5
	Right	1	5
	[Omission]	1	5

Category	Translation	Number of translations	Frequency (%)
Modernised	Civilised	15	75
	Orderly	3	15
	Courteous	1	5
	Polite	1	5
Accountable, responsible and environmentally-friendly	Civilised	14	70
	Good	6	30
Civilised	Civilised	20	100
Total		80	

As Table 12.8 shows, while the translators occasionally applied a cultural filter, e.g. by translating *wenming* in its 'Cultured, developed and well-mannered' use as 'model' and 'harmonious', they still mostly zeroed in on the overt translation 'civilised'. This outcome was surprising because the respondents were expert translators. One may venture to explain this phenomenon by referring to the category of Tenor: despite the private nature of the task, the official character of the text and the close connection between *wenming* and policy communication turned out to be dominant. Here is one example each for overt and covert translations of the use 'Cultured, developed and well-mannered':

EXAMPLE 18

Translator 2's overt translation

Task sentence:

统计数据是在上海电视台的颁奖典礼上宣布的。在仪式上，福州、西藏道路交叉口、黄皮公路、淮海路被列为"十大文明路口"，70条、49条公交线路被评为"十大文明公交线路"。

Translation:

The statistics were announced at the award ceremony of Shanghai TV. At the ceremony, Fuzhou, Xizang Road intersections, Huangpi Highway and Huaihai Road were listed as the "top ten civilised intersections", and 70 and 49 bus lines were rated as the "top ten civilised bus routes".

EXAMPLE 19

Translator 10's covert translation

Task sentence:

"星级文明户"评选、寻找"最美家庭" 等活动，促进社会主义核心价值观广泛传播，贫困地区文明程度显著提升。

Translation:

Activities such as the selection of "Model Households" and the search for "the most beautiful family" have promoted the wide dissemination of socialist core values and significantly improved the degree of civilisation in underdeveloped areas.

The following are excerpts from the interviews conducted with the translators of the above examples (18) and (19):

Translator 2 (overt translation of example 18)

"这个十大文明路口" … 我就觉得既然人家都这么使用了呢(.)，我就也这么使了。

Regarding this "top ten civilised intersections" … since others use this form (.) all the time, I opted for it as well.

Translator 10 (covert translation of example 19)

我觉得外国人会不理解文明指的是什么。

I feel that foreigners may not understand the meaning of wenming in this context.

As the second excerpt shows, translators who applied covert translations and cultural filtering usually referred to the fact that translating *wenming* as 'civilised' when announcing domestic Chinese policies may sound alien to foreigners.

The category of Tenor in my translation model (see Chapter 7), which captures the relationship between the writer/translator of the text and his addressees, has proved to be crucial for explaining the overriding frequency of overt translations of *wenming*. Since the corpus-based contrastive examination has revealed that most uses of *wenming* relate to communicating policies, it is obvious that in the

Chinese linguacultural context translators tend to shy away from 'tampering' with the officially decreed meaning of *wenming* because of the authority of the government. This is in line with the fact that many bilingual Chinese news outlets are designed essentially for domestic audiences, i.e. their main goal is to trigger alignment between the government and the local audience. It may be an awareness of the international relevance of certain news items that led translators to opt for using covert translation and cultural filtering. While this point cannot be proven on the basis of the bilingual media corpus, the interviews conducted with the translators appear to confirm this hypothesis.

The case study presented in this chapter has revealed the enormous complexity surrounding culturally embedded Chinese policy expressions like *wenming*. At this point, it is worth going back to the main question of this chapter, i.e. whether culturally embedded concepts can really be appropriately translated, or not. As quantitative and qualitative evidence in this case study has shown, in theory appropriate translations are possible provided translators make use of cultural filtering. However, in practice, appropriate translations are more an ideal than a reality because few translators apply cultural filtering due to various extralinguistic factors, such as respect for the context of the text.

THE ROLE OF TRANSLATION IN LANGUAGE LEARNING AND TEACHING

This chapter looks at how translation has been used in learning and teaching foreign languages over the past centuries. We will cast a critical eye over the role of translation in pedagogic contexts through the centuries and then consider a new, more creative view of translation in language learning and teaching. Concretely, we will carefully appraise the powerful monolingual myth in language learning and teaching which has resulted in either effectively banning translation from the classroom or 'misusing' it. We will then discuss a new way of creatively integrating translation activities in the foreign language classroom.

An important field for translation over many centuries and in many countries is pedagogy: in other words, translation is used as a means for teaching and learning a foreign language. Making use of the cross-linguistic and cross-cultural skill of translation seems, at first glance, a very sensible idea, because it is natural for people learning another language to relate it to a language they already know. And this is, of course, also in line with an important general pedagogic principle: in teaching anything, one should try to build on what one's learners already know. This principle has, however, not met with universal approval in the case of translation as a phenomenon that makes use of the learners' mother tongue. While translation has a long tradition as an easily administered exercise and test of learners' knowledge of foreign language vocabulary and grammatical structures, it has also been at the centre of a fierce controversy about the role of learners' mother tongue and the place of grammar in the foreign language classroom. In the next section, we

DOI: 10.4324/9781003355823-17

will look at this controversy and examine when, how and why the use of translation in foreign language teaching and learning has been viewed positively or negatively.

THE HISTORY OF TRANSLATION IN FOREIGN LANGUAGE LEARNING AND TEACHING

Translation has a long tradition in foreign language teaching and learning. Translation *from* the foreign language was probably first used in the third century bc by elementary school teachers of Latin in the Greek communities of the Roman Empire (Kelly 1969:172). During the early Middle Ages when Latin was still considered a 'living language' and the only medium of instruction in the schools, translation is hardly mentioned as a teaching tool. It only began to gain importance with the rise of the vernaculars when vernacular translations of the classics became popular. During the late Middle Ages, the technique of 'construing' was combined with translating into classical languages, i.e., dissecting words, phrases and sentences according to their grammatical function, establishing vernacular equivalents for them and gradually transforming the resulting 'literal translation' into an acceptable dialect sentence. This procedure became a keystone of all classical language instruction – and con- tributed to linking grammar and translation negatively for a very long time. During the Renaissance, 'simple translation' into a for- eign language was used to develop a sense of style in the foreign language and was often complemented by 'double translation', a combination of translation from and into the foreign language and intensive reading. At the end of the eighteenth century, the teach- ing of Latin had turned into a highly formalized ritual, the idea being to instil discipline into students' minds, often combined with an emphasis on grammar rules. This method of teaching Latin was then transferred onto the few modern languages that were then taught – mostly privately by native speakers in informal conversa- tions, which of course made translation superfluous. Translation *from* the foreign language was the most important form of exercise up to the last quarter of the eighteenth century, and translation *into* the foreign language rose to prominence as a means of applying grammatical rules: with this, the foundation of the so-called (in) famous 'grammar-translation method' was laid.

In the textbooks of the nineteenth century, translation became the single dominant feature of foreign language exercises. Grammar rules were mainly learnt through their application in the translation of artificially constructed, isolated, disconnected sentences. This practice, of course, did gross injustice to translation, giving rise to the type of textual and context-bound phenomenon which was discussed earlier in this book.

In the latter part of the nineteenth century, the 'grammar-translation method' met with strong opposition in foreign language teaching circles. The importance of the spoken language was now emphasized, and with this, the dominant role of translation in foreign language teaching was attacked. The so-called 'Direct Method' of foreign language teaching was born, featuring the exclusive use of the foreign language and the abolition of any form of translation. At the beginning of the twentieth century, theorists like Jespersen and Palmer and particularly Sweet (1964) were taking a more balanced view, refraining from a total ban on translation in language teaching and learning, recommending the judicious use of translation: translation *from* the foreign language might be used to make knowledge more exact, but translation *into* the foreign language should only be used in restricted circumstances since translating into an only partially mastered language was seen as doomed to fail. Translation *from* the foreign language was regarded as quite useful in promoting language comprehension and easily and economically testing it. Translation might also be a useful means of elucidating the meaning of foreign language items, whenever it included larger connected linguistic units with a specification of context.

While the Direct Method was extremely influential in excluding translation from the foreign language classroom, it never succeeded in completely banning it from the repertoire of language teaching techniques. In Higher Education, translation continued to be used in the foreign language departments in Europe, much less so however in Anglophone countries such as Britain and the United States. During the Second World War, the need to quickly bring US soldiers and government personnel to a level of fluency in a foreign language led to the establishment of the so-called 'Army Specialized Training Program'. This programme was based on the assumption that language is primarily oral, and that spoken communication is the main purpose of language learning and teaching, with translation being ruled out.

During the late 1950s, with the rise of structuralism and behaviourism in linguistics and psychology respectively, a new method, the 'Audio-Lingual Method' gained ground. As before, translation had no major place in it. Translation only featured occasionally in the early dialogues whose meaning needed to be known. As a major teaching technique, however, it continued to be discredited. It was thought to inhibit thinking in the foreign language and to produce the wrong kind of bilingualism.

In the more recent cognitive and communicative trends in language teaching and learning, conscious understanding and control of structures of the foreign language through study and analysis are emphasized as well as the ability to creatively use the foreign language. And with the recognition of the crucial role of the mother tongue in foreign language learning, came support for giving translation a more important role in language teaching (see here, for instance, Cook 2010).

Today, foreign language learning and teaching is no longer seen as an entirely monolingual undertaking but rather a bilingual one (see Widdowson 2014). If the foreign language is assumed to co-exist with the native language in learners' minds, then language learning becomes a sort of 'bilingualization process', i.e., a process promoting bilingualism. The ever-increasing importance of bilingualism, multilingualism and multiculturalism as a consequence of worldwide migration and globalization processes and technological progress further adds to the importance of using translation in foreign language learning and teaching.

Given this shift towards recognizing the role of learners' mother tongue and the need for explicit reference to the language(s) that learners already know, the advantages of translation can be summarized as follows:

1. Using translation helps to develop linguistic proficiency in a foreign language by economically and unambiguously explaining the meaning of foreign language items. Since learners' existing knowledge of mother tongue items can be referred to, knowledge of foreign language items can be made more exact.

2. In exploiting their knowledge of a language they already know, learners increase their confidence in learning the foreign language, whose intimidating strangeness can thus be reduced. Making explicit reference to learners' mother tongue is also a sign of appreciation of learners' previous knowledge. And since learners' native language is, of course, the medium in which learners were socialized and in which they developed their linguacultural identity, such an appreciation of their native language provides continuity of learners' linguacultural development. In concrete terms, translation promotes explicit knowledge about the foreign language and awareness of similarities and differences between the native and foreign language systems as well as conventional uses of these systems in different situations, genres and text types. Translation contributes to conscious learning, because it raises a general awareness of language and creates opportunities for reflection on differences and similarities at various linguistic levels. Comparative analysis and reflection in translation activities may also be used to unmask ideologies and other hidden agendas buried in texts. And it can confront learners with the limits of translatability in the form of connotations, humour and linguacultural regional and social variation described in Chapter 7.

Further, language awareness enhanced by translation also promotes cross-cultural understanding, in that translation can trigger discussions about language and culture specificity and universality, about forms and functions of culture-conditioned expressions of politeness, routine formulas and phenomena relevant for transitions from one language to another.

Despite these advantages of the use of translation in foreign language learning and teaching, a strong camp of theorists and practitioners still argue against it. They regard translation as an unnatural activity or a highly specialized art that is either not at all or negatively related to how learners use a foreign language, and they argue that translation does nothing for developing the standard four skills of speaking, writing, listening and reading in a foreign language. In other words, the controversy about the use of translation is still ongoing today. Major reasons for this continuing debate about the usefulness of translation for foreign language teaching and learning seem to be the following:

- The nature of translation is still little understood in language teaching circles. But any sensible discussion of the role of translation in language teaching needs to be based on theoretical understanding of translation.
- Translation was predominantly used to achieve linguistic competence only, and as a technique to (a) illustrate and explain grammar rules and exemplify them in sentences specially made up for this purpose, (b) help teachers establish if learners properly understand what teachers present to them and (c) provide teachers with a quick means of large-scale testing of knowledge and skills.

Such uses of translation fail to exploit the real pedagogical usefulness of translation as a complex cross-linguistic and cross-cultural activity. It is its strong pragmatic component that makes translation so potentially beneficial for language learners. If translation is used for establishing pragmatic equivalences by relating linguistic forms to their communicative functions, it may fulfil an important role in making learners communicatively competent.

In what follows, we will therefore explore some new and alternative uses of translation in the foreign language classroom.

NEW ALTERNATIVE USES OF TRANSLATION IN PEDAGOGIC CONTEXTS

First of all, the use of translation in the foreign language classroom should embrace a whole range of 'para-translation activities' – activities that involve (a) explicit comparisons of linguacultural phenomena in the source and target languages, (b) the creative production of source and target language texts, (c) modifying the make-up of original and translation texts by changing the situational dimension of the tests (following the model of translation quality assessment described in Chapter 7) and (d) engaging in context-sensitive evaluations of translations.

The objective of the new **alternative translation activities** is to improve receptive and productive aspects of communicative competence, and they should be restricted to advanced learners, who have a good overview of the equivalence relations between the two languages and cultures involved in translation. Priority is given to the communicative use of language, and translation should be conducted exclusively at the level of text. Only at this level can both linguistic and non-linguistic contexts be fruitfully considered, and only through using texts can the nature of equivalence relations in translation be fully recognized.

Given the complexity of translation, source texts should be carefully analysed using the procedures suggested in the translation assessment model detailed in Chapter 7 and discussed in class so that all learners can derive the maximum benefit from the reflections about the linguistic-pragmatic choices made by the author of the original text. All the texts chosen for translation should be fully contextualized for learners, and they should be presented as part of a communicative situation.

A first type of translation activity involves the selection of textual pairs (source and translation texts) that will be analysed, compared and evaluated according to the assessment model described above. Such contrastive activities are useful for sensitizing learners to the different repertoires of linguistic means through which a particular textual function is realized in learners' mother tongue and in the foreign language. In foreign language classrooms, the foreign language is usually learnt on the basis of previous knowledge of the native language. As mentioned above, this means that learners naturally contrast the uses of their native language for particular purposes with those of the foreign language. Learners also naturally compare cultural features of the two linguacultures in order to find out about similarities and differences. Such a comparison is a natural activity for all learners of another language. So we can say that translation used to compare explicitly and directedly the language in use in two different texts simply makes a virtue out of what has often been considered a vice in language teaching circles. Detecting and discussing mismatches as an outcome of textual analysis and comparison may involve a critical discussion of stereotypes and ideological assumptions.

In another translation activity, learners are asked to analyse a pair of source and target texts and to translate them. Here, it is important to fully contextualize the texts, i.e., provide learners with a motivating account of the origin and function of the text, and to make the task of translating as close as possible to fulfilling a real communicative need.

Here is a simple example: a neighbour, who does not know any French, has just received an email from a French girl written in French. She has noticed that frequent reference is made in this email to the name of her son, who is at present working for an international company in Paris. The neighbour is worried that the email contains bad news. So she asks you – a student of French – to give her a quick summary of the contents in English so that she may know at once what the email is about and afterwards a complete translation. In other words, the learner will first produce an oral (overt) version of the original and then a written overt translation.

In another example, a learner is similarly asked to produce an oral overt version and an overt written translation. The learner is, for instance, given the following scenario: during your summer holidays, you are working on a building site. Your supervisor has just received a new manual for the maintenance of one of the tractors. Unfortunately, the manual is written in English and translated into many other languages but not into Italian. He knows that you are competent in Italian and he asks you to provide an overt translation of this manual into Italian for him and to also give the other workers a quick idea of its main points, i.e., learners are asked to provide both a written overt translation and an oral summary, an overt version.

Along those lines, a whole range of scenarios can be used in teaching where a real need for a translation is simulated. It is important to introduce learners to many different domains and topics so that they can broaden their repertoire of language varieties. In the scenarios described above the resulting translations are evaluated, corrected and discussed in class with particular attention given to the reasons for and consequences of any mistakes and mismatch detected.

A more complicated type of scenario involves asking learners to change the original's function following the analysis and translation of the originals, i.e., learners are, for instance, asked to convert a specialist scientific text into a popular science text – this would be a type of intralingual version production. Various changes along the situational dimensions of the model will have to be undertaken by the learners, and on the basis of these, the original will be rewritten. Following this production of a new source text (a version of the original source text) in the learners' mother tongue, the learners translate this new source text. All changes along the entire textual profile will then be discussed in class with reference to both the original and the modified source texts and their translations.

Another type of translation activity makes use of learners' creative imagination and builds on their simulated needs. In these activities, learners do not start with a ready-made text but with the function of a text and they are asked to construct a text in accordance with this function, an outline of the content of the text and some other dimensional data contributing to this function. In one type of activity, learners are given an assignment such as the following: Write as email to the mother of a good friend of yours whom you have never met but who you would like to impress and make her like you. It is your task to make this email as polite, entertaining and attractive as possible. You will have to demonstrate your interest in her personal habits, her environment and interests. Following this first task, the teacher and the learners analyse the mother tongue email cooperatively in a group according to the translation evaluation model described above. In the second assignment, learners are asked to covertly translate the email into another language, i.e., write 'the same' email to the mother of another friend in another linguaculture making all the necessary changes as to the recipients' home, environment and interests.

Another translation activity involving the creation of a mother tongue text is the construction of advertisements. On the basis of a collation of a corpus of advertisements, learners will discuss the assumptions underlying the production of advertisements in the corpus as well as their grammatical, lexical and textual peculiarities. Learners are then asked to write advertisements in their native language and then covertly translate these advertisements into another language, making due allowance for linguistic and cultural differences between the two linguacultures. A discussion of stereotypes will naturally be part of this translation activity.

All the above translation activities feature a deliberate juxtaposition of verbal actions in the learners' mother tongue and in the foreign language, and they all include detailed analyses, comparison and criticism of original and translated texts.

TOWARDS A MORE REALISTIC VIEW OF TRANSLATION IN PEDAGOGIC CONTEXTS

In recent years, we have witnessed a more positive view of translation in the applied linguistics literature (cf. Cook 2010). Translation is now more often seen as an omnipresent general interpretative activity that plays an important role in realizing pragmatic meaning within and across languages, and translation is frequently regarded as a natural pragmatic process in acquiring a foreign language. This means that teachers of foreign languages need to encourage learners to actively engage in this pragmatic process by drawing on all the linguistic resources they have at their disposal, giving credit to what learners are able to achieve in their creative meaning-making. Translation activities are not teaching devices to get learners to conform, but they need to provide conditions that will stimulate the learning process, no matter how non-conformist the outcomes might turn out to be. While one tends to think of translation as an activity practised exclusively by professional translators, translation is really a very general, commonplace pragmatic process – something we all do when we interpret what other people say and write so as to accommodate this to our own discourse worlds. So translation is really a general human 'capability' of making meaning into and out of text. Translation is then not some extraneous activity but one that is intrinsic to the learning process itself.

Despite this development, which is increasingly favourable to translation, it is still often the case that language learning is understood not as a continuation of previous experience and an extension of an existing linguistic resource, but as the learning of some separate, new entity very much dissociated from the already known mother tongue. However, learners' mother tongues are clearly NOT separate in learners' minds.

Translation is thus a *normal* and natural process that occurs in all language use. In the foreign language classroom, learners are conventionally confronted with texts, and they will naturally seek to interpret them, and in so doing instinctively, and unavoidably, make reference to their own linguacultural reality. So, foreign language needs to be presented to learners not as something unrelated to their previous linguistic experience, but as something closely related to it and an additional resource in their multilingual linguistic repertoire. This is recently also emphasized by approaches which recognize translation as one of many other multilingual and plurilingual approaches in language learning and teaching (see here, for instance, Carreres et al. 2021; Galante 2021; Gonzalez-Davies and Soler Ortinez 2021). This means that in foreign language learning and teaching it is advisable to deliberately exploit learners' own multilingual experiences, to encourage them to recognize how other languages can be fruitfully used to realize meanings in alternative ways. For all this translation is indeed an excellent tool.

14

TRANSLATION AS A SOCIAL PRACTICE IN REAL-LIFE SITUATIONS

The final chapter of this book engages with the 'real world' of translation as a professional practice in different situations and in sites of potential conflict. We will first discuss the role of translation in multilingual institutions such as the European Union, multicultural societies and minority and migrant groups and then take up (again) the topic of ethics in translation practice, extending it to translation in areas of conflict and war as well as the increasing role of citizen media involving ad hoc translation. Finally, we will look at a type of translation which is fast growing in importance today: audiovisual translation.

TRANSLATION IN MULTILINGUAL INSTITUTIONS

Here, we will take a critical look at translation as a common practice that takes place in **international institutions** (see here, for instance, Pym 2000; Wagner 2003; Kang 2014). Institutional translation concerns organizational, ideological and historical aspects of an institution in which translations habitually occur, as well as the impact of an institution on translators and the process and product of their professional output. Translation in this context is seen as a socially situated practice, and studies of institutional translation include all texts that are translated in an institution, their structures and features, the official role of the translator in the institution as well as norms and conventions governing translators' work and the ideology underlying the functioning of the institution in question.

An institution that has been particularly well-studied is the **European Union** with its translation services – the largest of its kind in the world (see Wagner et al. 2002). The Finnish translation scholar Kaisa Koskinen (2000) has cast a critical eye over the EU's institutional ideology and its culture, which she characterizes as propagating an equality of all European languages, an equality which naturally feeds into a requirement of equivalence between source and target texts. The requirement of equivalence is to make EU texts function smoothly in the discourse of the institution, both internally and externally with the public at large. One effect of this belief in the necessity of equivalence is an overall attempt to hide the very fact that a translation is a translation. This denial of reality results in a consequent downplaying of the role and function of translators in the EU. Despite the institutional pressure for uniformity, translators seem to be able to retain their individual voice by engaging in numerous discoursal shifts and thus actively resisting the institution's equivalence-driven ideology.

In talking about the EU's 'illusion of equality', Koskinen has set out to unmask this institution's hypocritical ideology of multilingualism in the face of real inequality of the languages represented in the EU. Translations are a very important tool for implementing the EU's language policy. They are designed to safeguard the ideal of the equality of languages, and their symbolic value is high, eclipsing their real value and use. As Koskinen ironically remarks: 'Sometimes the primary function of the translation of a particular official document is simply to be there, to exist' (2000:51). And she goes on to state:

> Rather than just conveying a message or providing possibilities for communication, the role of the translation is then to stand as a proof of equality.... This could perhaps be called 'existential equivalence', i.e., all the language versions need to exist, any other features being irrelevant or at least subordinate to the symbolic function.
>
> (Ibid.)

In the case of translations from English in non-official working documents into minor languages documents, translators often suspect that no one will bother to read their translations anyway.

The official EU policy that all languages are equal has a further consequence: that translations are not really translations but 'language versions' (different from my own definition of a version, cf. Chapter 7) suggesting that the texts are produced simultaneously in all the EU languages. The built-in illusion of equivalence is one of the cornerstones of translation practice within the Commission (2000:54). This means, as Koskinen quips, that 'EU translators miraculously produce eleven [now 24, J. H.] similar versions of a document'. In Koskinen's (2000:58) opinion, a fruitful approach to the specific nature of EU translations would start from the assumption that EU institutions form a culture of their own, such that the institutional framework has its own specific frame of reference with its own shared system of knowledge, aims and norms – much like a community of practice. This would hold more or less, I propose, for all institutions in which translations are produced.

Another characteristic of institutional translations is that they routinely involve teams of translators who draft the translations collectively in working groups and committees. This is of course not only a characteristic of institutional translations but is probably most marked here. Another characteristic of institutional translations is their anonymity. Texts are produced by the institution, which of course makes translators invisible both inside and outside the institution. So Umberto Eco's (2001) famous dictum: 'The language of Europe is translation' is oddly not held in great esteem in the EU. And, as Koskinen (2000:61) points out, the other side of this invisibility is paradoxically the visibility of the 'translatedness' of the translations, and this is revealed in a kind of 'eurorhetoric', EU terminology and unidiomatic structures with which most EU citizens are quite unfamiliar.

TRANSLATION IN MULTILINGUAL AND MULTICULTURAL SOCIETIES

Another new field of translation studies is exploring the interface between translation and migration, minorities and the larger issues of power and inequality or the role translation plays in shaping the relation between majority and minority groups in society (see here, for instance, Cronin 1998). It is now recognized what an important role translating plays in the context of present day multi-ethnic, multilingual and multicultural societies. Translations into minority languages are crucial in that they can help to ensure the recognition and survival of these languages and also help reinforce the confidence and pride of their speakers. Many, if not most, societies today are multilingual and multicultural and this means that, given the growing presence of multilingual speakers around the world, a monolingual perspective is no longer tenable and should be replaced by a multilingual perspective in education and many other domains of contemporary life (see here for instance Kramsch 2009). Migration and the globalized economy as well as increased access to the Internet and to global means of communication make translation a subjective experience for many ordinary citizens and also increase the need for professional translations in various domains.

The demand for such translations, e.g. into Kurdish, various varieties of Arabic, Pashtu or Farsi, has greatly increased in Europe, particularly in Germany, where several millions of refugees have arrived, and need to be integrated, from 2015 onwards. Apart from teachers of the language of the receiving countries, translators and interpreters are now more in demand than ever before. They play a crucial role in avoiding linguistic and cultural misunderstandings and in helping migrants to feel more at home in a foreign environment. Especially necessary in these circumstances is the translation of bureaucratic paperwork, providing crucial assistance in filling out these forms and generally helping refugees to better understand the maze of bureaucracy through the provision of translation of foreign concepts and procedures.

MICRO-HISTORY IN TRANSLATION

Another recently emerging interest in translation studies is what Munday (2014) has called 'the microhistory of translation and translators', which examines the use and value of manuscripts, archives, personal papers and post-hoc accounts and interviews with translators in order to come up with a sort of 'micro-history' of actual translations and the everyday work of translators in the past and the present to improve our understanding of an individual translator's everyday life as a starting point for arriving at a bigger picture of a social and cultural history of translation and translators in a particular social, political and cultural context. Apart from meticulous documentation, this approach can generate new narratives of translator behaviour and reveal and challenge dominant historical discourses of text production and reception.

THE WORKING ENVIRONMENT OF TRANSLATORS

Another further area of interest in translation studies which has a direct bearing on the translator's work concerns the translator's immediate workplace and conditions of work as well as the influence exerted by the nature of her working environment on her cognitive processing and job satisfaction (see here, for instance, Halverson 2014; Ehrensberger-Dow and O'Brien 2015). We see here a new trend for studies to be carried out in the translators' technologically equipped workplaces, in their natural habitat, by observing translators when they are working on real-life, authentic tasks. Such observations have been carried out in both large translation agencies and companies with translation departments as well as with freelance translators. Studies of translators' working environments give access to the situated, embedded aspects of what translators are thinking when they are involved in their translations. But with such real-life studies, one also manages to gain an insight into how the various agents, aids and tools work together to contribute to a translator's work. The translator's workplace today is characterized by an intensive interaction with a computer. Translators are therefore subject to spatial, temporal and technological constraints that can be relativized by the design of the workplace in which a translator's work is embedded. We have here an interaction of physical, cognitive, emotional, organizational and technological aspects of the situated workplace of the translator. This view of the situated activity of translation can only be captured with a multi-method methodology including, for instance, screen and video recordings, interviews with translators that try to tap into their personal evaluation of their feelings about their workplace environment, health issues and general job satisfaction.

As mentioned in Chapter 1, computer-aided or computer-assisted translation (CAT) is common today in any translator's workplace. **CAT tools** enable cooperation between the human translator and a computer: a translational computer output currently needs to be post-edited by the human translator to make its quality acceptable.

The range of CAT tools currently available is large; those most commonly used by translators at present are the following:

- translation memory tools that have a database for routinized text passages in a source language and their expert translations in a selected target language;
- electronic dictionaries in a selected language pair;
- grammar checkers as add-on programs or programs built into the word-processing software;
- terminology managers that the translator can use to electronically manage their own special terminology bank;
- terminology databases;
- full-text search tools with which the translator can access previously translated texts in a multitude of genres useful to her;
- concordancing programs with which a translator can access words and phrases in context in different types of corpora;
- project management software designed to help translators to plan, structure and monitor translation projects in the form of 'work-flow' charts. This allows a translator to assign different tasks to colleagues in teams as well as enabling her to monitor the development of each person and each task.

As briefly mentioned in Chapter 10, translators need to be aware today of the need in the translation industry and in their daily tasks for localization, i.e. adapting output for local target conditions by using special programs for a specific audience. As stated in Chapter 7, localization is similar to the concept of a 'cultural filter' in covert translation processes. Just like cultural filtering, localization is used to make a text have the feel and look of being designed especially for a particular target audience (see also 'audience design' in Chapter 4). This cultural adaptation is often undertaken to make a product sell better and generally to boost its success in the context of the receiving culture.

ETHICS IN THE PRACTICE OF TRANSLATION

Another recent influential concern in translation studies – as indeed in many other fields of contemporary life – is the socio-philosophical issue of **ethics** (see e.g. Inghilleri 2008). This question is, of course, intimately tied up with the current focus not on the texts to be translated but on the person of the translator and her responsibility for, and awareness of, the ethics of her textual actions. Such thinking has been mostly associated with post-modern, post-colonial, feminist and post-structuralist trends in translation studies described above in Chapter 3. The work by the philosopher Emmanuel Levinas (for instance, 1989) on subjectivity and ethical responsibility of the individual has been influential here. The idea is to help translators to gain a heightened transcultural consciousness, causing them to reflect on their translational actions and the complicated ethical relationship between author, text and translator.

While ethical issues faced by the translator were not given much attention in the early days of translation studies, they are now increasingly popular in scholarly reflection on translator actions. But issues of ethics are clearly most relevant for the person of the practising translator, because it is the translator who most acutely feels the ethical responsibility of her task and the conflicts that often arise. Recent concerns with ethical issues relate to individual translators' ethical responsibilities to some superordinate standards of justice, morality and, last but not least, their own conscience. The customary 'codes of ethics' and 'codes of professional conduct' issued by governments and professional translation organizations mainly existed to protect translators from exploitation by employers and also to professionalize their translational practice. They often emphasized the necessity of the translators' fidelity to the message of the original and admonished translators to be impartial and refrain from letting their personal or political opinion affect their translation. In the current climate in translation studies this very 'fidelity' and 'impartiality' is, however, increasingly challenged as overly naive. Propagators of the idea that translators are honest mediators and innocent builders of bridges between languages and cultures are today confronted with the reality of the more ambiguous role of translators and interpreters in situations of conflict that involve unequal power relationships, exploitation and injustice. Translators in such situations are urged to resist translating texts and to refuse to be complicit in propagating such views. Existing norms and conventions need to be understood as invariably reflecting certain biases, hidden agendas and interests of influential groups or individuals. Translators should stop acting in conformity with expectations and normative behavioural standards so as to liberate themselves from, and actively resist, the perpetuation of ethnocentric values and the seamless integration of the foreign into one's own cultural system. In following this resistant and liberating agenda, translators would also cease to be 'invisible', and they would be in a position to play a more important role in their day-to-day business of translating.

The idea that translators can never function totally neutrally, impartially and *in vacuo* but are frequently implicated in political, economic, military and power relations that strongly affect their mediating role, is today accepted by many practitioners. This means that the translator's task of mechanically transferring messages, acting as a sort of 'slave to the original text' is seen as no longer tenable. The translator's seemingly simple role as mediator may in fact camouflage the expected conformity with the expectations of the powerful commissioner of the translation. So the limits of the traditional code of ethics for translators are reached whenever the expected neutrality and impartiality comes into serious conflict with an individual translator's conscience and his personal code of ethics, leading him to construct and defend his very own 'code of ethics' in order to preserve his personal integrity.

What this means for the translator is, first and foremost, a heightened personal and transcultural sensibility which takes account of the norms and conventions of the culture into which the original's translation is 'entering'. Questions of ethics relate to an individual translator's choice and her individual accountability, affecting of course also the personal and social identity of the translator. This type of ethical choice by the individual translator clearly transcends the linguistic-cultural choices involved in any translation (see here also Pym 2001). One might argue that because the individual element in this type of ethical choice necessarily defies generalization, it cannot form part of a theory. That is applicable to many different cases. However, at a very basic level, generalizations may be possible, for instance, the need for 'understanding' as a superordinate

ethical principle, suggesting that translators in their quest for facilitating cross-cultural understanding need not only to understand the
text they are to translate but also need to consider the expectations
of potential recipients of the translation.

In their day-to-day work, translators are often faced with sexist,
colonialist, imperialist or otherwise offensive and discriminatory
texts that they are asked to translate. It is one thing to preach resistance and personal integrity, but quite another thing when it comes
to translators' situation in the real world, where they are inevitably
not at all independent in their actions but rather subject to a commissioner's brief and the need to keep a job in order to survive. So
a translator often faces a very real dilemma: should she follow her
conscience and, for instance, refuse to translate 'faithfully' disturb-
ingly sexist descriptions of women in an original, opting instead for
a more enlightened, 'ethical' description – a strategy that may well
cost her her job – or should she act as a neutral medium and quietly
get on with her translating task? There can be no general rules for
the translator about how she ought to behave in such situations.
The translator's choice will depend on her own culturally, histori-
cally and experientially defined individual values, her conscience
and her willingness and determination to live with the consequences
of her choice.

One of the often quoted attempts to come to grips with the issue
of ethics in translation is Andrew Chesterman's (2001) suggestion to
divide the role that ethics can play in translation into four distinct
but clearly overlapping models: the ethics of representation (of the
source text or of the author), an expanding ethics of service (based
on fulfilling a brief negotiated between the translator and a client),
a philosophical type of ethics of communication (focused on
exchanges with a member of another culture) and a norm-based
ethics (where ethical stances and behaviours depend on particular
expectations of a specific cultural location), as well as a fifth model,
namely an 'ethics of commitment', an attempt to define 'the good'
residing in a general code of professional ethics for translators. All of
these 'models' are only partially valid, covering only a limited part
of any ethical action, and, as Chesterman admits, they are inadequate on their own.

So in the last analysis, it remains up to the individual translator
and her conscience which type of ethics she will heed, first and

foremost. For instance, how should a devout Muslim translator act when he is confronted with the translation of an issue of the French satirical magazine *Charlie Hebdo* in which the head of the Prophet Mohammed is unmistakably shown with male sexual organs? How should the translator proceed in a context of strong international approval of such a representation in the name of the freedom of the press? In this situation, a translator who refused to be part of the commissioned translation team because his belief made him object to a depiction of the Prophet, let alone a pornographic one, would face not only financial and professional retribution but also run the risk of being caught in the international surveillance net of secret services hunting terrorists.

Ethical issues cannot be solved by recourse to supposedly agreed and generally acceptable standards, certainly not those of 'political acceptability'. Ethical action depends to a large degree on liberating oneself from the politically acceptable mood of the day if our conscience tells us to do this. It is the translator's conscience which frees the translator to decide on the right and responsible course for her translation.

For some, acting ethically means that the translator must have the courage to act on her convictions even in the face of adverse consequences. There are no general guidelines in the realm of ethics which would be valid in all imaginable contexts, because we are here concerned with human beings who vary so much that any generalization would be preposterous.

As opposed to this extremely relativistic view, Andrew Chesterman (2001:153) proposes what he calls a 'Hieronymic Oath' for the practice of translation consisting of nine commitments or 'suboaths' that range from loyalty to the profession, understanding, truth, clarity, trustworthiness, truthfulness and justice to the striving for excellence. These principles that are meant to go beyond genuinely personal and subjective ethical positions and choices certainly offer themselves for generalization.

But, given Chesterman's ethical oath, are we now in a position to say of a given translation that it is 'ethical' or 'unethical'? Who is to decide whether a translation is 'unethical', for whom and why? These simple questions show how complex and still ultimately subjective statements about ethics are now and will remain in the future. Coming back to the above example of *Charlie Hebdo*, if a translator refuses to translate a text that offends her own and others' religious feelings, is she acting unethically because she steps outside the ethical consensus of 'freedom of the pen', 'freedom from censure', 'freedom of speech'?

To use another example: does the translator who translated the philosopher Ted Honderich's book *After the Terror* (2002) into German act 'unethically' when he faithfully translated a paragraph of the book in which Honderich reflected on what he called 'liberation–terrorism':

> The principle of humanity, being serious and arguable, does not give an automatic verdict on all terrorism. It is a principle that takes account of the world in its differences. It struggles with facts and probabilities, with the difficulty of rationality. To my mind, still, it does issue one conclusion of a certain generality, this being about *liberation-terrorism*, terrorism to get freedom for a people when it is clear that nothing else will get it for them.

> (2002:150–151)

In this paragraph, Honderich refers to the Palestinian people. Would it have been 'ethical' either to leave this paragraph out or to change its offending content and tone? As it happens, the German translation of the book was almost immediately withdrawn from the market, so the ethical decision by the translator to translate the book including this statement by the original author was reversed.

While it is, of course, extremely difficult to give any clear, non-ambivalent guidelines and general statements about a concept of ethics relating to an individual translator's responsibility, her conscience and sense of social justice in a variety of different contexts, a much more modest conceptualization would be to simply view an ethics of translation as a striving for professionalism in the practice of translation – at the expense of the individual and subjective part of the translator as a person and a responsible human being. To unite the two, the professional and the individual, is a daunting task, indeed.

Related to the concern about a translator's ethical concerns and practices in translation is the recent interest on the part of translation scholars in applying narrative theory to translation. In her **narratological approach** to the practice of translation, Mona Baker

(2006, 2014), for one, assigns a central place to narratives – as distinct from some abstract ideals and values human beings have come to embrace about the world they inhabit. Ethical choices and practices are found to be grounded in forms of rationality which are inherently subjective. The underlying assumption is here that human beings never have direct, unmediated access to reality. Rather, their access to reality is filtered through the stories (or narratives) we narrate to ourselves and others about the world around us. Further, in narrative theory, these stories also participate in configuring this reality. The practice of translation is then seen as a form of (re)narration which constructs rather than represents events, states of affairs and human beings renarrated in another language. This means that a translator participates actively in configuring intercultural encounters, which are embedded in the existent narratives and also contribute to changes and dissemination of these narratives through the translations.

For the practice of translation, this means that the unit of analysis is the narrative, i.e., a story and its participants, settings, plot, etc. The focus is here on the ways in which individuals and institutions configure and disseminate the narratives that make up our world and how translators intervene in this process. Such a methodology assumes that narratives can in principle be realized in a variety of different media where narrators can rely on an open-ended set of resources for elaborating stories: written and spoken text, images, diagrams, colour, layout, lighting in theatre, choice of setting and so on. Individual narratives can have both immediate, local significance and are able to function as parts of larger narrative entities which they can undermine, challenge and so on. Translations always function in a particular local environment, but they also contribute to the multitude of other narratives circulating around this environment. Narratives have no objectively delineable borders, as they are constructed out of a continuous stream of consciousness and experience. Baker (e.g. 2010a) has distinguished four types of narratives: personal narratives, public narratives, conceptual narratives and metanarratives. Personal narratives are stories which we tell ourselves and others about our own personal experience and our world. Public narratives are stories which we share with others and which can be and often are in this sharing process elaborated or otherwise changed. Conceptual (or disciplinary) narratives are theoretical constructs designed in a particular discipline. Metanarratives are narratives at a high level of abstraction which are often highly pervasive and influential and taken for granted. Examples are communism, terrorism or democracy.

Narratives are useful for orienting a translator in her world and for guiding her actions. In short, narratives construct the world for the translator. Baker attempts to replace a view of translation as mediation by a view of translation as intervention. In her view, no translation can ever be totally neutral and objective as it invariably depends on some type of interpretation on the part of the translator, who is never a passive recipient but an active participant. As Baker states,

> [b]eing neutral is of course an illusion of theory; indeed, given the impossibility of being neutral and the nature of power relations, one may ask who the translator or interpreter is expected to be neutral *against* when they are fed the disciplinary narrative of neutrality.
>
> (Baker 2009:223)

In terms of how the sociologist and linguist Erving Goffman (1981) sees it, the translator is never simply an 'animator' (of another person's thoughts), rather he is his own author who may undermine the principal's, i.e., the commissioner's, brief. This is particularly relevant when translators are involved in situations of violent conflict where they need to develop a high degree of self-reflexivity. This means that translators – as professionals and citizens – need to reflect on how and why they arrive at a decision regarding what is ethical for them in a given conflictual situation so as to be ethically accountable not only to themselves but also to their professional community of practice, the community at large and to humanity – over and above their traditional responsibility to authors and commissioners. In her work, Baker (see, for instance, Baker 2007) refers to groups of committed, **activist translators** and interpreters like Babels, Tlaxcala, ECOS, Translators for Peace and others who together follow a particular political agenda resisting mainstream interpretations of social and political issues. They can assist individual translators in difficult ethical decisions they face in certain translation tasks, when it comes to uncritically reproducing existing ideologies or to courageously resisting them.

In her article entitled 'Translation as an Alternative Space for Political Action', Baker (2013) looks at the origin, development and positioning of activist groups of translators and interpreters. She finds that, in the type of activism engaged in by many of these groups, linguistic skills are used to extend narrative spaces made invisible by the dominance of Global English and the politics of language in late modernity. In this context, translation is regarded as providing spaces of resistance through the deliberate use of a hybrid language to break the dominant English agenda.

Narrative theory allows the translator to recognize the varied, negotiable positioning and footing they need to assume vis-à-vis the texts they are translating, their authors and recipients, societies and majority ideologies.

With regard to the concept of equivalence, Baker seems to reinterpret it as referring not to a relationship between source text and translation text but to relationships of both source and target texts to events in the world around us and an ethically responsible stance on the part of the translator.

TRANSLATION AND CONFLICT IN THE PRACTICE OF TRANSLATION

The increasing concern about ethics in translation studies can also be seen in the context of a growing interest in the social and political role of translators, intimately related to (as yet unresolved, as we saw above) issues regarding what constitutes a code of ethics and ethical practice. This seems particularly relevant when translators are involved in communities of practice set up in hospitals, prisons, courts of law, business and diplomatic contexts, and conflict and war zones (see Salama-Carr 2007, 2013).

Over the past decades, interest in the connection between the practice of translation and conflict and war has increased (see here, for instance, Baker 2010b; Baker and Maier 2011; Inghilleri and Harding 2010) and with this growing interest has come a focus on texts that are ideologically laden, featuring a dominant discourse on 'terrorism', 'security' and 'intelligence'. Several factors are responsible for this interest in the 'politics of translation' and in a view of a translator's action as a space for political action and activism. One of these factors is a move away from a naïve model of communication, where the objectivity and neutrality of mediation used to be taken for granted, towards a recognition of the important role of translation in constructing and representing, as well as resisting, the dominant framing of such discourses of conflict and war. This new interest is, of course, also fuelled by the increasing influence of post-colonial studies and by the ideological and political engagement of many contemporary translation scholars who are part of the so-called 'Committed Approach' to translation. This approach can be linked to the discourse on human rights in general and to the conflicts in the Arab and Islamic world in particular.

War and conflict and the dangers to which translators are exposed have foregrounded the centrality and complexity of the practice of translation. Important in this respect is the work of various non-governmental organizations (NGOs) and activist groups of translators, such as 'Translators without Borders', as well as the 'framing' of global news and ways of reframing and resisting mainstream discourse. The concept of 'frame' and **'framing'** is seen here as an active process of meaning construction and a means of explaining how narratives are differently framed by different narrators and translators. Framing is part and parcel of activist agendas, it is used to question, problematize and undermine dominant narratives of a political conflict and as a snowballing strategy for creating and expanding communities of practice of activists.

When translators work in situations of conflict, they are invariably confronted with their own personal, professional and political beliefs, and they are required to fully reflect on and understand the conflict situation. This situation is, however, dynamic and unpredictable, demanding that the translator continuously critically examines her allegiance. In situations of war in particular, translators face enormous ethical challenges, given the general atmosphere of uncertainty and ambivalence, with shifting positioning inside political narratives. The translators' task is an important, if highly ambiguous one. Various parties need or fear them, trust or mistrust them, respect or despise them. They are seen as either trustworthy allies or dangerous security risks. In situations of violent conflict and war, translators are often confronted with persons whose human rights have been constrained or violated by national or international interest groups. Here, translators must make ethical and political judgments for which they are very often ill-prepared. To provide such preparation is an urgent desideratum for translator training institutions.

The translator's work is also often crucial in negotiations that make aggression and war acceptable, effectively constructing the other party as an evil enemy, thus legitimizing invasion and destruction for a country's citizens. An example is the translations of the statements of both Israeli and Palestinian spokesmen in the July 2014 war between Israel and Gaza. In the German news, the stories told by Israeli citizens who had been kept awake by sirens announcing Palestinian rockets were consistently framed as those of victims of serious attacks although no one was actually hit. By contrast, stories by inhabitants of Gaza, if not suppressed completely, were always connected with militant Islamist fighters. So translators are often forced in their work to construct evil enemies in order to maintain current conceptions of worthwhile friends. Certain genres in the practice of translation that lend themselves particularly to such work are news reporting or political speeches.

In the course of digitalizing communication, activities involving volunteer translation and informal translation and interpreting activities have increased over the past decades. Along with a general distrust of the way in which selecting, reporting and commenting on news is carried out in the established media, with their tendency to produce and spread 'fake news' and fall into the trap of 'alternative truths' and 'post-truth' reports, groups of activists as well as ordinary citizens are now doing their own alternative reporting and commenting, which relies heavily on translating and interpreting actions. An increased distrust of the mainstream media, which many view as manipulated by political and economic powers, has now given rise to massive alternative means of action and participation that has come to occupy a prominent place in the public awareness around the world. As a new trend, unaffiliated, non-professional and non-institutionalized volunteer translators and translation collectives now play an important part in translating texts in both physical situations (e.g. in informal translating and interpreting in activist workshops and conferences) or virtual platforms (blogging, fansubbing, mockumentaries) or across newly formed hybrid environments which combine embodied and digital activities. In producing and disseminating such citizen media content, individuals and collectives reclaim physical and digital spaces where they are free to express their very own concerns. For more detailed information, I refer the reader to the new Routledge Series: *Critical Perspectives on Citizen Media*, edited by Luis Pérez-González, Bolette Blaagard and Mona Baker (2015 and following).

A field in which the active participation of ordinary citizens in translation activities is particularly striking is audiovisual translation. This will be discussed in the next and final section.

AUDIOVISUAL TRANSLATION AS A SITE OF COLLABORATIVE PRACTICE

Audiovisual translation is one of the most innovative and fastest growing fields of action for translators worldwide. It is also an important professional practice that presents new challenges for translators given the multimodality of the texts involved here and the semiotic complexity of audiovisual texts.

Many people all over the world are today exposed to a great variety of different audiovisual texts. They use established media such as films and the so-called new media with its evolving audiovisual genres used by millions for relaxation and adventure. And disadvantaged and disempowered people across the globe can make use of global TV broadcasts with their programmes for sensory impaired persons. For all these contexts, translation is an integral part whenever texts travel across time, space, languages and cultures and need to be re-contextualized.

Audiovisual translation has grown exponentially in recent decades, propelled by the galloping technological advances, which have made the fast spread and mediation of audiovisual material across the world possible. From early uses of translation in 'film dubbing' or 'film translation' to televised broadcasting as a mass medium in 'media translation' to the more recent computerization of audiovisual texts in electronic or digital media, audiovisual has now spread far beyond its original scope providing excellent opportunities for the practising translator. The following paragraphs distinguish the major types of audiovisual translation.

SUBTITLING

We speak of **'subtitling'** when short bits of written target text are superimposed on source speech visual footage that is to be rendered in synchrony with the corresponding original spoken language. Subtitling involves a shift from oral language to written language. However, subtitles will usually only account for about 60% of the spoken original simply because speaking is, as a rule, faster than reading. This means that the written translated texts are usually more condensed than the original speech, which in turn leads to losses of ambiguity and indirectness. Such losses are likely to change the personality of the characters who are portrayed as much more complex in the original than the subtitled version insinuates. With the development of new digitization techniques and new practices of distribution and use of audiovisual translations, a new subtitling culture has recently arisen. Members of this new trend look critically upon the traditional commercial way of subtitling. They are committed to **'fansubbing'**, i.e., subtitling of televised films by networks of amateur fan communities. Fansubbers distribute their subtitled versions via the Internet to fellow fans. Their aim is to provide more 'faithful' subtitles and give viewers a more authentic experience. A subgroup of fansubbers consists of the virtual community of committed political activists and political cybercultures united in their fight against global capitalism, economic exploitation and political suppression.

With the ever-growing demand for subtitling services for a great variety of texts and genres, e.g. videogames, documentaries or commercial and promotional productions, we see current moves towards automatization of subtitle translation based on large corpora of existing high-quality human-translated subtitles as a basis for automated production.

Another recent development in subtitling facilitated by technological progress is subtitling for 3D films, a challenging technique that needs to accommodate the three-dimensional space of the scenes.

REVOICING

Revoicing refers to a variety of different spoken translation techniques, such as narration, simultaneous interpreting and free commentary as well as voice-over and lip-synchronized dubbing.

The technique of narration is a live (but sometimes also prerecorded) form of oral transfer that aims at faithfully summarizing the original speech. The delivery of this narration is timed so as to avoid clashes with the original programme.

Simultaneous interpreting is a live transfer method used for films and at film festivals whenever more expensive and time-intensive methods of revoicing are unavailable or inaccessible. Interpreters are frequently engaged to dub the voices of all the characters in a film.

Free commentary is a revoicing method used by commentators in important social, cultural and political events. As the name 'free commentary' suggests, this is no faithful rendering of an original speech but a comment on it. Here, we have to do with an adaptation or free version of the content of the original speech for a different linguacultural audience. Free commentary can therefore contain many additions, omissions and explanations of various kinds.

In the voice-over technique, also sometimes referred to as 'half-dubbing', the original soundtrack and the translated soundtrack overlap. The original voice tends to be heard exclusively at the beginning, and a few seconds into this original soundtrack the translated voice becomes louder while the volume of the original is diminished but remains somewhat audible in the background. The idea behind this 'double voicing' is for the translation to retain a touch of authenticity. Voice-over practices are frequently used in televised interviews or documentaries. Voice-over is sometimes regarded as a less expensive version of full dubbing, and it was used with high frequency in many former Communist countries and also in several Asian and Middle Eastern countries. In each of these contexts distinct traditions of voice-over were developed. They ranged from a completely self-effacing style of the voice-over speakers to a more prominent and more intrusive rendering of the translation by voice-over speakers.

Lip-synchronized dubbing is the replacement of the original speech by a voice-track that mimics the original speech as closely as possible. This technique was first used in the film industry during the 1930s as a means of producing dialogues in a foreign language that would fit an actor's lip movements.

Over the past decades, the use of audiovisual translation techniques has also been employed for assisting minority groups, helping them to lead a fuller life and making it possible for them to integrate into the majority society. Thus, subtitled programmes may help immigrants improve their mastery of the language of the host country. Subtitled programmes may also be useful for the hard-of-hearing. Subtitling for the hard-of hearing provides them with a text display of the original speech, mixed with written descriptions of the sound features of the action. While such an elaborate transfer of information from speech to written subtitles was originally only available for films and pre-recorded messages, the audiovisual industry has now vastly extended its use of live subtitling practices.

Real-time subtitling for the hard of hearing and for the deaf is also often referred to as 're-speaking'. This is a procedure where the re-speaker first listens to a live programme and then re-speaks it, including specific features for a deaf and hard-of-hearing audience, to a special speech recognition software which converts utterances into subtitles on screen.

The technique of audio-description, which consists of a spoken account of all those visual aspects of a film that are vital to its plot, has become an important means of making audiovisual products accessible to the visually impaired. In transferring information from the visual channel to the acoustic channel, from images to spoken narrations delivered in between spoken dialogue, audio-describers must constantly make decisions about which information their audience primarily needs and which information can be left out without major consequences for understanding.

DIGITALIZATION AND THE RISE OF A NEW PARTICIPATORY CULTURE IN TRANSLATION

One of the most exciting developments in the field of audiovisual translation today is the involvement of cybercultures as sites of interventionist practices. These are made possible through the rapid developments in digital technology with its de-materialization of space (see the excellent description of this development in the book by Pérez-González 2014). Pérez-González argues that audiovisual translation, which used to be a site of simple representational practice, is now fast becoming a site of intervention and regular audience participation. Through these new developments, the power of the big media corporations is increasingly eroded in processes of translation. Viewers are then no longer passive consumers, rather they become co-creators of the translation.

Digital technologies have been responsible for effecting lasting changes in the production, distribution and consumption of digitized media. Digital communication and information technologies are empowering ordinary citizens to become actively involved in the production and distribution of media content to a hitherto unheard-of degree. Viewers can now participate in audiovisual translation activities such that formerly passive consumers now become active producers. Active media users collaborate with one another to intervene in the texts and often set out to deliberately flout traditional media standards. Collaborative technologies facilitate new transnational, networked collectivities that de-territorialize the formerly nation-based linguacultural space and add to the hybrid linguistic-cultural identification of the global citizen. Volunteer and amateur translators of audiovisual material are responsible for a growing displacement of commercial media content, both in space and time, due to a general discontent with fake news, alternative truths and post-truth preferences.

Along with bottom-up consumer-driven processes of production and consumption of digital media content in translation, a new participatory culture is emerging worldwide. This culture succeeds in blurring the lines between production and consumption, making consumers into co-creating translators. The involvement of amateurs in the process of co-creation is, however, not restricted to manipulating media content: co-creation also involves earlier steps of selecting media content as well as distributing the re-mediated content.

The creative involvement of ordinary citizens in audiovisual translation cannot be ignored by commercial companies and public organizations. The non-professional organization TED (Technology, Entertainment, Design) has launched an Open Translation Project that distributes TED talks across the world, offering subtitles, time-coded transcripts and the possibility that any talk can be translated by international volunteers into many different languages.

In the era of digital cultures, audiovisual translation can no longer be monopolized by professional translators. Rather, the field of audiovisual translation is now becoming a de-centralized field of hitherto unknown diversity and accessibility. The production of audiovisual content and its translation is today increasingly influenced by the participatory involvement of audiences, more often than not in the form of co-creational, networked cyber communities. With this, the question arises, of course, as to whether the continuous spread of amateur and participatory activities in audiovisual translation threatens the profession of audiovisual translators. Since this development is so new, no definite answers can be given at the present time. Suffice it to say, however, that many commercial enterprises will in all likelihood prefer professionally certified translators in the future as well, so translators will continue to be employed.

Finally, a recent transdisciplinary development with relevance to translation needs to be briefly mentioned: **translation beyond translation studies** (Marais 2022). Translation is here used as a concept in other disciplines, e.g. in medicine (see Boettger and House submitted). Here, the differences and similarities between translation in language and 'translational medicine' relating for instance to the transfer from animals to humans in the development of certain drugs are investigated to the mutual benefit of fostering conceptual and terminological clarity and preciseness.

GLOSSARY

acceptability
Refers to the nature of a text that makes the text acceptable to addressees and their socio-cultural background because the text predisposes addressees to 'accept' it as coherent and cohesive

afterlife
Of a text through its translation(s). This term refers to the importance of translations to guarantee the continued 'life' of an original text and to prevent its sinking into oblivion

animator
A person reading or producing a text or a translation for which she is not responsible (see **principal**)

audience design
The way a text is constructed to fit addressees' expectations

audio-description
A spoken account of visual material

audiovisual translation
Transfer of multimedia texts into another language (see **multimedia translation**)

back translation
A translation whose purpose is to inform about foreign language material that readers are assumed not to know

black box
Part of the brain whose functioning is unknown

brief
The task description given to a translator to enable her to carry out her translation

case study
A qualitative research study emphasizing in-depth inquiry into particular cases of phenomena

cloze test
A test where certain words are removed which the test taker is asked to fill in

co-creation
A term used in literary translation studies to characterize the translator as a co-author alongside the original text's author

coherence
A quality of a text that makes parts of the text hang together because they are semantically meaningful

cohesion
A quality of a text denoting the syntactic and lexical linking of parts of the text

collocation
A term used particularly in corpus linguistics to denote a sequence of words that co-occur more often than is expected by chance

commissioner
The person responsible for ordering a translation to be carried out by a translator

communicative equivalence
The relation between an original text and its translation characterized by a comparable use in a communicative situation (see also **functional equivalence**)

comparable corpus
In corpus linguistics, this is a corpus holding texts similar in genre, content and function to those in another corpus (in translation studies often holding original texts)

computer-mediated translation
A type of translation in which a computer does parts or the whole of a translation

connotation
Cultural and/or affective shades of meaning carried by a word or phrase (see also **denotation**)

context of situation
A term denoting the immediate situational context in which a word, phrase or text is embedded

co-occurrence
A term used particularly in computer linguistics to characterize more frequent occurrence of two words or phrases in immediate proximity than chance would indicate

corpora
Plural of corpus

corpus
A collection of texts that can be analysed fully or partially automatically

co-text
The immediate linguistic environment of a word or phrase in a text

covert translation
A type of translation in which the function of the original text is maintained (see **overt translation**)

covert version
A non-equivalent 'translation' in which the cultural filter (see below) was applied arbitrarily with no recourse to an established set of contrastive pragmatic studies of the language pair involved (see **overt version**)

critical discourse analysis
A branch of linguistics which examines texts as forms of social practice focusing on how social power is reinforced in language use

critical incident
In intercultural communication, this term refers to a situation regarded by one or more participants as problematic, confusing and indicative of a culture clash

cultural filter
A procedure used in covert translation (see above) by a translator in order to make the translation compatible with target culture discourse norms and preferences

declarative knowledge
Conscious knowledge which involves THAT something is the case (see also **procedural knowledge**)

deep learning
A part of computerized learning which aims at the highest possible level of abstraction in a dataset

deictic
Specifying the identity, or spatial or temporal location from the perspective of one or more participants in an act of speaking or writing

denotation
The explicit, referential meaning of a word or phrase (see also **connotation**)

descriptive translation studies
Aim to set up an empirical, scientific and non-prescriptive discipline within translation studies

diachronic
In linguistics and translation studies relating to studies of phenomena in one or more language(s) across time (see also **synchronic**)

digitalization
A process of transforming analogue bits of information into digital bits. Also used in a broader sense to refer to the many domains of everyday life that are restructured to fit digital communication

diglossia
Refers to situations in which two languages or dialects are used in a group, one being the vernacular (see below), or 'low' variety used in ordinary conversations, the other being the 'high' variety used in formal contexts such as education, administration etc.

directionality
Refers to the different directions of translations: either into the foreign language or into the mother tongue of the translator

direct method
A method used in language teaching in which the foreign language is employed exclusively and both the use of learners' mother tongue and translation are banned

discourse analysis
A discipline which focuses on the analysis of texts as phenomena of language use and communicative events

domestication
A procedure in translation where a text is adapted to the norms of the target culture (see also **foreignization**)

double linkage
The relation of a translated text both backwards to its original and forwards to the communicative needs of the target addressees

dubbing
A method of audiovisual translation in which the entire audio information of a film is reproduced in another language

dynamic equivalence
A term coined by Eugene Nida which refers to the quality of a translation in which the message of the original has been rendered

in the target language in such a way that the response of the receptors is essentially like that of the original receptors

eco-translatology
A branch of translation studies that originated in China and that emphasizes the embeddedness of translational activities in the situational and socio-cultural contexts

English as a lingua franca (ELF)
A worldwide use of the English language for communicative purposes by non-native speakers of English

equivalence
In translation studies this term refers to the relation between a translation and its original text where both texts fulfil a similar function

equivalent response
A response by target addressees that is similar to the response by addressees of the original text

ethics in translation
Refers to the idea that translators are accountable for their translations

event-related potential (ERP)
A technique in which electrical potentials generated by the brain that are related to specific internal and external events are monitored. This technique has become a common method in psychological research

eye-tracking
A method used in translation process research in which the movements of participants' eyes are analysed in order to find out about difficulties in the process of translation

fansubbing
A technique in audiovisual translation in which non-professional translators ('fans') engage in the task of dubbing (see **dubbing**)

field
In Hallidayan linguistics, a Register dimension that captures the content of a text, its subject matter

foreignization
A procedure in translation where the translated text is translated in such a way as to maximally resemble its original

formal correspondence   (also often called 'literal translation')
Refers to the relationship of an out-of-context equivalence between items of a source language text and items of a target language text (see also **dynamic equivalence**)

frame
An often conventionalized scheme of interpreting and thus assigning importance to events, themes and texts

framing
A process of embedding events, themes and texts in a subjective frame of interpretation

free translation
A translation which gives priority to preserving the meaning of an original text (see **Word-for-word translation**)

function
Of a text refers to the use or application of the text in a certain situation

functional equivalence
Refers to the fact that an original text and a translated text have equivalent application in comparable communicative situations (see also **communicative equivalence**)

functional magnetic resonance tomography (fMRT)
A technique used in cognitive neuroscience, in medicine and applied disciplines to measure brain activity by detecting changes associated with blood flow

functions of language
Basic uses of language as suggested by scholars in linguistics and philosophy. All these suggestions featured these two uses: an informative use and an affective-interpersonal use

genre
In systemic functional linguistics and diverse applied sciences, the term refers to a collectivity or category of texts that represent recurrent configurations of meaning and enact the social practices of a given culture

globalization
A worldwide movement towards economic, financial, trade, cultural and media integration and aiming at an interdependent and interconnected world transcending national borders

grammar-translation method
A method in language teaching in which typically translations of isolated sentences are used to illustrate and explain grammatical phenomena

hermeneutic school of translation studies
A school of translation studies which emphasizes the necessity for a translator to identify with the author of the original text, and giving priority to understanding and interpreting the original text

ideology
A body of conscious or unconscious ideas entertained by an individual, a group or a society, which underlie goals, motives and expectations

informativity
Refers to new information presented in a text and/or information which was previously unknown

institutional translation
Translation which occurs within the framework of an institution

intentionality
Refers to the purpose of a text's author

interlingual translation
Translation proper, i.e., translation from one language into another language

internationalization
A term that refers to the tendency of businesses to operate across national borders and to designing products and services that easily adapt to different linguacultures

interpreting
Is the oral mode of translation

intersemiotic translation
Translation across different semiotic systems, for instance, 'translations' of written text into films

intertextuality
Is the relationship between a text and other relevant, similar texts encountered in previous experience

intralingual translation
Refers to changing a given text by comments, paraphrases, summaries, style modifications, etc. and is not really a 'translation' in the sense in which translation is commonly understood

introspection
A method of self-observation and reporting used in psychology and in translation studies designed to 'look into' and find out what goes on in, a person's mind

keystroke logging   (also called keylogging)
A procedure used to study human–computer interaction and which is also used in translation process research to monitor the translator's strikes on the keyboard

language for communication
A language such as English as a lingua franca that is used only as means for communication, not as a means for affective identification

linguaculture
A term which emphasizes the fact that language cannot be separated from culture

linguistic-cultural relativity
The idea that the cultural embeddedness of the language a person speaks may have an impact on her thought processes and behaviour

linguistic diversity
A term that signifies that many different languages are present in a given group

linguistic relativity
The idea that a person's mother tongue influences her thinking and behaviour

literal translation
A translation in which, as far as possible, the target text is translated word for word (see **word-for-word translation** and see **sense-for-sense translation**)

literary text
A text that belongs to a national literature (see **pragmatic text**)

localization
A procedure in which a translated text is adapted to the local, socio-cultural norms of the target culture

longitudinal study
A study which encompasses two or more time windows following trends of a phenomenon over time

machine translation
A term which refers to the fact that computers take on the task of translation either partially or entirely

metalinguistic knowledge
Knowledge about language

mode
In Hallidayan linguistics, a Register dimension referring to the nature of a text in terms of, e.g., orality versus writtenness, coherence and cohesion, theme–rheme sequences

multilingual institutions
Institutions such as the European Union in which many different languages are present and respected

multimedia translation
A translation which involves the movement from one medium to another medium, such as from texts available in written form to oral script and pictures in films

narrative
Another term for a story

narrative theory
A theory in which it is emphasized that we are not able to perceive reality directly but always mediated through certain narratives

natural translation
Translation conducted by bilingual persons who are assumed to be 'naturally' competent translators

norms of translation
A term usually associated with descriptive translation studies and referring to a category of descriptive analysis of translation phenomena

observer's paradox
The phenomenon that the behaviour of persons is different when they are being observed from when they are not being observed

orders of indexicality
A term that refers to the fact that indexical meanings, that is connections between linguistic signs and contexts, are ordered and closely related to other social and cultural features of social groups

overt translation
A type of translation in which the original text is, as far as possible, preserved such that the linguistic forms and structures of the original often 'shine through' the target text

overt version
A textual operation in which a text is transferred into another language and an additional function is added onto the function of the original, resulting for instance in summaries of the original, or adaptations of the original for children or foreign language learners

parallel corpus
A corpus of translated texts

polysystem theory of translation
A literary theory suggesting a multiple system of various systems that intersect with each other and partially overlap, but functioning as one structured whole

positron emission tomography (PET)
A nuclear medicinal functional imaging technique used to observe metabolic processes of the body

post–colonial translation studies
A branch of translation studies that looks at translations as sites of necessary intervention revealing power differences and social injustice, particularly with regard to post-colonial contexts

post-editing
A procedure in which a translation produced by a computer is 'edited', i.e., examined for mistakes in the computer translation and corrected

pragmatic text
A text that does not belong to the domain of literature (see **literary text**)

pre-editing
A procedure in which a text which is to be translated by a computer is edited before the translation is effected

principal
In translation studies, this term refers to a person who is responsible for the translation but does not normally undertake it (see **animator**)

procedural knowledge
A type of knowledge that refers to HOW something is done (see **declarative knowledge**)

qualitative research
This type of research aims at in-depth inquiry and understanding of certain phenomena and examines the why and how of their behaviour; typical methods are case studies (see **case study**)

quantitative research
This type of research refers to the systematic empirical investigation of selected phenomena via statistical techniques

re-contextualization
A concept in translation studies that refers to the fact that a text in a source language context is inserted into a new context in the target language

Register
A term from Hallidayan linguistics which refers to a variety of a language used in a particular socio-cultural context for a particular purpose

retrospection
A method used in translation studies where the translator is interviewed about her translation process after it has occurred

revoicing
A method in audiovisual translation which refers to spoken translation techniques like narration, simultaneous interpreting, free commentary and voice-over and lip-synchronized dubbing

screen-recording
A method used in translation process research where pictures of a computer screen are taken and recorded

semiotic
Of, or relating to, signs

sense-for-sense translation
Refers to the translation of the meaning of sentences (see **word-for-word translation**)

short-term memory
A type of memory that is able to hold for a short period of time (commonly defined as 4 plus or minus 1 second) a small amount of information

situationality
Refers to the relationship of a text to a particular socio-temporal and local context

Skopos
In translation studies, this term refers to the purpose of a translation

source language
The language in which the original text is written

source text
A different term for 'original' or 'original text' (see **target text**)

subtitling
A method in audiovisual translation which shifts from spoken language (for instance in a film) to written language. Subtitles are short bits of written target text superimposed on source speech visual footage that is to be rendered in synchrony with the corresponding original spoken language

superdiversity
A phenomenon referring to the hitherto unknown tremendous increase in worldwide migration that leads to many different languages, ethnicities, religions and their effects on interests, motives, housing and labour markets of host societies

synchronic
In linguistics and translation studies, relating to the study of phenomena in one or several language(s) at only one point in time (see **diachronic**)

target language
The language into which a source text is translated (see **source language**)

target text
An alternative term for 'translation' or 'translated text' (see **source text**)

Tenor
In Hallidayan linguistics, a Register dimension that refers to inter-personal factors such as attitude, stance, role relationship

tertium comparationis
The third part in a comparison of two entities and the quality that these entities in a comparison have in common. In translation studies, this term is used to describe categorial schemes that function as superordinate, neutral means of comparison between an original text and a translated text

text linguistics
A branch of linguistics that examines the way texts are constructed, typically focusing on ways of creating coherence or cohesion and other standards of textuality

text type
A categorization of texts in translation studies, for instance informative texts, expressive texts, etc.

textual equivalence
A type of equivalence that holds at the level of text

textuality
What makes a text a text, i.e., a unified meaningful whole rather than a string of unrelated words, phrases or sentences

theme–rheme
Theme refers to facts either to be taken to be universally known, taken for granted or given from the context as 'old information', i.e., information that does not contribute to the new information conveyed by the entire sentence. Rheme contains the main 'new' information to be transmitted by the sentence

thinking-aloud protocols (TAPs)
A method in translation process research in which participating translators talk aloud about their thoughts while they are in the process of translating, and this talk is recorded

topic and comment
Alternative terms for theme–rheme (see above)

transfer competence
The central competence needed for a translator in her translation activities. It distinguishes a translator from a bilingual person. Transfer competence is essentially about mediating *between* languages and cultures rather than being merely proficient *in* two languages

translanguaging
The fluid and dynamic practices which transcend the boundaries of discrete, named languages, language varieties and other semiotic systems

translatability
Refers to the fact that translation in the case of certain texts or genres is possible

translation memory
Refers to a database which stores linguistic units in the form of sentences or other segments, which stem from previous human translations and can be used in software programs for computer-assisted translation but also as an aid in non-computer-aided translations

translation process
The translator's cognitive process of translation, or more informally put: what goes on in a translator's mind

translation product
The text in a target language that results from the process of translation

translation unit
A concept from translation process research associated with cognitive effort expended and attention foci. It can be defined as source text segments that attract a translator's focus of attention at any given time in the translation process

translog
A keystroke logging tool that records the keys pressed down by a translator during her translation and produces a log which can be systematically analysed

universals of translation
Phenomena in translation that are assumed to occur regularly with all language pairs and in both translation directions

verbal reports
The output of thinking-aloud activities of a translator

vernacular
The native language or dialect of a particular group

version
The result of a textual operation that does not result in a translation but a different type of text

voice-over
A technique in audiovisual translation often used in televised interviews in a foreign language in which the original soundtrack and the translated soundtrack overlap

word-for-word translation
A type of translation in which, as the name suggests, word after word is translated irrespective of meaning

working memory
A memory with limited capacity responsible for keeping, processing and manipulating information for a limited amount of time. While similar to short-term memory, it is a central executive function and thus different from short-term memory that only stores information (see **short-term memory**)

world-view
An assumed attitude towards and conception of reality, often believed to be rooted in a particular language

REFERENCES

Adorno, Theodor W., Else Frenkel-Brunswik, Daniel Levinson and R. Nevitt Sandford (1950) *The Authoritarian Personality*. New York, NY: Harper and Brother.

Aijmer, Karin, Juliane House, Daniel Kadar and Hong Liu (eds) (2022-) *Contrastive Pragmatics. A Cross-Disciplinary Journal*. Leiden: Brill.

Almanna, Ali and Juliane House (2023a) *Linguistics for Translation Students*. London/New York, NY: Routledge.

Almanna, Ali and Juliane House (eds) (2023b) *Translation Politicised and Politics of Translation*. Berlin: Peter Lang.

Alves, Fabio, Adriana Pagano, Stella Neumann, Erich Steiner and Silvia Hansen-Schirra (2010) 'Translation Units and Grammatical Shifts. Towards an Integration of Product- and Process-based Research', in Gregory Shreve and Erik Angelone (eds) *Translation and Cognition*. Amsterdam: Benjamins, 109–142.

Alves, Fabio and Daniel Vale (2011) 'On Drafting and Revision in Translation: A Corpus Linguistics-oriented Analysis of Translation Process Data', *Translation: Computation, Corpora, Cognition 1*: 105–122.Anderson, John (1976) *The Architecture of Cognition*. Mahwah, NJ: Erlbaum.

Baker, Mona (1992/2011) *In Other Words: A Course Book on Translation*. London: Routledge.

Baker, Mona (1993) 'Corpus Linguistics and Translation Studies: Implications and Applications', in Mona Baker, Gill Francis and Elena Tognini-Bonelli (eds) *Text and Technology: In Honour of John Sinclair*. Amsterdam: Benjamins, 233–250.

Baker, Mona (1995) 'Corpora in Translation Studies. An Overview and Suggestions for Future Research', *Target 7:2*: 223–243.

Baker, Mona (2006) *Translation and Conflict: A Narrative Account*. London: Routledge.

Baker, Mona (2007) 'Reframing Conflict in Translation', *Social Semiotics* 17:2: 151–169.

Baker, Mona (2009) 'Resisting State Terror: Theorizing Communities of Activist Translators and Interpreters', in Esperança Bielsa Mialet and Chris Hughes (eds) *Globalisation, Political Violence and Translation*. Basingstoke: Palgrave Macmillan, 222–242.

Baker, Mona (2010a) 'Translation and Activism: Emerging Patterns of Narrative Community', in Maria Tymoczko (ed) *Translation, Resistance Activism*. Amherst/Boston: University of Massachusetts Press, 23–41.

Baker, Mona (2010b) 'Interpreters and Translators in the War Zone', *The Translator* 16:2: 197–222.

Baker, Mona (2013) 'Translation as an Alternative Space for Political Action', *Journal of Social, Cultural and Political Protest* 12:1: 23–47.

Baker, Mona (2014) 'Translation as Re-narration', in Juliane House (ed) *Translation: A Multidisciplinary Approach*. Basingstoke: Palgrave Macmillan, 158–177.

Baker, Mona and Carol Maier (eds) (2011) *Ethics and the Curriculum*. Manchester: St. Jerome.

Baker, Mona and Gabriela Saldanha (eds) (2019) *Routledge Encyclopdia of Translation Studies*. 3rd ed. London/New York, NY: Routledge.

Bassnett, Susan and Harish Trivedi (eds) (2002) *Post-colonial Translation in Theory and Practice*. London: Routledge.

Baumann, Gerd (1996) *Contesting Culture: Discourses of Identity in Multi-Ethnic London*. Cambridge: Cambridge University Press.

Baumgarten, Nicole (2007) 'Converging Conventions? Macrosyntactic Conjunction with English *and* and German *und* ', *Text & Talk* 27: 139–170.

Baumgarten, Nicole (2022) 'Contrastive Pragmatics', in Federico Zanettin and Christopher Rundle (eds) *The Routledge Handbook of Translation and Methodology*. London/New York, NY: Routledge, 172–189.

Baumgarten, Nicole, Juliane House and Julia Probst (2004) 'English as a Lingua Franca in Covert Translation Processes', *The Translator* 10: 83–108.

Baynham, Michael and Tong King Lee (2019) *Translation and Translanguaging*. London/New York, NY: Routledge.

Becher, Viktor (2010) 'Abandoning the Notion of "Translation-inherent" Explicitation: Against a Dogma in Translation Studies', *Across Languages and Cultures* 11: 1–28.

Becher, Viktor (2011) *Explicitation and Implicitation in Translation: A Corpus-based Study of English–German and German–English Translations of Business Texts*. PhD thesis, University Hamburg. Available online at http://ediss. sub.uni-hamburg.de/volltexte/2011/5321/pdf/Dissertation.pdf (accessed 25 May 2017).

Becher, Viktor, Juliane House and Svenja Kranich (2009) 'Convergence and Divergence of Communicative Norms through Language Contact in Translation', in Kurt Braunmüller and Juliane House (eds) *Convergence and Divergence in Language Contact Situations*. Amsterdam: Benjamins, 125–152.

Behrens, Bergljot and Cathrine Fabricius-Hansen (2009) 'Introduction to Contributions in Structuring Information: The Explicit/Implicit Dimension', *Oslo Studies in Language* 1: 2–10.

Bellos, David (2011) *Is That a Fish in Your Ear? The Amazing Adventure of Translation*. London: Penguin Books.

Benjamin, Walter (1923/1977) 'Die Aufgabe des Übersetzers', in Hans-Joachim Störig (ed) *Das Problem des Übersetzens*. Darmstadt: Wissenschaftliche Buchgesellschaft, 182–195.

Biber, Douglas (1988) *Variation across Speech and Writing*. Cambridge: Cambridge University Press.

Biber, Douglas, Stig Johansson and Geoffrey Leech (1999) *The Grammar of Spoken and Written English*. London: Longman.

Blommaert, Jan (2005) *The Sociolinguistics of Globalisation*. Cambridge: Cambridge University Press.

Blommaert, Jan (2013) *Ethnography, Superdiversity and Linguistic Landscaping*. Bristol: Multilingual Matters.

Blommaert, Jan and Ben Rampton (2011) 'Language and Superdiversity', *MMG Working Papers*, 36 pages.

Blum-Kulka, Shoshana (1986) 'Shifts of Coherence and Cohesion in Translation', in Juliane House and Shoshana Blum-Kulka (eds) *Interlingual and Intercultural Communication*. Tübingen: Narr, 17–35.

Blum-Kulka, Shoshana, Juliane House and Gabriele Kasper (eds) (1989) *Cross-Cultural Pragmatics: Requests and Apologies*. Norwood, NJ: Ablex.

Boettger, Michael and Juliane House (submitted) 'Speaking the Same Language? Translation in Language and Science', *Contrastive Pragmatics*.

Bolinger, Dwight (1979) 'To Catch a Metaphor: *You* as a Norm', *American Speech 54*: 194–209.

Brown, Roger and Albert Gilman (1960) 'The Pronouns of Power and Solidarity', in Thomas Sebeok (ed) *Style in Language*. Cambridge: MIT Press, 253–276.

Bühler, Karl (1934/1965) *Sprachtheorie. Die Darstellungsfunktion der Sprache*. Jena/Stuttgart: Fischer.

Bührig, Kristin, Juliane House and Jan ten Thije (eds) (2009) *Translational Action and Intercultural Communication*. Manchester: St. Jerome.

Calzada-Pérez, María (2007) 'Translators and Translation Studies Scholars as Inoculators of Resistance', *The Translator 13*:2: 243–269.

Calzada-Pérez, Maria (2014) *Apropos of Ideology: Translation Studies on Ideology. Ideologies in Translation Studies*. London: Routledge.

Carl, Michael, Srinivas Bangalore and Moritz Schaefer (eds) (2015) *New Directions in Translation Process Research*. Berlin/New York, NY: Springer.

Carreres, Angeles, Maria Noriega-Sanchez and Lucia Pintado Gutierrez (2021) 'Introduction: Translation and Plurilingual Approaches to Language Teaching and Learning', *Translation and Translanguaging in Multilingual Contexts* 7:1: 1–16.

Catford, John C. (1965) *A Linguistic Theory of Translation*. Oxford: Oxford University Press.

Chafe, Wallace (2000) 'Loci of Diversity and Convergence of Thought and Language', in Martin Pütz and Marjolijn Verspoor (eds) *Explorations in Linguistic Relativity*. Amsterdam: Benjamins, 101–123.

Chesterman, Andrew (2001) 'Proposal for a Hieronymic Oath', *The Translator* 7:2: 139–154.

Chomsky, Noam (1965) *Aspects of the Theory of Syntax*. Cambridge: MIT Press.

Comrie, Bernard (2003) 'On Explaining Language Universals', in Michael Tomasello (ed) *The New Psychology of Language*. Vol. 2. Mahwah, NJ: Erlbaum, 195–209.

Cook, Guy (2010) *Translation in Language Teaching*. Oxford: Oxford University Press.

Coulmas, Florian (ed) (1979) *Conversational Routine*. Berlin: Mouton de Gruyter.

Cronin, Michael (1998) 'The Cracked Looking Glass of Servants: Translation and Minority Languages in a Global Age', *The Translator* 4:2: 145–162.

Cronin, Michael (2003) *Translation and Globalization*. London: Routledge.

de Beaugrande, Robert and Wolfgang Dressler (1981) *Einführung in die Textlinguistik*. Berlin: de Gruyter.

Derrida, Jacques (1985) 'Des Tours de Babel', in Joseph Graham (ed) *Difference in Translation*. Ithaca, NJ: Cornell University Press, 165–208.

Eco, Umberto (2001) *Experiences in Translation*. Toronto, ON: University of Toronto Press.

Ehrensberger-Dow, Maureen and Sharon O'Brien (2015) 'Ergonomics of the Translator's Workplace: Potential for Cognitive Friction', *Translation Spaces* 4: 98–118.

Ericsson, K. Anders and Herbert Simon (1984) *Protocol Analysis: Verbal Reports as Data*. Cambridge: MIT Press.

European Commission Directorate-General for Translation (2009) *Translating for a Multilingual Community*. Luxembourg: Office for Official Publications for the European Communities.

Even-Zohar, Itamar (1990) 'Polysystem Studies', *Poetics Today* 11: 9–26.

Fairclough, Norman (1995) *Critical Discourse Analysis: The Critical Study of Language*. Cambridge, MA: Blackwell.

Fedorov, Andrei (1958) *Introduction to the Theory of Translation* (in Russian). 2nd ed. Moscow: Izdatel'stvo literartury na inostrannikh yazykakh.

Foucault, Michel (1977) *The Archaeology of Knowledge*. London: Tavistock.

Galante, Angelica (2021) 'Translation as a Pedagogical Tool in Multilingual Classes: Engaging the Learner's Plurilingual Repertoire', *Translation and Translanguaging in Multilingual Contexts* 7:1: 106–123.

Galtung, Johan (1985) 'Struktur, Kultur und intellektueller Stil', in Alois Wierlacher (ed) *Das Fremde und das Eigene*. München: iudicium, 151–193.

Geertz, Clifford (1973) *The Interpretation of Cultures: Selected Essays*. New York, NY: Basic Books.

Goffman, Erving (1974) *Frame Analysis*. London: Harper & Row.

Goffman, Erving (1981) *Forms of Talk*. Philadelphia: University of Pennsylvania Press.

Gonzalez-Davies, Maria and David Soler Ortinez (2021) 'Use of Translation and Plurilingual Practices in Language Learning: A Formative Intervention Model', *Translation and Translanguaging in Multilingual Contexts* 7:1: 17–40.

Goodenough, Ward (1964) 'Cultural Anthropology', in Dell Hymes (ed) *Language in Culture and Society*. New York, NY: Harper & Row, 36–39.

Göpferich, Susanne and Riitta Jääskeläinen (2009) 'Process Research into the Development of Translation Competence: Where Are We and Where Do We Need to Go?', *Across Languages and Cultures* 10: 169–191.

Greenberg, Joseph (ed) (1963) *Universals of Language*. Cambridge: MIT Press.

Hall, Edward T. (1976) *Beyond Culture*. New York, NY: Doubleday.

Halliday, M. A. K. (1961) 'Categories of the Theory of Grammar', *Word* 17:3: 241–292.

Halliday, M. A. K. (1973) *Explorations in the Functions of Language*. London: Arnold.

Halliday, M. A. K. (1994) *An Introduction to Functional Grammar*. 2nd ed. London: Arnold.

Halliday, M. A. K. and Christian M. I. M. Matthiessen (2011) *An Introduction to Functional Grammar*. 4th ed. London: Arnold.

Halliday, M.A.K. and Ruqaiya Hasan (1976) *Cohesion in English*. London: Longman.

Halliday, M. A. K. and Ruqaiya Hasan (1989) *Spoken and Written Language*. Oxford: Oxford University Press.

Halverson, Sandra (2014) 'Reorienting Translation Studies: Cognitive Approaches and the Centrality of the Translator', in Juliane House (ed) *Translation: A Multidisciplinary Approach*. Basingstoke: Palgrave Macmillan, 116–139.

Hansen-Schirra, Silvia, Stella Neumann and Erich Steiner (2007) 'Cohesive Explicitness in an English–German Translation Corpus', *Languages in Contrast* 7:2: 241–265.

Harris, Brian (1976) 'The Importance of Natural Translation', *Working Papers in Bilingualism* (University of Toronto, OISE) *12*: 96–114.

Hatim, Basil and Ian Mason (1990) *Discourse and the Translator*. London: Longman.

Hatim, Basil and Ian Mason (1997) *The Translator as Communicator*. London: Routledge.

Hawkins, Roger (1994) *A Performance Theory of Order and Constituency*. Cambridge: Cambridge University Press.

Hermans, Theo (ed) (1985) *The Manipulation of Literature. Studies in Literary Translation*. London: Croom Helm.

Hofstede, Geert (1980) *Culture's Consequences*. London: Sage.

Holliday, Adrian (1999) 'Small Cultures', *Applied Linguistics 20*: 237–267.

Holliday, Adrian (2012) *Intercultural Communication*. London: Routledge.

Honderich, Ted (2002) *After the Terror*. Edinburgh: Edinburgh University Press.

House, Juliane (1977) *A Model for Translation Quality Assessment*. Tübingen: Narr.

House, Juliane (1997) *Translation Quality Assessment: A Model Revisited*. Tübingen: Narr.

House, Juliane (2000) 'Linguistic Relativity and Translation', in Martin Pütz and Marjilijn Verspoor (eds) *Explorations in Linguistic Relativity*. Amsterdam: Benjamins, 69–88.

House, Juliane (2003) 'English as a Lingua Franca: A Threat to Multilingualism?', *Journal of Sociolinguistics* 7: 556–578.

House, Juliane (2004) 'Linguistic Aspects of the Translation of Children's Books', in Armin Paul Frank, Norbert Greiner, Theo Hermans, Harald Kittel, Werner Koller, José Lambert and Fritz Paul (eds) Übersetzung – Translation – Traduction: An International Handbook. Berlin: Mouton de Gruyter, 683–697.

House, Juliane (2005) 'Politeness in Germany – Politeness in Germany?', in Leo Hickey and Miranda Stewart (eds) *Politeness in Europe*. Clevedon: Multilingual Matters, 13–29.

House, Juliane (2006a) 'Text and Context in Translation', *Journal of Pragmatics 38*: 338–358.

House, Juliane (2006b) 'Communicative Styles in English and German', *European Journal of English Studies 10*: 249–267.

House, Juliane (2008) 'Beyond Intervention: Universals in Translation?', *transkom 1*: 6–19.

House, Juliane (2009) *Translation*. Oxford: Oxford University Press.

House, Juliane (2010) 'A Case for "Globish"', *The Linguist* June/July 2010: 16–17.

House, Juliane (2013) 'Translation and English as a Lingua Franca', *The Interpreter and Translator Trainer* 7: 279–298.

House, Juliane (2015a) *Translation Quality Assessment: Past and Present*. London: Routledge.

House, Juliane (2015b) 'Global English, Discourse and Translation: Linking Constructions in English and German Popular Science Texts', *Target 27:3*: 370–387.

House, Juliane (2016) *Translation as Communication across Languages and Cultures*. London/New York, NY: Routledge.

House, Juliane and Danie Kadar (2021) *Cross-Cultural Pragmatics*. Cambridge: Cambridge University Press.

House, Juliane, Bo Wang and Yuanyi Ma (2022) 'Developing Translation Studies as an Applied Linguistic Disciplines' in Bo Wang and Yuanyi Ma (eds) *Key Themes and New Directions in Systemic Functional Translation Studies*. London/New York, NY: Routledge, 87–97.

Hu, Gengshen (2013) *Eco-Translatology: Construction and Interpretation*. Beijing: The Commercial Press.

Huntingdon, Samuel (1997) *The Clash of Civilizations and the Remaking of the World Order*. New York, NY: Simon & Schuster.

Inghilleri, Moira (2008) 'The Ethical Task of the Translator in the Geo-political Arena', *Translation Studies 1:2*: 212–223.

Inghilleri, Moira and Sue-Ann Harding (2010) 'Translating Violent Conflict', *The Translator 16:2*: 165–173.

Jääskeläinen, Riitta (2011) 'Back to Basics: Designing a Study to Determine the Validity and Reliability of Verbal Report Data on Translation Processes', in Sharon O'Brien (ed) *Cognitive Explorations of Translation*. London: Continuum, 15–29.

Jakobsen, Arnt Lykke and Lasse Schou (1999) 'Translog Documentation', in Gyde Hansen (ed) *Probing the Process in Translation: Methods and Results*. Copenhagen Studies in Language 24. Copenhagen: Samfundslitteratur, 151–186.

Jakobson, Roman (1959) 'On Linguistic Aspects of Translation', in Reuben Brower (ed) *On Translation*. New York: Oxford University Press, 232–239.

Jakobson, Roman (1960) 'Closing Statement: Linguistics and Poetics', in Thomas A. Sebeok (ed) *Style in Language*. Cambridge: MIT Press, 350–377.

Jensen, Kristian (2008) 'Assessing Eye-tracking Accuracy in Translation Studies', in Susanne Göpferich, Arnt Lykke Jakobsen and Inger Mees (eds) *Looking at Eyes: Eye Tracking Studies of Reading and Translation Processing*. Copenhagen: Samfundslitteratur, 157–174.

Kang, Ji-Hae (2014) 'Institutions Translated: Discourse, Identity and Power in Institutional Mediation', *Perspectives. Studies in Translatology 22:4*: 469–478.

Kaniklidou, Themis and Juliane House (2018) 'Discourse and Ideology in Translated Children's Literature: A Comparative View'. *Perspectives 26*:2: 232–245.

Kelly, Louis (1969) *25 Centuries of Language Teaching*. Rowley, MA: Newbury House.

Kim, Mira, Jeremy Munday, Zhenhua Wang and Pin Wang (eds) (2021) *Systemic Functional Linguistics and Translation Studies*. London: Bloomsbury Academic.

Koller, Werner (1995) 'The Concept of Equivalence and the Object of Translation Studies', *Target 7*: 191–222.

Koskinen, Kaisa (2000) 'Institutional Illusions: Translating in the EU Commission', *The Translator 6*:1: 49–65.

Kramsch, Claire (2009) *The Multilingual Subject*. Oxford: Oxford University Press.

Kranich, Svenja, Juliane House and Viktor Becher (2012) 'Changing Conventions in English and German Translations of Popular Science Texts', in Kurt Braunmüller and Christoph Gabriel (eds) *Multilingual Individuals and Multilingual Societies*. Amsterdam: Benjamins, 315–335.

Krein-Kühle, Monika (2013) 'Towards High-quality Translation Corpora: The Cologne Specialized Translation Corpus (CSTC)', in Monika Krein-Kühle and Ursula Wienen (eds) *Kölner Konferenz zur Fachübersetzung 2010*. Frankfurt/Main: Lang, 3–17.

Krein-Kühle, Monika (2014) 'Translation and Equivalence', in Juliane House (ed) *Translation: A Multidisciplinary Approach*. Basingstoke: Palgrave Macmillan, 15–35.

Krings, Hans (1986) *Was in den Köpfen von Übersetzern vorgeht*. Tübingen: Narr.

Kroeber, Alfred and Clyde Kluckhohn (1952) *Culture: A Critical Review of Concepts and Definitions*. Harvard University Peabody Museum of American Archaeology and Ethnology Papers 47.

Kruger, Alet, Kim Wallmach and Jeremy Munday (eds) (2011) *Corpus-based Translation Studies*. London: Continuum.

Kunz, Kerstin, Ekaterina Lapshinova-Koltunski, Jose Manuel Martinez Martinez, Katrin Menzel and Erich Steiner (2021) *GECCO- German English Contrasts in Cohesion. Insights from Corpus-Based Studies of Languages, Registers and Modes*. Berlin: de Gruyter Mouton.

Langacker, Ronald (1967) *Language and Its Structure*. New York, NY: Harcourt.

Laviosa-Braithwaite, Sara (1998) 'Universals of Translation', in Mona Baker (ed) *The Routledge Encyclopedia of Translation*. London: Routledge, 288–291.

Levinas, Emmanuel (1989) *Ethics as First Philosophy*. London: Routledge.

Li, Wei (2018) 'Translanguaging as a Practical Theory of Language', *Applied Linguistics 39*:1: 9–30.

Longacre, Robert E. (1956) 'Review of W. B. Urban "Language and Reality" and B. L. Whorf "Four Articles of Metalinguistics"', *Language 32*: 298–308.

Lucy, John (1992) *Language Diversity and Thought*. Cambridge: Cambridge University Press.

Lucy, John (1997) 'Linguistic Relativity', *Annual Review of Anthropology 26*: 291–312.

MacKenzie, Ian (2018) 'Bilingualism, Translation and Anglicization', in Ian MacKenzie (ed) *Language Contact and the Future of English*, chapter 7. London/New York: Routledge, 102–126.

Macnamara, John (1970) 'Bilingualism and Thought', in James Alatis (ed) *Georgetown University 21st Round Table*. Washington, DC: Georgetown University Press, 25–40.

Mair, Christian and Geoffrey Leech (2006) 'Current Changes in English Syntax', in Bas Aarts and April Macmahon (eds) *The Handbook of English Linguistics*. Oxford: Blackwell, 318–342.

Malamatidou, Sofia (2018) *Corpus Triangulation: Combining Data and Methods in Corpus-based Translation Studies*. London/New York, NY: Routledge.

Malinowski, Bronislaw (1935) *Coral Gardens and Their Magic*. London: Allen & Unwin.

Marais, Kobus (ed) (2022) *Translation beyond Translation Studies*. London: Bloomsbury Publishing.

Mason, Ian (2010) 'Discourse, Ideology and Translation', in Mona Baker (ed) *Critical Readings in Translation Studies*. London: Routledge, 83–95.

Mason, Ian (2014) 'Discourse and Translation: A Social Perspective', in Juliane House (ed) *Translation: A Multidisciplinary Perspective*. Basingstoke: Palgrave Macmillan, 54–81.

Mauranen, Anna (2021) 'ELF and Translation as Language Contact', in Anna Mauranen and Svetlana Vetchinnikova (eds) *Language Change. The Impact of English as a Lingua Franca*. Cambridge: Cambridge University Press, 95–122.

Mauranen, Anna and Pekka Kujamäki (eds) (2004) *Translation Universals – Do They Exist?* Amsterdam: Benjamins.

Munday, Jeremy (2007) *Translation as Intervention*. London: Continuum.

Munday, Jeremy (2014) 'Using Primary Sources to Produce a Microhistory of Translators and Translations', *The Translator 20:1*: 64–80.

Muñoz Martín, Ricardo (2010) 'On Paradigms and Cognitive Translatology', in Gregory Shreve and Eric Angelone (eds) *Translation and Cognition*. Amsterdam: Benjamins, 169–187.

Nida, Eugene (1964) *Toward a Theory of Translation*. Leiden: Brill.

Nida, Eugene and Charles Taber (1969) *The Theory and Practice of Translation*. Leiden: Brill.

Nord, Christiane (1997) *Translation as a Purposeful Activity*. Manchester: St. Jerome.

O'Brien, Sharon (ed) (2011) *Cognitive Explorations of Translation*. London: Continuum.

PACTE Group (2009) 'Results of the Validation of the PACTE Translation Competence Model. Acceptability and Decision-making', *Across Languages and Cultures 10*: 207–230.

PACTE Group (2011) 'Results of the Validation of the PACTE Translation Competence Model: Translation Project and Translation Index', in Sharon O'Brien (ed) *Cognitive Explorations of Translation*. London: Continuum, 30–56.

Paradis, Michel (2004) *A Neurolinguistic Theory of Bilingualism*. Amsterdam: Benjamins.

Paradis, Michel (2009) *Declarative and Procedural Determinants of Second Languages*. Amsterdam: Benjamins.

Pérez-González, Luis (2014) *Audiovisual Translation: Theories, Methods and Issues*. London: Routledge.

Pérez-González, Luis, Bolette Blaagard and Mona Baker (eds) (2015) *Critical Perspectives on Citizen Media*. New York: Routledge..

Piller, Ingrid (2013) *Intercultural Communication: A Critical Introduction*. Edinburgh: Edinburgh University Press.

Pym, Anthony (2000) 'The European Union and Its Future Languages: Questions for Language Policies and Translation Theories', *Across Languages and Cultures 1*: 1–18.

Pym, Anthony (ed) (2001) 'The Return to Ethics: Special Issue of The Translator', 7:2.

Reiss, Katharina (1971) *Möglichkeiten und Grenzen der Übersetzungskritik*. München: Hueber.

Robinson, Douglas (2014) *Translation and Empire: Postcolonial Theories Explained*. London: Routledge.

Ruzicka Kenfel, Veljka and Juliane House (eds) (2020) *Death in Children's Literature and Cinema and Its Translation*. Berlin: Peter Lang.

Said, Edward (1993) *Culture and Imperialism*. London: Chatto & Windus.

Salama-Carr, Myriam (2013) 'Conflict in Translation', in Mona Baker and Gabriela Saldanha (eds) *Handbook of Translation Studies*, Vol. 4. Amsterdam: Benjamins, 31–35.

Salama-Carr, Myriam (ed) (2007) *Translating and Interpreting Conflict*. Amsterdam: Rodopi.

Sapir, Edward (1921) *Language: An Introduction to the Study of Speech*. New York, NY: Harcourt.

Sapir, Edward (1949) *Selected Writings on Language, Culture and Personality.* Edited by David Mandelbaum. Berkeley: University of California Press.

Schleiermacher, Friedrich (1813) 'Über die verschiedenen Methoden des Übersetzens', reprinted in Hans-Joachim Störig (ed) *Das Problem des Übersetzens.* Darmstadt: Wissenschaftliche Buchgesellschaft, 38–70.

Searle, John (1977) 'Reiterating the Differences: A Reply to Derrida', *Glyph 1*: 198–208.

Shreve, Gregory and Erik Angelone (eds) (2010) *Translation and Cognition.* Amsterdam: Benjamins.

Simon, Sherry (1996) *Gender in Translation: Cultural Identity and the Politics of Transmission.* London: Routledge.

Slobin, Dan (1997) 'Mind, Code and Text', in Joan Bybee, John Haiman and Susan Thompson (eds) *Essays in Language Function and Language Type.* Amsterdam: Benjamins, 437–467.

Slobin, Dan (2009) 'Verbalized Events: A Dynamic Approach to Linguistic Relativity and Determinism', in Susanne Niemeier and Rene Diven (eds) *Evidence for Linguistic Relativity.* Amsterdam: Benjamins, 107–138.

Snell-Hornby, Mary (2010) 'Mind the Gab', *The Linguist* June/July 2010: 18–19.

Sperber, Dan (1996) *Explaining Culture.* Oxford: Blackwell.

Steiner, Erich (1998) 'A Register-based Translation Evaluation: An Advertisement as a Case in Point', *Target 10*: 291–318.

Steiner, Erich (2004) *Translated Texts: Properties, Variation and Evaluation.* Frankfurt/Main: Lang.

Steiner, Erich (2008) 'Explicitation: Towards an Empirical and Corpus-based Methodology', in Jonathan Webster (ed) *Meaning in Context.* London: Continuum, 235–278.

Steiner, George (1975) *After Babel: Aspects of Language and Translation.* Oxford: Oxford University Press.

Stolze, Radegundis (1992) *Hermeneutisches Übersetzen: Linguistische Kategorien des Verstehens und Formulierens beim Übersetzen.* Tübingen: Narr.

Sweet, Henry (1964) *The Practical Study of Languages.* Oxford: Oxford University Press.

Terkourafi, Marina (2011) 'Thank You, Sorry and Please in Cypriot Greek: What Happens to Politeness Markers When They Are Borrowed across Languages?', *Journal of Pragmatics 43*: 218–235.

Thomas, Alexander (1986) *Kulturvergleichende Psychologie.* Göttingen: Hogrefe.

Tirkkonen-Condit, Sonja (2004) 'Unique Items: Over- or Underrepresented in Translated Language', in Anna Mauranen and Pekka Kujamäki (eds) *Translation Universals –Do They Exist?* Amsterdam: Benjamins, 177–184.

Toury, Gideon (2001) *Probabilistic Explanations in Translation Studies: Universals – Or a Challenge to the Very Concept?* Paper at the 3rd EST Congress, Copenhagen.

Toury, Gideon (2012) *Descriptive Translation Studies and Beyond.* Rev. ed. Amsterdam: Benjamins.

Tymoczko, Maria (2000) 'Translation and Political Engagement: Activism, Social Change and the Role of Translation in Geopolitical Shifts', *The Translator 6:1:* 23–47.

Tymoczko, Maria (2007) *Enlarging Translation, Empowering Translators.* Manchester: St. Jerome.

Venuti, Lawrence (ed) (1992) *Rethinking Translation: Discourse, Subjectivity, Ideology.* London: Routledge.

Venuti, Lawrence (1995) *The Translator's Invisibility.* London: Routledge.

Vermeer, Hans (1994) 'Hermeneutik und Übersetzungswissenschaft', *TEXT-conText 9*: 161–182.

Vieira, Else (1999) 'Liberating Calibans: Readings of *Antropofagia* and Haroldo de Campos' Poetics of Transcreation', in Susan Bassnett and Harish Trivedi (eds) *Postcolonial Translation: Theory and Practice.* London: Routledge, 95–113.

von Flotow, Luise (1997) *Translation and Gender.* Manchester: St. Jerome.

von Flotow, Luise and Joan W. Scott (2016) 'Gender Studies and Translation Studies', in Yves Gambier and Luc van Doorslaer (eds) *Border Crossings: Translation Studies and Other Disciplines.* Amsterdam: Benjamins, 349–374.

Wagner, Emma (2003) 'Why International Organizations Need Translation Theory', in Luis Pérez-González (ed) *Speaking in Tongues: Language across Contexts and Users.* Valencia: Valencia University, 91–102.

Wagner, Emma, Svend Bech and Jésus M. Mártinez (2002) *Translating for the EU Institutions.* Manchester: St. Jerome.

Wang, Bo and Yuanyi Ma (eds) (2022) *Key Themes and New Directions in Systemic Functional Translation Studies.* London/New York, NY: Routledge.

Weinreich, Uriel (1953/1963) *Languages in Contact.* The Hague: Mouton.

Wenger, Etienne (1989) *Communities of Practice.* Cambridge: Cambridge University Press.

Whorf, Benjamin Lee (1956) *Language, Thought and Reality.* Edited by John Carroll. Cambridge: MIT Press.

Widdowson, Henry (2014) 'The Role of Translation in Language Learning and Teaching', in Juliane House (ed) *Translation: A Multidisciplinary Approach.* Basingstoke: Palgrave Macmillan, 222–240.

Wilss, Wolfram (1996) *Knowledge and Skills in Translator Behaviour.* Amsterdam: Benjamins.

Wodak, Ruth (ed) (2013) *Critical Discourse Analysis*. Thousand Oaks, CA: Sage.

Wu, You (2021) 'Revisiting Translation in the Age of Digital Globalization', *Babel* 67:6: 819–844.

Zanettin, Federico (2014) 'Corpora in Translation', in Juliane House (ed) *Translation: A Multidisciplinary Approach*. Basingstoke: Palgrave Macmillan, 178–199.

INDEX

Printed in the United States
by Baker & Taylor Publisher Services